Pandemic Economics

To Andrew M. Cuomo who made me plan ahead of the curve

Pandemic Economics

Peter A.G. van Bergeijk

Professor of International Economics and Macroeconomics, International Institute of Social Studies at Erasmus University Rotterdam, The Hague, the Netherlands

 Edward Elgar
PUBLISHING

Cheltenham, UK • Northampton, MA, USA

Cover image: Peeter Burgeik

Published by
Edward Elgar Publishing Limited
The Lypiatts
15 Lansdown Road
Cheltenham
Glos GL50 2JA
UK

Edward Elgar Publishing, Inc.
William Pratt House
9 Dewey Court
Northampton
Massachusetts 01060
USA

A catalogue record for this book
is available from the British Library

Library of Congress Control Number: 2020952724

This book is available electronically in the **Elgar**online
Economics subject collection
http://dx.doi.org/10.4337/9781800379978

Printed on elemental chlorine free (ECF)
recycled paper containing 30% Post-Consumer Waste

ISBN 978 1 80037 996 1 (cased)
ISBN 978 1 80037 997 8 (eBook)

Printed and bound in the USA

Contents

Preface

Tuesday March 10, 2020 was my last 'normal day' in The Hague. I remember teaching my 'Global Economy' course on a pressure-cooking Tuesday in which I had stuffed as many individual meetings as possible. On Wednesday I finished field research with the last interviews in Rotterdam. Erasmus University came to a standstill on Thursday, when lectures and meetings with students were forbidden.

Staff and students adapted to the new situation overnight and during the next week classes were already over the internet. Research also picked up quickly and within a few weeks we re-started capacity building projects, were writing and peer-reviewing and organized virtual research seminars. So academic work continued in a new format but with similar, if not more, intensity as before the outbreak. In these weeks the idea for this book emerged as an afterthought in an email exchange with Caroline Kracunas at Edward Elgar on April 1, 2020. I started writing April 10. Writing was not 'normal'. Over the past decade I have written nine books while commuting and on international trips. I learned to appreciate airports, train stations and hotel rooms as places to write. Planes and trains and their delays became opportunities. It turns out that the lock-down also has its merits: this book was written at home.

To most people it would seem to be very unwise to write a book on one of the largest economic crises since the Second World War while we are still amid the storm. It is indeed difficult and exhaustive to analyse a moving target. There is an information overkill and new and challenging perspectives are developed on a daily if not hourly basis. For a pure scientist it would probably make a lot of sense to wait until all the data are in so that theories and hypotheses can be tested.

It is, however, necessary to write this book, because humanity for the first time in history has been able to deeply hurt the economy by its own response to a pandemic. These costs have stimulated a debate between those that give priority to the economy and those that give priority to health. This antithesis at the same time is both correct and, to a large extent, false, depending on the epidemiologic features and pathogenicity of a new virus. It is correct because health protection obviously comes at an economic cost. It is wrong because a high-mortality-high-contagion pandemic would mean economic disaster and the economy, indeed, could only survive if health was protected vigorously.

The COVID-19 pandemic as such is, of course, serious, but certainly not without historical precedent and not exceptionally severe in terms of mortality. It appears that, unlike other pandemics such as the Spanish Flu and HIV/AIDS, the death toll is not among children and young adults. The response to the pandemic, however, has been exceptionally costly for the world economy and has hurt the poor and those that had just escaped from poverty in the past decade. Since pandemics occur with a frequency of roughly seven to eight events per century, it is vital to look beyond the apex of the COVID-19 pandemic and the trough of the ensuing recession, and to investigate how prevention and mitigation can become more cost effective. The only way to beat the future contagious diseases – that will without any doubt emerge – is to plan in a rational way for the Big One.

We have witnessed responses that were induced by neglect, ignorance and fear. This triumvirate has led to the worst possible outcome for the world, an outcome that is not sustainable if only because killing the economy is neither helpful for the necessary investments in health care systems (diagnosis and monitoring) nor for the Research and Development that is necessary for curing and preventing the next pandemic.

So, our response to the next pandemic must be better, more efficient and especially more rational. I live in the Netherlands, four meters below sealevel, and when you think about this it is a much stranger and riskier way of living than the new normal of the COVID-19 world. The Netherlands has managed to protect its way of living by means of the Delta Works, a massive and long-term engineering project that started in 1953 and is supported by law from the vagaries of short-termism of politics. If the water comes, the policy is that I should not flee. I must evacuate vertically as my attic is sufficiently high, and horizontal evacuation (to get out of the risk area) would be dangerous because of the congestion. The Delta Works and the Dutch vertical evacuation policy offer a real-world example of how we can use planning to construct rational protection at acceptable levels, and also against pandemics.

The Dutch, incidentally, needed a disaster, the North Sea Flood of 1953, to start preparing. Most important perhaps, while they were willing to invest in protection against the sea, the Dutch did not act on warnings that the Dutch Intensive Care capacity was too low in the case of a pandemic (ANV, 2016).

Nobody has the perfect recipe and neither do I, but I do hope that this book can be of help by offering building blocks and a framework to think about the challenges of pandemic economics.

De Koog, August 1, 2020

Acknowledgements

I am not an expert; nobody is yet an expert in the new field of pandemic economics. I may, however, have been a bit more mentally prepared than most economists.

I had to think about pandemics while COVID-19 was still beyond the horizon, when I was a member of ANV Netherlands Network of Safety and Security Analysts. Most of that work by its nature has been in Dutch, but an English translation of the major all-hazard report in which severe pandemic scenarios also feature has appeared as ANV (2016). This book, as my other work on disasters, has benefitted from comments by people that I have worked with in ANV, in particular, Peter Scheepstal and Leendert Gooijer.

My thinking, pre COVID-19, had also been stimulated because I work at a development studies institute. The major recent almost-pandemics (or 'international epidemics', in WHO speak) have been in Africa, namely Ebola and HIV/AIDS. Development economists cannot avoid the impact of contagious diseases on the economy: one of my students had been in lockdown quite recently during the outbreak of Ebola. As always, I learned a lot from the institute community, also – during the outbreak – about the daily experiences of lockdowns in Barcelona, Tel-Aviv and Dar-es-Salaam.

The economics of natural disasters was not a new topic either. I have worked on natural disasters for quite some time and produced one of the first meta-analyses on the economic impact of natural disasters in developing countries (Lazzaroni and van Bergeijk 2014). The key finding of the meta is that disasters are not by definition bad for the economy and may actually stimulate productivity. Later work on trade and disasters (Li and van Bergeijk 2019) revealed that the trade impact of disasters is not as negative as is often assumed and may sometimes stimulate trade. I do, of course, not claim that these findings on natural disasters such as floods, earthquakes and droughts are valid for the COVID-19 pandemic, because such a generalization would be both 'out of sample' and an example of the Fallacy of Hasty Generalization. Still I have benefitted from this research experience because it has forced me to keep an open eye for unexpected and counterintuitive developments during the pandemic.

Even in the Dutch society, with its rational outlook and consensus-based approach, it is not easy to start planning for the more distant future. Therefore, I wanted to engage with the debate and wrote quite a lot and often in Dutch that was later useful for this book. Short economic essays appeared in *ESB*, Me Judice, ElgarBlog, Bliss, *Nederlands Dagblad* and *NRC Handelsblad*. As always, I benefitted a lot from the comments of editors and readers of the Dutch contributions. *Pandemic Economics* re-uses some adapted and updated texts and diagrams from earlier books (van Bergeijk 2010, 2013 and 2019).

I benefitted from comments during virtual seminars at the ISS Development Economics Seminar (May 26, 2020), especially Georgina Gomez, the University Higher School of Economics of Moscow (June 11, 2020), in particular, Leonid Grigoryev and Igor Makarov and RIVM Netherlands National Institute for Public Health and the Environment (July 13, 2020), expressly Marcel Mennen.

Ksenia Anisimova competently provided editorial assistance.

A special word of thanks to Hanneke Sassenburg for social closeness and to my economist-friends Frank Kalshoven, Dick Kabel, Selwyn Moons and Rolph van der Hoeven who helped me by disagreeing with earlier concepts.

1. Introduction

For decades scientists all around the world have steadily predicted that a new pandemic with significant loss of life would occur within a generation. The case is clear. Pandemics have been with us for a long time. The father of medicine, Hippocrates, already discusses the bubonic plague and the 'Cough of Perinthus' in the fifth century BC.[1] Since 1580, when the first detailed description of an influenza pandemic occurred, 32 such pandemics (including COVID-19) have been recorded, or once every fifteen years. The twentieth century was no exception with four influenza pandemics: the severe Spanish Flu of 1918–20, the Asian Flu of 1957–60, the Hong Kong Flu of 1969 and the rather mild Swine Flu of 2009.

Table 1.1 Four centuries of pandemics

	Influenza	Other[#]	Total
18th century	4	1	5
19th century	2	7	9
20th century	4	2	6
21st century[*]	2	1	3
Total	12	11	23
Average per century	3.8	3.4	7.2

Notes: * 2000 – 2020
            # Yellow fever, Cholera, HIV/AIDS and Zika
Sources: Cunha (2004), Smith (2017)

The track record seemed to have improved as the last serious case was half a century ago and some analysts argued that this was due to improved health care.[2] Still the consensus amongst national security experts was that there was a significant possibility that an influenza pandemic would occur in the next five years. Most analyses of pandemics focussed on influenza, but other pandemics and international epidemics could also have been considered (Table 1.1), roughly doubling the frequency of pandemics. Even so, the expected number of influenza pandemics is 3.8 in a century; so, the probability that an influenza pandemic would occur in a specific decade is 38% and the number for a five-year-period would be almost twenty percent. If we look at all pandemics, the probability of a pandemic in a decade is 72% or roughly thirty-five percent over a five-year period. This was true before the outbreak of COVID-19 and it will be at least equally true again once all Corona containment restrictions are relaxed.[3] The anatomy of pandemics, moreover, implies that the frequency of pandemics will increase, due to intensification of global travel, increasing human–wildlife interaction, intensification of global food production and densification of population.[4]

Pandemic Economics investigates the role, contribution and functioning of economic science and practice in the context of pandemics. When the world was hit by the outbreak of COVID-19, pandemics could be seen as complex and, in a sense, underexplored problems in mainstream economics. Firstly, a pandemic predominantly is a global supply shock with initially no impact on the capital stock while recent recessions have been demand-side phenomena with a significant role for private investment. Secondly, the policy timing is fundamental and has a number of new elements including the strictness and severity of interventions regarding economic and societal freedom. Thirdly, international cooperation is essential to fight pandemics, but the reality is one of 'save ourselves'. Economic science has put a lot of energy and thinking into this topic recently and *Pandemic Economics* fits into that emerging literature. The focus is broad, although with a strong macroeconomic component, and in the spirit of (International) Political Economy. This emphasis obscures to some extent what a pandemic means in individual lives and also that humanity is facing a triple crisis that potentially carries a risk of extinction due to the simultaneous occurrence of three mutually reinforcing ruin problems.[5]

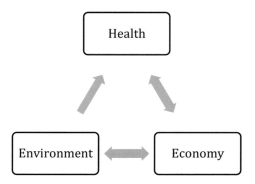

Diagram 1.1 Three reinforcing ruin problems

Norman et al. (2020, p. 1) define ruin problems as high impact events with 'a very high probability for humanity surviving a single such event [but] over time, there is eventually zero probability of surviving repeated exposures to such events.' This definition relates to the *reoccurrence* of the phenomenon of pandemics – so that is the frequency over time – that in itself is also a powerful motivation for this book. There is, however, a need to broaden the definition of the ruin problem to include the *concurrence* of different hazards – that is, the frequency at a point in time (Martin and Pindyck, 2019). In the area of health, the pandemic takes the front seat, but at stake is the breakdown of global and local health care systems. For the environment, Global Warming, climate change and the extinction of species provide a complex but recognizable ruin problem. In the economic arena the fallout from the Great Recession – Secular Stagnation and the World Trade Slowdown – had already made the system vulnerable to the last straw that could break the camel's back. These are, moreover, reinforcing ruin problems which makes their concurrence the more problematic. The pandemic is bad for the economy. A sour economy drives people into poverty providing a spreading ground for pandemics and also threatens health care funding. Environmental degradation threatens economic sustainability and a recession puts the required massive investments for the transition to environmental sustainability under pressure. A direct link from pandemic to environment does not exist, but indirect links via the economy are clear, as is the fact that Global Warming and an increasing ecological footprint are conducive to the occurrence and global transmission of new diseases. Realizing these interdependencies is not a reason for despair but illuminates the challenge of moving simultaneously into the right direction in these three areas. Once we get into reverse, reinforcement will strengthen recovery for health, the environment and the economy. We can be somewhat optimistic because a common shared risk provides strong incentives to overcome holdup-problems and generate collective action. Indeed, we need to be optimistic and work hard to make something good from something bad.

I have organized this book in three parts. My treatment of time prevents the material from becoming outdated before the book is printed. Part I focusses on the past which consists of the pre-COVID-19 period (Chapter 2) and the outbreak (Chapter 3) which is identified in a down-to-earth manner: restrictions on economic activities reached their peak in April 2020 and the forecasts for global economic growth in 2020 reached their apex in July 2020, the cut-off date for the book. The benefit is that these are relevant periods of roughly three to four months in which the pandemic plays out along different dimensions (the forecasts start to deteriorate around March 2020) and brings out all elements of the policy reaction; the cost is that Part II misses the period of relaxation of lockdowns and related measures, the shift of the hotspot to Latin America and the historic Second Quarter numbers for the GDP of advanced economies. Part II focusses on the now. Rather than engaging with the stream of daily data and developments, the focus is on the issue of how to deal with such an information pandemic. This focus is relevant both for the first and for the later phases of the pandemic: how to deal with uncertainty, measurement error and the tsunami of heterogenous opinions and often contradictory scientific analyses? Part III is about another distinct period: the future, that is the post-COVID-19 era. This period is both post-pandemic *and* pre-pandemic. It is a time when lessons can and will be learned and where preparations need to be stepped up for the next pandemic. Because the next pandemic is a certainty – only its timing is uncertain.

1.1 THE PAST: PREPAREDNESS AND PANDONOMICS

We have witnessed a lot of chaos and fear, and the lack of a clear strategy has already given rise to a lot of criticism. Ecks has called COVID-19 not only a viral pandemic, but 'a pandemic of epistemic unpreparedness':

> The scale and severity of the coronavirus pandemic is a shock to health systems. It is a shock to economies and governments. It is also a shock to the life sciences, which were meant to anticipate a pandemic of this magnitude, but failed to do so. The "life sciences" in question are virology, epidemiology, biomedicine and pharmacology. But the social, political, and economic life sciences were also unprepared for COVID-19 (Ecks, 2020b).

Now you may wonder: why were we not prepared if this kind of a health disaster occurs so frequently? The answer to that question is – paradoxically – that we were mentally prepared, but we were unfortunately not physically equipped. As discussed, in Part I (that deals with the past), scientific and policy communities (in particular the health authorities and national security experts) were well aware of the risks of a future pandemic and created institutional structures (for example, outbreak management teams), prepared playbooks and scenarios and organized trainings and exercises. The paperwork and drills prepared for a similar pandemic (contagion and mortality) as the COVID-19 pandemic, but the reality was different – of course.[6]

Policy free scenarios
The difference was not only due to the fact that COVID-19 is spread by asymptomatic infected people (which makes monitoring and isolation extra difficult), but also because most of the scenarios were 'policy free' (nobody intervenes), assuming that other countries would not act. In other words, such scenarios typically assumed that the pandemic would run its course without restrictions and that the death toll would be accepted. Not because that would be the reality, but because it was needed as training material. The benefit of 'policy free' scenarios was that they provided good training for health and

policy professionals, especially because such scenarios illuminated that the existing health infrastructure in many countries was insufficient to meet the extraordinary demands of a pandemic. The most prominent amongst these studies is probably the report *The Neglected Dimension of Global Security* by the Commission on a Global Health Risk Framework for the Future (CGHRFF, 2016) that assessed the need for an additional $4.5 billion annual investment in global, regional and national health capabilities and an accelerated R&D programme. The CGHRFF (2016, p. 8) wrote,

> $4.5 billion is not a small sum, but neither is it beyond reach. In the context of estimated expected economic losses from pandemics of over $60 billion per year, it is very good investment. Considering the potential threat to human lives, the case is even stronger.

Thanks to such studies, pandemic risk was well understood and plans for action had been prepared.[7] Economic analyses also delivered significant inputs for the scenarios, providing estimates of the costs of pandemics that had occurred in the past as well as forecasts of the expected economic outfall from a future pandemic. Chapter 2 provides an overview of the state of economic knowledge before the outbreak of COVID-19.

The limitations of the 'policy free' scenario approach were, however, significant and costly. Firstly, these scenarios did not take into account that all countries would act in the same manner, thus creating scarcity for medical equipment, and would lockdown economies that reduced economic activity domestically but also decreased global activity further due to leakage and spillovers across borders. Secondly, the 'policy free' scenarios did not invite thinking and preparation from the social sciences. While the medical urgency was well illustrated by the predicted risk of breakdown of the health care system, the social impact of the pandemic was limited in these scenarios because policy interventions were often not implemented by assumption. In particular, the economics profession was therefore not sufficiently equipped for the COVID-19 pandemic as mainstream economics had simply not thought about the possibility of a massive worldwide use of lockdowns and business closures. It had considered the negative economic impact of a pandemic without intervention, but not the negative use of the economy (that is, the rationing of labour and restrictions on demand) to contain a pandemic.

Pandonomics

This cost – the lack of preparedness of economists – became apparent after the emergence of COVID-19. Diagnosis, advice and treatment of the economic condition during a pandemic was haphazard, monopolized by health policy considerations, influenced too much by overly pessimistic expectations, and confusing with a clear risk of self-fulfilling predictions.

It is not an issue that economists did not understand directly all the characteristics of the 'pandonomics virus' that spread when governments around the world shut down large parts of their economies and ordered their citizens to go in isolation. Why is this not an issue? Because economists, just like the medical profession, had to learn and cope with the new virus and all its characteristics. Building knowledge is only possible by means of trial and error and therefore wrong analyses are just as much part of learning as 'the' right analysis. We can live with errors – in a broad philosophical sense we live thanks to the errors of the past – provided that we learn. We will encounter many of the wrong interpretations, from an 'economic coma' to a 'war economy' and from a fundamental misinterpretation of uncertainty to a lack of understanding of the need for counterfactuals. Chapter 3 documents the outburst of the pandonomics virus and the response of our profession. Economists, like the proverbial generals, were waging the previous war as their recipes were by and large based on the experiences of the Great Recession (the financial crisis that started in 2008). The economic fallout of a pandemic is, however, completely different from a traditional recession. One important goal of this book is to prepare and equip economists better for the next pandemic.

1.2 THE PRESENT: STATISTICS AND ECONOMIC TOOLS

Writing about the present is illusive. The moment you write, the present has become the past – and even more so when you are being read. So, Part II is about how we perceive the world and act on that perception, knowing that our acts will have an impact on the future. We will also take up the issue of the economist's toolbox. Two issues are important: firstly, the availability and reliability of data and, secondly, the appropriateness of economic theories. Chapter 4 discusses issues related to data. Evidence-based policy advice requires data and unfortunately economists were flying blind during the first part of the pandemic – or perhaps more accurately eye-patched, distorting the perspective. Complete lockdowns, although novel for current generations, could be understood without much analytical complication, but for 'light' or 'intelligent' lockdowns interpretation of the economic condition was difficult. The sectors that came to a standstill were outspoken and in the media, so that the problem areas were easily identified and well known in the public domain: catering, hospitality, cultural activities and international travel were shut down overnight. In contrast, about a third to half of the workforce continued because these workers were providing essential services in health care, the food chain, distribution and security. Importantly, many other sectors were able to return to business-as-usual levels of activity, although they often needed to pioneer new forms of organization and management. In many countries tele-working became a standard overnight and significant parts of services, including banking, insurance and the government, did what only a few decades ago would have been impossible with staff working from home. Importantly, ICT, logistics, drive throughs and home delivery services blossomed. These growth sectors of the Corona economy were not observed by the statistical apparatus that accurately measured the shrinking old economy, but not the new economy, and lost track of the dynamism and entrepreneurship that led in a Schumpeterian sense to *neue Kombinationen*: new ways to combine products, technology and delivery. Growth also occurred where it was unavoidable, namely in the Covid care sector[8] and in funeral services, and, although it is perhaps strange to consider such activities as production, this is exactly what we should do when calculating Gross Domestic Product according to the System of National Accounts. Also, the new activities to counteract COVID-19, including testing and tracing and the development and use of a vaccine count as production, generate employment and will be innovative and more effective and efficient overtime.[9]

Chapter 5 focusses on economic analysis. As is always the case during the initial phase of a crisis, economic analyses and recipes are heterogeneous and often contradictory. Convergence of focus and analysis always takes quite some time. It is therefore important to understand that the validity of economic theories depends on conditions of time and place. Economic theories are not necessarily right or wrong but are – given time and place – appropriate or inappropriate and the art of economics is to select those theories that are appropriate. As will become clear in Chapter 5, the economics of pandemics can make good use of the basic tools of economic analysis (if properly applied) and, therefore, we do not need new economic theories.

1.3 THE FUTURE: SETTINGS AND LESSONS FOR THE NEXT PANDEMIC

Part III looks at the future. The aim is not to predict, but to investigate different societal contexts in which a new pandemic will hit the world. Any strategy for pandemic preparedness needs to consider the social context, because it is a key element of resilience that determines the potential and effectiveness of policy instruments. These settings are consistent descriptions of the possible dimensions of the societal, philosophical, political and economic responses to the next pandemic(s). It is common to use the term 'scenario' for such a description, but I want to avoid that term in this book, because we need to investigate societal response to the *same* event in different social contexts. My settings are thus fundamentally different from the available scenarios of pandemics, also because the latter typically have been 'policy free'.

The Darwinian Society

The first setting (prepared unpreparedness) is that of a Darwinian Society that accepts, so to say, the pandemic attack as part of nature. In this society the basic philosophy is that of the survival of the fittest. Ask this society the holdup question 'your money or your life' and expect that the choice is for the money. Preference is given to economic wellbeing and therefore loss of human life and suffering are accepted as unavoidable collateral damage – in the Global South of survival and in the Global North of a way of living that values the benefits of globalized production networks and freedom of travel. The orientation is individualistic in nature rather than based on solidarity or fairness.

Deglobality

The second setting is strictly nationalistic in orientation. This is the world of deglobality, a state of mind of shrinking social, economic and political cross-border linkages and this impacts on how we live and work. The multilateral and supranational organisations have lost both their authority and their support. Border controls, tariffs and non-tariff barriers have been reinstalled at the levels of the early 1960s, physical production has been localised and international travel is restricted and expensive. This setting is, however, not a look-alike of the decade after the Great Depression of the 1930s: exchange of ideas and international collaboration via the Internet continues to be an important aspect of our daily life.

Benevolent Big Brother

The third setting is that of the benevolent Big Brother. Pandemic control is difficult and requires the kind of draconian measures that are problematic to implement in a Western decentralised market-oriented economy. The use of strict quarantine, especially if this amounts to forced isolation, does not relate well to human rights and basic liberties but appears to have been effective in Vietnam especially in terms of the countrywide death toll. Big Brother could be benevolent in the sense that it saves lives. Also, the use of digital surveillance, drones and Big Data may have been effective tools to combat the spread of the COVID-19, but again it comes at a loss of privacy. In this setting decision-making is less democratic and more autocratic in order to achieve as effective as possible a defence against future pandemics.

Autocratic Autarky

The fourth setting brings what could technically look like the most efficient policy mix since contacts with the world at large are limited and the authorities have a battery of measures that can be applied in a much stricter way than in modern open democratic market economies. However, while autarky and economic self-isolation can delay, they cannot stop a virus. Especially those diseases that originate domestically or are transmitted by migrating wildlife, birds and vectors (mosquitoes, ticks, fleas, and so on) will occur anyway. Autocracy makes the use of restrictions on daily life easier to achieve, but, in general, the lack of transparency and reliability of statistics that is associated with autocratic systems is not conducive for identification and early response, both at the national and at the global level.

Article 3 trilemma

The fifth setting zooms in on societies that try to maintain the lifestyle, norms and values, including privacy, democracy and openness, at levels that are comparable to those reached before the COVID-19 pandemic. This is a permanent policy puzzle as adjustment to the reality of recurring pandemics involves, sometimes diabolical, trade-offs along many dimensions. The COVID-19 pandemic has, for example, featured isolation of the weak and vulnerable living in nursing homes and this has been condemned as inhumane by many. Self-isolation and sheltering at home have caused anxiety and psychological disorders, and lifting the measures against the virus has had similar effects, but – and this is a highly relevant point – for different parts of the population. Freedom to move and meet have been restricted at unprecedented levels but with the aim of respecting other elements of Article 3 of the Universal Declaration of Human Rights. 'Everyone has the right to life, liberty and security of person.' Life, liberty and security form a pandemic policy trilemma with health, freedom and the economy as poles that require a balancing act at the centre of this setting.

The investigation of a pandemic in these five settings is not an exercise in forecasting or a method to speculate about the future, but rather a tool to investigate the components and building blocks of a sustainable strategy to reduce the impact of pandemics on life and living conditions. We need that strategy urgently. The outbreak of a new pandemic is a certainty, only the timing is uncertain. This time we should be prepared ... and equipped.

Chapter 7 takes up the challenge of preparation. Preparation needs to be organized at the individual level (households and firms), at local levels (this is important for mega-cities and other conglomerates with a high population density), as well as at national, international and global levels. Individual preparedness is important because individual defence reduces the speed with which an epidemic develops, because it is cheap and because individual measures provide a line of defence against the breakdown of systems at higher levels of aggregation. Importantly, higher level measures will also not work or work less well if the basis of individual preparedness is insufficient. A second level to organize preparation and resilience is local. Here a distinction needs to be made between measures that can be taken in the short to medium term and the long run, as the former is about using existing structures differently while the latter will strive for changes in, for example, the design of city plans, infrastructure and housing. National planning is the next level that we will consider. Health care is an area where policy is essentially national (and in federations often at the level of the member state), because of the political implications of the direct impact on the voters. Delegation of tasks to higher levels of (supra) national governance has and will continue to be difficult and therefore it is realistic to pay attention to preparation in a national context too, also because national isolation has been used effectively in, for example, China, Vietnam, New Zealand and Taiwan to tackle the outbreak of COVID-19. National planning, however, cannot provide a line of defence against pandemics. Healthwise isolation might, under the right kind of circumstances, be possible for a longer period, but economic interdependency and the forces of nature imply that the fallout of a pandemic will ultimately reach the shores of all countries in the world.

Clearly, a pandemic necessitates preparation and mitigation at all levels – individual, local, national, regional and global. Without these activities at all levels, it will be impossible to beat the next pandemic. The chain of defence against the next pandemic is as strong as the weakest shackle.

Key takeaways of Chapter 1

- Pandemics occur frequently. Over the last 4 centuries the world experienced a pandemic every 14 years, on average.
- A pandemic is a ruin problem: a high impact event that humanity can survive per occurrence, but with eventually zero probability of surviving repeated exposures.
- COVID-19 is a special case because of the simultaneity of three mutually reinforcing ruin problems: the pandemic, the aftermath of the Great Recession and Global Warming.
- Pandemic scenarios were 'policy-free' because they were meant to train policy makers and thus did not investigate the massive use of lockdowns and their economic consequences.
- The economic impact of a pandemic is fundamentally different from a recession.
- A strategy for pandemic preparedness needs to consider the social context because it is a key element of resilience and the potential and effectiveness of policy instruments.

> • Preparation needs to be organized at the individual level (households and firms), at local levels (this is important for mega-cities and other conglomerates with a high population density), at national levels, internationally and globally.

ENDNOTES

[1] See Pappas et al. (2008). Hippocrates also provided us with the analytical distinction between an endemic disease (ἔνδημος meaning 'native, among the people') and an epidemic disease (ἐπιδήμιος meaning 'upon the people'). The term pandemic occurred later (the late Latin *pandere* means to spread).

[2] See Tognotti (2009) and Hays (2005). Note that Ebola and HIV/AIDS have been classified as 'international epidemics' reflecting the World Health Organization's more restrictive use of the word 'pandemic' during the Swine Flu of 2009, when 'the WHO came under attack from several quarters accused of succumbing to the pressures of the pharmaceutical industry to "fake" a pandemic in order to drive up profits from vaccine production' (Rubin, 2011, p. 13). But see Gilman (2010) for a more nuanced view.

[3] This frequency does not apply during a pandemic because lockdown and social distancing hinder the spread of new viruses as well. Incidentally, some of those measures like washing your hands, no handshakes and high fives, and working from home may stay with us for a long time after the lifting of restrictions, thus reducing the pandemic risk for some time to come (see also Chapter 7).

[4] See Daszak (2012) and O'Callaghan-Gordo and Antó (2020).

[5] Some like Caruso (2020) see a fourth ruin problem emerging with the rise of authoritarianism and (armed) conflicts threatening world peace. See, however, Bloem and Salemi (2020) who find that, so far, COVID-19 has been associated with lower levels of inter-group conflict.

[6] There is a more general lesson and that is that mortality and contagion of future pandemics will be different. Preparation for pandemics cannot rely on the past but needs to take a broader look at different forms and patterns of contagious diseases.

[7] Also, the willingness to pay for the avoidance of pandemics was established to be remarkably high (see Martin and Pindyck, 2019).

[8] The evaluation of the impact of COVID on health care production and health care productivity is complicated by four factors: (*i*) the extent of unpaid overwork that is nowhere reflected in statistics, (*ii*) the reduction of non-COVID care which leads to a cost explosion in terms of QALYs (Quality Adjusted Life Years), because equipment is not used, (*iii*) the enormous improvement in the treatment of a new disease and (*iv*) technological

innovation in diagnosis and treatment over the internet. Compare Gupta Strategists (2020).

To the non-economist these activities may seem unproductive, but the distinction between productive and non-productive is conditioned by time and place. The distinction dates back to Smith (1776) who defined productive labour as activities that enlarge prosperity (growth). Unproductive labour often is essential (e.g. the military, government) but the production cannot be sold (it does not generate further prosperity). Modern management theories still use the same sort of distinction by their focus on value adding activities (for example, Young et al. 2000). Mainstream economics no longer makes this *a priori* distinction anymore although it recognizes the possibility of unproductive activities and value destruction rather than value creation.

PART I

THE PAST

2. Prepared, but not Equipped

With hindsight the larger part of the post Second World War period probably has been an exceptional blessed period in which mankind has not been confronted with significant global disasters. World Wars were avoided, the major economic crisis (the Great Recession) did not develop into a full-blown depression and natural disasters, by and large, remained local in nature (although their frequency increased due to Global Warming). Future generations will undoubtedly observe that the generations that grew up since the 1950s healthwise were extremely lucky.[1] Luck makes lazy and is a disincentive to invest in risk reduction. Our posterity will also wonder how it was possible that humanity ignored the risk of pandemics and did not take the necessary precautions and did not prepare. This lack of investment in prevention, early identification, mitigation and treatment capacities is perhaps best illustrated by the finding of the Commission on a Global Health Risk Framework for the Future (CGHRFF, 2016, p. 23) that

> even countries with highly developed economies and sophisticated health systems have failed to invest in the infrastructure and capabilities necessary to provide essential public health services.

This finding is further substantiated by the 2019 *Survey on pandemic influenza preparedness* organized by the World Health Organization amongst its member states. The survey pointed towards two important areas: (a) Preventing illness in the community (pharmaceutical and non-pharmaceutical interventions) and (b) Status of national pandemic influenza preparedness plans. According to the WHO (2019, p. 37),

> Member States on average scored about 51% for these sections, indicating that almost half of the preparedness capacities identified as being necessary in these areas are not established in countries.

The situation may have been even worse. The global response rate for the survey was only 54%; a very low response rate for a multilateral survey of governments.

15

Even more telling perhaps is that 36% of the High-Income Countries did not respond, including Germany, Russia, Switzerland and the Netherlands. The fact that countries did not respond may offer an indication of the low importance that their governments attached to the occurrence of a pandemic and their preparedness for such an event. The WHO identified that many countries were not equipped to meet an influenza pandemic; Textbox 2.1 provides a chilling account of what should have been done before COVID-19 entered the world.

Textbox 2.1
The priorities for strengthening pandemic influenza preparedness according to WHO (2019, p. 8)

- Updating pandemic influenza preparedness plans and making them publicly available;
- Conducting simulation exercises to test and validate pandemic preparedness plans;
- Establishing mechanisms to secure access to pandemic influenza vaccine during a pandemic and defining regulatory pathways for the emergency use of pandemic influenza vaccine;
- Including and specifying non-pharmaceutical public health measures for pandemic response in preparedness plans;
- Preparing mechanisms to conduct risk communications and community engagement during a pandemic;
- Developing plans to manage excess mortality during a pandemic;
- Establishing standard operational procedures for conducting systematic influenza risk using surveillance data.

Also, the economic profession apparently did not prepare. One reason is that the major financial institutions in their flagship publications did not sufficiently recognize the issue of a pandemic threat. The point is not that they did not pay attention to pandemics, because, for example, relevant all-hazard overviews by the OECD (2011) and World Bank (2014b) covered pandemics in detail and especially the studies underlying reports by these institutions are very informative (for example, Rubin, 2011 and Jonas, 2013). The point is that these studies did not become part and parcel of the risk factors covered in the many economic outlooks that are provided by leading economic institutions. Sands et al. (2016), for example, point out a lack of analyses of the economic impact of pandemics by both global institutions (IMF, OECD, World Bank), regional institutions (the African, Asian and Inter-American Development Banks), as well as private institutions and rating agencies. Sands et al. (2016)

analyse three well-known economic publications regarding fifteen countries that were most severely hit by SARS, MERS, Ebola and Zika distinguishing between the two years before the outbreak and the two years after the outbreak. Figure 2.1 illustrates their main findings for the country reports of the Economic Intelligence Unit and the Article IV Consultations of the IMF.[2]

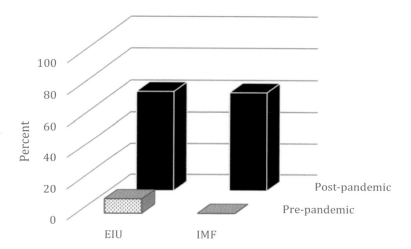

Source: Based on Sands et al. (2016), p. 2444

Figure 2.1 Share of infectious disease terms in total risk terms for Economic Intelligence Unit country reports and IMF Article IV Consultations (2001–2016)

Academia did not fare much better. In a short (4 page) overview article in the *American Economic Review*, Rasul (2020, p. 265) characterized the literature on viral outbreaks as a 'nascent literature'. Figure 2.2 provides a very rough picture of the academic discourse by means of a Google-Scholar-based analysis. The figure reports year by year the number of hits for the combination of the three search terms 'pandemic', 'health' and 'economic'. Combining 'health' and 'pandemic' is necessary to avoid the analysis becoming contaminated by the metaphorical use of pandemic for economic phenomena that spread globally very quickly. The picture is rough because this combination also identifies studies that have these words in the titles of the references so that a cautious interpretation of the reported numbers is in order. What we do find is an *indication* of the literature that pays attention to or connects the economic and health aspects of pandemics. With this caveat in mind, the literature thus identified tends to grow exponentially between 1990 and 2010. This growth may be the consequence of the unprecedented growth in academic studies in general that is stimulated by the Internet and the publish-or-perish culture in the academic world. Against that background, however, the breakdown in the growth rate of the annual number of hits is even more noteworthy. Economists might be inclined to attribute this to the Great Recession that started in 2008 and that may have drawn the energy and attention of the profession, but it is equally probable that the limited impact of the Swine Flu in 2009 drives this trend-break since the slowdown in the number of hits also occurs for the general pandemic hits. Even so, Figure 2.2 drives home the message that academic research on economic aspects of pandemics had passed the apex in the second decade of the 21st century.

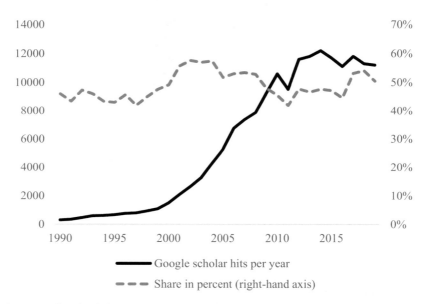

━━━ Google scholar hits per year

━ ━ ━ Share in percent (right-hand axis)

Notes: Google scholar hits are for 'pandemic health economic'. Share is calculated in percent of annual hits for 'pandemic health'

Source: Google scholar date accessed April 30, 2020

Figure 2.2   Attention for economic aspects of pandemics (Annual scholar hits, 1990–2019)

The flattening of the curve, however, was not specific for economics. Flattening also occurred for pandemic-related research in general as the share of economy-related in total pandemic hits remained more or less stable at some fifty percent.

2.1 WHY DID THE WORLD UNDERINVEST?

There are many reasons why countries did not invest sufficiently in pandemic preparedness. Let's consider six main reasons: risk perceptions, the invisibility of preparedness, a distorted view on the preparedness of the advanced economies, competition with other categories of government spending, the assumed policy response regarding an emerging pandemic and the global public good nature of pandemic preparedness.[3]

Firstly, it is difficult to recognize risks properly. Indeed, in general, disaster myopia and the neglect of Black Swans (low frequency events with a very high societal impact) are a general aspect of human behaviour.

> Despite widespread availability of information at the global level on the evidence of climate change, disasters, or the possibility of yet another pandemic, individuals and governments continue to overlook their potential exposure to what they view as rare or distant events, take a parochial view of, hence underestimate, the potential cost of inaction, and fail to insure against them or take preventive action (Ötker-Robe, 2014, p. 11)

On both counts the general public as well as policy makers consider many types of disasters to be unlikely. The downward distortions in the risk perceptions were in this case stimulated because the frequency of pandemics was historically low in the period after the Spanish Flu of 1918 with only two high impact pandemics in the 1950s and 1960s, a low impact pandemic in the 2000s and two major international health crises that did not develop into truly global pandemics (in WHO-speak Ebola and HIV/AIDS are international epidemics and not pandemics). Often these events were perceived as African problems only. Finally, the level and quality of the health sector in the advanced economies was deemed so good that both the public at large and policy makers had difficulty in imagining that they could ever be in a life-threatening situation that the modern medicine men could not cure.[4]

Secondly, the production of the facilities and services that are necessary during a pandemic is essentially intangible and invisible (Ötker-Robe, 2014). This is because the utility of preparation can only be demonstrated during an actual outbreak of sufficient scale. If the disease risk pool does not deliver new dangerous contagious diseases, then the preparations and investments in the health care sector may look like a waste of money *ex post*.[5] If epidemics that could develop into pandemics are contained, then the preparations in other continents look like a waste. Last and not least: the most effective form of production in the pandemics industry is a health crisis averted – so something that does not happen. Non-events are invisible by their very nature.

Thirdly and relatedly, many advanced economies may have been under the impression that they were well prepared for pandemics, because international organizations had pointed out that the problem for lacking preparedness was mainly a problem of the non-OECD countries. An example is the 2017 World Bank study *Disease Control Priorities: Improving Health and Reducing Poverty,* that reports:

> A geographic analysis of preparedness shows that some areas of high spark risk also are the least prepared. Geographic areas with high spark risk from domesticated animals (including China, North America, and Western Europe) have relatively higher levels of preparedness although China lags behind its counterparts. However, geographic areas with high spark risk from wildlife species (including Central and West Africa) have some of the lowest preparedness scores globally, indicating a potentially dangerous overlap of spark risk and spread risk. (Madhav et al., 2017), pp. 320 – 321)

Figure 2.3 illustrates the extent of these perceptions and although the relationship between low income and unpreparedness may not have been causal, the impression was that the advanced economies would not fall victim to a pandemic.[6] Awakening from this illusion was hard. Importantly, before COVID-19, collective action was difficult to organize due to perceived differences in national interests.

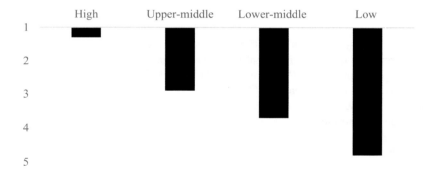

Sources: Based on Madhav et al. (2017), p. 321

Figure 2.3   Mean epidemic preparedness score, by country income group, 2017 (1 = most prepared; 5 = least prepared)

Fourthly, prevention and preparedness always compete with the everyday policy needs that have a direct and visible impact on citizens. Education, employment, housing and environmental policy compete with the preparation for disasters. Competition, moreover, also relates to preparedness for other disasters as well. This is even true within the health care sector itself where clusters of diseases may not only reflect contagious diseases but may also be of a chemical or radio nuclear nature or be related to health security breaches in the food chain. It is especially true if one considers the many components of national security. It is unwise to analyse the preparedness for pandemics in isolation, because we live in a world with many hazards. National security analyses need to be 'all hazard' and cover other disasters, be they natural (such as floods, droughts, hurricanes, earthquakes, sun storms, and so on) or man-made (wars, terrorism, financial crises, cyber-attacks, and so on). In an all-hazard approach, the approach is multi-risk and multidisciplinary, so typically both the medical and the economic profession provide inputs. To some extent the national (health) security analyses that are prepared on a regular basis in most countries helped to create awareness for pandemics, and the majority of such analyses pointed out both the fact that a new pandemic was a certainty with an uncertain timing, and the issue that Intensive Care facilities would not be sufficient to meet the requirements during a pandemic. These findings were reported transparently, but did not draw a lot of attention, neither from the public nor from policymakers, nor from politicians:

> For far too long, our approach to pandemics has been one of panic and neglect: throwing money and resources at the problem when a serious outbreak occurs; then neglecting to fund preparedness when the news headlines move on (International Working Group on Financing Preparedness, 2017, p. *xix*).

Fifthly, and relatedly, the analyses that *inter alia* clearly showed these problems mostly assumed that the solution would be sought in light forms of social distancing and a significant use of triage. Triage is a form of medical rationing that determines access to health care based on the probability for survival after treatment, as is common practice during disasters and mass accidents. Most analysts involved in national security analyses, in other words, assumed that countries would not opt for a complete lockdown and certainly not of long duration in the case of an influenza type of pandemic with comparatively low mortality. The policy-free approach, therefore, with hindsight appears to have underestimated the costs of a pandemic *cum* policy. As such the approach did not underestimate the economic impact of the pandemic, but rather of the policy response to the pandemic as it assumed that countries would not be willing (in the words of Lars Jonung) 'to commit economic hara-kiri'.[7] The point is that the all-hazard approach to national security risks ignored the problems that occurred in the policy process itself.

Sixthly, pandemic preparedness requires collective action. Olson's (1965 and 1982) theory of collective action is still one of the main references on the provision of public goods and the mechanism of cooperation between governments. Olson argued that collective action is plagued by the free rider problem. If the public good (pandemic preparedness by all other countries) is provided, then rational selfish beneficiaries that cannot be excluded from its use have no incentive to share in the costs of its provision. Why pay for something that you will get anyhow? Kindleberger (1986, p.2) pointed out that while domestic public good provision is already difficult, it is even 'a more serious problem in international political and economic relations in the absence of international government'. If more countries decide to deflect and/or to invest less than necessary in pandemic preparedness, then the global public good of pandemic preparedness can turn into a global public bad of an uncontrollable outbreak.

2.2 MACROECONOMIC ANALYSIS AND PREDICTIONS PRE-COVID-19

Before we take a look at the numbers that were published in academic studies and leading policy papers, it is worth noting that a great many different methods have been used since the turn of the Millennium to estimate the potential economic impact of a pandemic. We will restrict our attention, by and large, to macroeconomic studies. The reason to steer clear of the microeconomic studies is that aggregating the microeconomic findings in order to arrive at a total impact for an economy is problematic due to the Fallacy of Composition, a logical flaw that assumes that what is true of a member of a group is true for the group as a whole.[8]

The first approach is historic and backward looking. Typically, historical data have been used to get an idea of the expected costs and frequency of future pandemics. This is a very broad and abstract approach. A more concrete idea of what one can expect from a new pandemic can be derived from the past by looking at specific cases (typically the Big Four: The Spanish Flu, HIV/AIDS, SARS and Ebola). Case studies of previous international epidemics use descriptive statistics and econometrics to establish the impact during episodes of pandemics and international epidemics. In addition to historic data forward looking analyses have been used that are based on economic snapshots of the current (that is pre-pandemic) economy and well-established economic reactions to shocks such as natural and manmade disasters. The methods run from rules of thumb used in National Accounting (that gives useful indications of the order of magnitude of the economic costs) via input output analyses (that provide details for specific industries and intermediate production) to macroeconomic models (that enable analysis of behaviour and general equilibrium effects). Each approach has its specific focus, but in combination these different research strategies also give an idea of the robustness of the findings. The analyses typically have been done at different levels of aggregation, so we have individual country studies, studies related to geographical regions (such as Europe or the European Union), studies that report impact by level of development (for example, the OECD countries *versus* developing countries and emerging markets) and at the world level. Finally, a third dimension of heterogeneity is caused by different assumptions about the severity of the disease and the speed of the pandemic.

In sum, differences in estimation technique, geographical coverage, case specific characteristics and assumptions lead to ranges for the reported economic impacts. These ranges are actually useful because they signal the extent of uncertainty (rather than so-called point estimates that suggest that we are omniscient) and transparently show that economists did not know and do not know the exact costs. The ranges communicate the order of magnitude and give a good indication of what the economic damage of an uncontrolled pandemic could be. We will use the different methodologies that have been applied to assess the impact of pandemics to organize our discussion of the estimates that were available at the outbreak of the COVID-19 pandemic.

Historic frequencies as a basis for expected economic damage
The basic philosophy that stimulates broad based historic research in the frequency and impact of pandemics is solidly grounded in two well-known fields: insurance (Smith, 2017) and homeland security, a.k.a. national security (Givens et al., 2018). Both fields need to know the frequency of an event and its impact. Insurance needs these two variables to calculate the premium; homeland security in order to set priorities for prevention and mitigation against other risk areas, such as natural disasters, Global Warming, terrorism, large scale industrial accidents and so on. Most reports and academic articles start with an overview of literature and a short discussion of cases, but although informative this does not provide aggregate evidence that is needed for decision making. An important issue for policy makers is the frequency with which pandemics occur. Table 1.1 provided a rough indication based on four centuries: for influenza this is 3.8 pandemics per century on average and for other diseases 3.4 pandemics per century yielding a total of 7.2 pandemics per century or once every fourteen years.

Figure 2.4 on the next page by way of illustration shows the binominal distribution of the number of pandemics (the occurrence of a pandemic statistically is a yes – no question). The curves are drawn for the associated probability 3.8/100 = 3.8% for influenza pandemics and 7.2% for all pandemics.[9] For influenza the mode is 3 pandemics per century and the probability that a century provides three or less pandemics is 47% – this also helps to understand the implication that Earth had centuries with relatively few influenza pandemics. Moreover, Figure 2.4 also gives a feeling about the probability that things could be worse. For example, five or more influenza pandemics can be expected in about a third of the centuries.

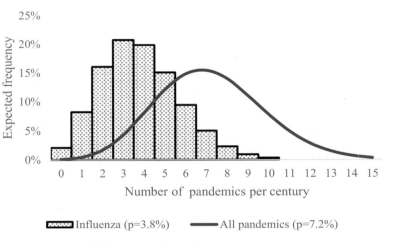

Figure 2.4   Expected frequency of pandemics per century

Not all pandemics are equally harmful. The health and economic impacts depend on the specifics of the disease, including mortality, the average duration of sickness and the speed by which the disease spreads, but also on the underlying economic conditions, such as inflexible structures, high indebtedness and substantial inactivity.

So, researchers also needed to take these uncertainties into account. El Turabi and Saynisch (2016) combine the historic frequency of pandemics and their historic economic impacts in a Monte Carlo experiment and find an average annual loss of $64 billion per year and if added up over a century this amounts to $6.4 trillion per century. Since this is the average value, they also report the 9th decile loss that arrives at double the amount with a ten percent chance of occurring. Fan et al. (2017, 2018) arrive at a higher expected value of about $500 billion per year because they also include a valuation of the lives lost due to the higher mortality of a pandemic. Benchmarking their findings (see Figure 2.5), Fan et al. (2018, p. 313) conclude that their 'estimate of total pandemic related losses (0.6% of Gross National Income (GNI)) falls within the corresponding Intergovernmental Panel on Climate Change's estimates of the costs of Global Warming (0.2–2.0%).'

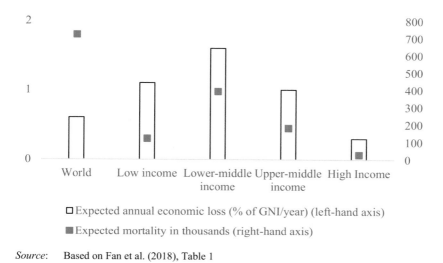

Source: Based on Fan et al. (2018), Table 1

*Figure 2.5   Annual expected economic losses and mortality of influenza-
pandemics*

This approach clarifies that the annual costs of pandemics are roughly comparable to the costs of Global Warming. This finding, however, needs to be interpreted with caution. While the perspective is correct from an investment perspective, the issue with pandemics is that the costs are concentrated in the year of the outbreak. Assuming four pandemics per century the costs of a pandemic outbreak would amount to roughly 25 x 0.6% or 15% of world income per pandemic on average.

Case studies
Four case studies feature in most of the pre-COVID-19 narratives, either because these cases relate to a pandemic with an exceptional global death toll (the Spanish Flu) or because they constitute relatively recent cases that, although small by global standards, locally had a strong impact and could have developed into pandemics.

Spanish Flu
By many considered to be the mother of influenza pandemics, the episode of the Spanish Flu has been investigated a lot but continues to provide puzzles that still need to be solved (Spinney, 2017; Morens and Fauci, 2007) as well as an important warning that a severe and not well understood pandemic could happen again:

Even with modern antiviral and antibacterial drugs, vaccines, and prevention knowledge, the return of a pandemic virus equivalent in pathogenicity to the virus of 1918 would likely kill >100 million people worldwide. A pandemic virus with the (alleged) pathogenic potential of some recent H5N1 outbreaks could cause substantially more deaths (Taubenberger and Morens, 2006, p.18)

The Spanish Flu that was delivered in three waves was exceptional, firstly, because of its mortality – estimates vary from twenty to one hundred million (with a world population of about two billion that amounted to some one to five percent mortality) and, secondly, the speed by which the disease led to death (sometimes a few days after infection). Probably the scariest thing about the Spanish Flu was its ability to reach even the most remote corners of our planet – in a world without mass tourism, global production networks and refugee flows that characterize modern life. The most devastating aspect was that the virus, unlike other influenza pandemics, did not hit older generations but young adults. The economic profession has especially been interested in the 1918 pandemic because it provided a shock to labour supply and this 'natural experiment' offered a testing ground for theories suggesting that the negative labour supply shock would increase wages, a thesis confirmed for the United States (Garrett, 2009), but not for Sweden (Karlsson et al., 2014).[10]

Table 2.1 Annual real GDP growth rates 1918–20

	1918	1919	1920
Western Europe	-4%	-8%	2%
Latin America	4%	3%	6%
North America and Oceania	7%	1%	-1%
Japan	1%	10%	-6%

Source: Maddison (2006)

It has been difficult to find evidence of the macroeconomic impact of the Spanish Flu also because of the confluence with the end of the First World War (Table 2.1). Sharp recessions that could be noted for some countries were deep, but also short-lived (e.g., Dahl et al., 2020 for Denmark). The long run impact of the 1918 influenza pandemics is still an issue for debate, even up to the point that some have uncovered a counterintuitive positive impact (e.g., Brainerd and Siegler, 2003). Bell and Lewis (2005, p. 22) argue that the Spanish Flu 'had very limited macroeconomic effects in relative terms, as the impact on aggregate mortality was relatively small. Even though [it] caused great individual suffering, with some households and communities incurring dramatic economic losses, it was still a small event when viewed globally.'

Ebola

The 2013 outbreak of Ebola that started in Guinea and then spread to Liberia and Sierra Leone did not bring a new and unknown disease. Outbreaks of Ebola have occurred since 1976, but the 2013–2016 outbreak was the largest in four decades. Being concentrated in Africa Ebola does not meet the WHO definition of a pandemic[11], but this case is worth discussing because it is highly instructive to see how a deadly (the average case fatality rate is 50%) and contagious disease can have catastrophic impact and because of its potential to develop into a pandemic (Elmahdawy et al., 2017).

In the midst of the outbreak, the World Bank (2014a) provided a detailed description of the impact, both for key sectors that were hit by the outbreak and for the economy (Figure 2.6). Estimates were also provided in two scenarios for the midterm with an annual reduction of GDP growth by 3.4 percentage points in West Africa over 2014–15 (the worst case scenario would reduce GDP growth in Liberia by 12 percentage points in 2015 and in Sierra Leone by 8.9 percentage points; Figure 2.6).

Huber et al. (2018) provide a systematic review that in addition to peer reviewed material also includes grey literature (reports by governments, international organizations and NGOs). Based on their review they arrive at a cost of 53 billion (2014 USD). One of the most important impacts of the outbreak that is often neglected in assessments of this case consisted of non-Ebola related deaths (a cost of US$ 19 billion) due to closure of facilities, illness and death of health workers and prioritisation of Ebola containment.

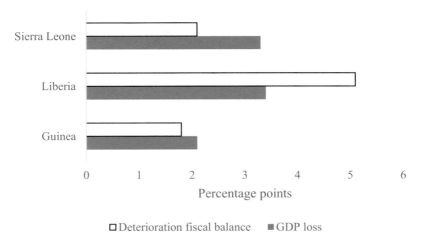

Source: World Bank 2014, pp. 9 – 32 and 56 – 7

Figure 2.6 Estimated economic impacts of Ebola

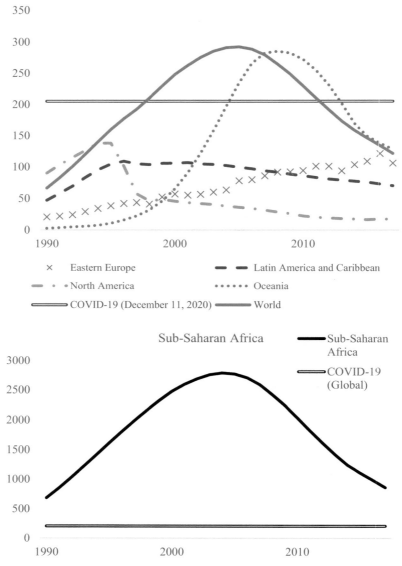

Note: Do not let your eyes trick you: the axis for bottom panel is a tenfold of the top panel

Source: Ourworldindata.org accessed December 11, 2020

*Figure 2.7   HIV/AIDS age-standardized death rate per 1,000,000 people
              (1990–2017)*

HIV/AIDS

Although the World Health Organization has always called HIV/AIDS an 'international epidemic' rather than a pandemic, common sense dictates to see this as a pandemic. It was recognized as such by the national security community when the UN Security Council stated that 'the HIV/AIDS pandemic, if unchecked, may pose a risk to stability and security' (Resolution 1308).

Figure 2.7 shows the annual number of age-standardized deaths and the international spread of the disease. For purpose of reference the COVID-19 death rate at the day this book went to print was added. HIV/AIDS moved less fast globally but did spread across all continents with very significant death rates. The disease has hit Sub-Saharan Africa especially hard and over a long period and therefore a lot of studies are available of the impact of HIV/AIDS on African economies. At the height of the pandemic Dixon et al. (2002) performed a structured review of the macroeconomic impact of the HIV/AIDS pandemic and identified 11 studies.[12] The early studies find a median growth reduction of 0.7% per annum; their most recent study (Dixon et al., 2001) estimates the reduction in long run per capita growth at 2% to 4% per annum.

Some analysts, however, have pointed out that the impact of pandemics on growth works via many channels some of which are negative, but others positive. Analysing 42 Sub-Saharan countries for the years 1990–2013 with a Solow panel model, Maijama'a et al. (2015) make a distinction between HIV which is associated with high levels of illness absenteeism and has a negative impact on productivity and AIDS which is associated with death and through the denominator effect exerts a positive impact on per capita GDP. Young (2005, p. 423 and 460), in the case of South Africa, has found:

> On the one hand, the epidemic is likely to have a detrimental impact on the human capital accumulation of orphaned children. On the other hand, widespread community infection lowers fertility, both directly, through a reduction in the willingness to engage in unprotected sexual activity, and indirectly, by increasing the scarcity of labor and the value of a woman's time. I find that even with the most pessimistic assumptions concerning reductions in educational attainment, the fertility effect dominates. The AIDS epidemic, on net, enhances the future per capita consumption possibilities of the South African economy [...] The AIDS epidemic is a humanitarian disaster of millennial proportions, one that cries for assistance. It is not, however, an economic disaster.

SARS

The outbreak of the Severe Acute Respiratory Syndrome in 2003 offers a particularly interesting case, because predictions of its macroeconomic impact have been analysed retrospectively by Keogh-Brown and Smith (2008). Although the globally expected effects were small in relative terms to the tune of about 0.3% of Gross Planetary Product (about US$100 billion in current prices), the predicted effects according to Lee and McKibben (2004) were significant in Taiwan, Singapore and especially in Hong Kong and China (Figure 2.8).

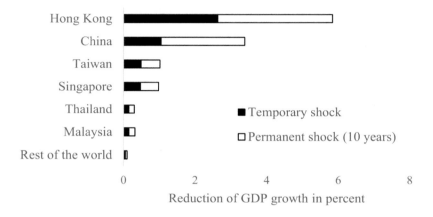

Notes: Reported countries show at least twice the impact on the world economy
            Temporary shocks assume a quick V-shaped recovery
Sources: Lee and McKibben, 2004, Table 4, p. 124

Figure 2.8 Predicted impact of SARS (reduction of GDP growth)

On the lower side of the spectrum, Fan (2003) expected a GDP growth reduction by 0.4 to 1.4 percentage points in Asia (depending on the duration of the outbreak: one versus two quarters) although for Hong Kong and Taiwan the predicted loss in GDP growth was also of comparable size. Keogh-Brown and Smith's (2008) detailed post-mortem uncovered that the impact of the pandemic had been serious in China and Hong Kong and minor in Canada and Singapore but that the catastrophe predicted by models and media had not occurred.

In a sense, however, Keogh-Brown and Smith created a straw man when they focussed on the non-occurrence of economic hardship, because their findings for GDP (for example, reductions for China and Hong Kong by 3 and 4 ¾ percentage points, respectively) are in line with the model predictions:

> Overall, the largest economic impact of SARS was related to overall GDP and investment, and sectors representing hotels and restaurants and tourism. [...] these losses rarely affected more than one quarter's data and often only adversely affected the economy for a single month. It should also be noted that in many cases the losses were succeeded by (often equivalent) gains in

the following month, quarter or year, such that over a year the effect was marginal at best. The impact from SARS, where it occurred, was therefore usually very short-term. (Keogh-Brown and Smith 2008, pp. 113-4)

Overall, the case of SARS is an example of a pandemic that was contained quickly so that its economic impact remained regional and, due to a quick V-shaped recovery, also concentrated in time. SARS did have a strong impact in the national security community raising the awareness that contagious disease could – if unstopped – have significant economic repercussions (Elbe, 2011).

All in all, the case studies provide key insights into pandemics. The parameters of the Spanish Flu have been used in most of the recent pre-COVID-19 studies. Judged against our current understanding of the mortality rates of COVID-19 (Verity et al., 2020), these parameters may presently appear to be over-pessimistic and it should be noted that the impact of a specific mortality pattern also depends on the outbreak's moment in time because of the ageing of the world population as illustrated in Figure 2.9.

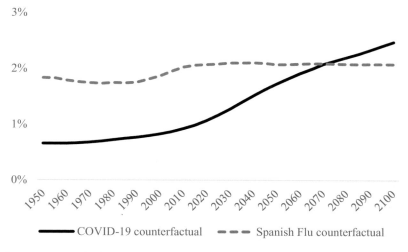

Source: Calculations based on UN DESA (2019) and mortality patterns by age

Figure 2.9   Hypothetical death rate of Spanish Flu and COVID-19

Figure 2.9 shows some crude calculations based on historic data and forecasts for the world population by age. The figure is not a prediction of the final outcome of COVID-19 but simply applies estimates of current mortality as approximated in the first phase of the pandemic to the world population at large. It is a counterfactual, a 'what if' and the 'what if' is applied to both pandemics. The figure illustrates thus the crude answer to the question 'what would have happened if the Spanish Flu/COVID-19 had hit the world in a specific year and the whole world population had become infected'.

The comparison of the counterfactuals shows that the death rate of the Spanish Flu variant is less sensitive for the moment in time that the disease hits Earth and that COVID-19 would have been much less intrusive in the Twentieth Century. Importantly, the death rate would triple in the hypothetical world at the end of our century. The Spanish Flu had an atypical age pattern and COVID-19 is more 'normal' (Cunha, 2004) so Figure 2.9 provides both a piece of the puzzle as to why the other post Second World War influenza pandemics did not trigger such massive policy interventions and a warning that the impact of previous pandemics cannot be extrapolated just like that.[13] Figure 2.9 points out that we can expect that the impact of pandemics in terms of death rate will increase over time. Living longer makes you more vulnerable.

Even so, mortality of HIV/AIDS and Ebola exceed that of the Spanish Flu, but the spread of these diseases (like SARS) remained limited in comparison to the Spanish Flu and therefore their global economic impact was limited. The case studies, however, by highlighting national and regional impacts also provide a first glimpse of the global impact of pandemics and thereby a basis for comparison of the analytical analyses of pandemics that informed policy makers in the years before the outbreak of the Corona virus.

National Accounting (working days and input output analyses)
In contrast to other natural disasters, pandemics do not have a major impact on the capital stock. The virus attacks people that become sick for some time in different degrees and a certain percentage will die. Epidemiological models can be used to establish both the temporary loss of working time (due to sickness) and the permanent loss of labour supply due to the loss of lives.[14] The latter needs to consider several factors, including the age profile of deaths due to the pandemic as well as the extent of unused labour reserves, such as a significant pool of unemployed. If death occurs especially in the working population, such as with the Spanish Flu, the impact is stronger than when death is concentrated in older generations as is more usual for influenza. Likewise, if enough spare capacity exists to hire workers to temporary or permanently replace the infected, then the economic impact will be less severe. National Accounting procedures have a standard approach to correct for working days, for example, to make correction for the occasional February 29 and for different patterns in public holidays that sometimes do and sometimes do not reduce working times (for example, when Christmas is on a Sunday). In European countries a working day lost roughly costs a quarter of a

percentage point of GDP (CPB Netherlands Bureau for Economic Analysis, 2010, van Bergeijk and Mennen 2014) and a working week in which the whole population would not work would thus amount to 1.5 percentage points of GDP loss. Typically, many if not most people continue to work even during a serious flu because they (have to) ignore the disease, for example, if they are low income earners and/or essential workers and/or work in the informal sector.[15]   In the studies of influenza pandemics, roughly a third of the population was assumed to be absent for a three-week period (not only to be sick, but also to care for the sick at home). To this the structural reduction of the working population needs to be added. This is a midterm effect as new generations grow up and help to increase labour supply up to pre-pandemic levels. Elementary calculus then yields a loss of some 2 to 3 percent of GDP for a pandemic that infects roughly half the population with a mortality concentrated in older generations. Admittedly a rough number, but the general picture is more important than a very detailed analysis.[16]

An influential study by the US Congressional Budget Office (2005) adds demand effects to these supply side effects. Demand effects are important because during a pandemic (inter)national travel will endogenously come to a halt and because people fearing contagion will avoid crowds and public places – also when no formal restriction would have been imposed by the government. In all likelihood many people would self-quarantine to a large extent, avoiding non-essential activities with high levels of interaction or even important activities such as going to school. So, these demand effects are important, but they cannot simply be summed with the supply side effects to arrive at a total. If, for example, a quarter of the population is sick then economic activities are reduced by a quarter. Supply would be reduced by a quarter and demand would be reduced by a quarter, but obviously adding up in this example results in a nonsensical halving of activities.

An important aspect of an economy is the interdependence of firms. A final product is a composite where many sectors of an economy are involved. Even for primary products such as raw materials and agricultural products other sectors are necessary, including, for example, logistics, energy and banking (Barrot et al., 2020). These interdependencies are best studied using input output models that show how the products of one sector become inputs for another sector (a further extension Social Accounting Matrices, see Kotsopoulos et al., 2019, is to include all money flows). These interdependencies mean that a pandemic moves as a ripple through the economy with one sector infecting the next (Santos et al., 2009), not only because the work force gets infected but also because the demand and supply of the different actors are linked. Stand-alone applications of input output analysis are easy to do and will be part of applied work in order to get an idea of the first shock.

Macroeconomic models

Macroeconomic modelling comes with a lot of benefits. In comparison to the methods related to National Accounting (working days and input output) that are mechanical and ignore adjustment in the economy, macroeconomic models allow for flexibility, substitution and behaviour. In a business-as-usual economy mechanical methods such as those based on national accounting are appropriate, but during sharp and significant shocks these approaches can at best guesstimate the maximum order of magnitude. Moreover, these methods do not provide insights on how the economy develops over time and thus do not provide an answer when and where policy makers must intervene. In order to understand behaviour, timing and adjustment, we need macroeconomic models.

Essentially, two different approaches to macro modelling exist: traditional large-scale econometric models and Computable General Equilibrium (CGE) models. The macro econometric models are based on historical data and estimated economic relationships and as such use the experience of the past as a basis for the analysis of future developments. These models may be less relevant for two reasons. First, the recent history of most countries does not contain a sufficiently large number of epidemics/pandemics. Second, the Lucas Critique (Lucas, 1976) that structural change and transformation impact on the coefficients that drive the model and thus affect the results may be relevant since the pandemic significantly changes behavioural patterns. CGE models are also vulnerable to this critique but to a lesser extent because they derive relationships from theory and optimizing behaviour and can be calibrated without the enormous data requirements of macro econometric models (although for very detailed CGE models the data requirements are also significant). Since the key parameters of a CGE model are 'deep' (for example, substitution elasticities), structural change is often assumed to be less of a problem and if problems emerge then sensitivity analysis is an accepted method to show the extent of uncertainty. CGE models are less capable of showing the dynamics of an economy and most economists would assume that CGE models provide answers for the long run or perhaps the mid-term (so up to 5 years).

Table 2.2 provides an overview of the findings of macro-modelling exercises that on balance seem to suggest that the costs of a pandemic would be severe but manageable (the study by McKibben and Sidorenko, 2006, with a loss of 12.6% is the exception but this is the only study that assumes mortality in excess of the Spanish Flu). Most studies are policy free although some of the more recent studies also include specific scenarios for school closures and significant (prophylactic) absence from work that increase the costs of the pandemic significantly.

Table 2.2 Impact on GDP of pandemics in macroeconomic models (most severe disease scenario)

Study	Coverage	Method	Loss
McKibben and Sidorenko (2006)	Global	CGE	12.6%
Smith et al. (2011)	UK	CGE	3.7%
Chang et al. (2007)	Taiwan	CGE	2.4%
Keogh-Brown et al. (2010)	UK, France, Belgium and The Netherlands	CGE	1 to 2%
Dixon et al. (2010)	USA	CGE	1.6%
Jonung and Roeger (2006)	EU	Quarterly macro	1.6%
Smith and Keogh-Brown (2013)	Thailand, Uganda and South Africa	CGE	<1%
Verikios et al. (2012)	Australia	CGE	0.6%
McDonald et al. (2008)	EU	CGE	0.5%
Prager et al. (2017)	USA	CGE	0.4%

A problem with modelling pandemics is that the accuracy of the predictions ('potential impacts of a pandemic') cannot be checked due to the infrequent occurrence of the event. Keogh-Brown (2014, p. 180), evaluating predictions and realisations of the 2003 SARS breakout for China and Hong Kong, finds

> Although this is not proof of the accuracy of macroeconomic models, it provides some evidence of their usefulness in the context of communicable disease modeling.

Overlapping generations models (for example, Bell and Gersbach, 2009 and Bairoliya and Imrohoroglu, 2020) are at the boundary of the short and medium term covered by macroeconomic models and the long run which is covered by growth models. Modelling generations is especially relevant for pandemics that hit younger generations because of the impact on human capital formation.

Growth models
Growth models are a completely different class of models, if only because of the possibility of both positive and negative effects. Macroeconomic growth can be decomposed into two components: population growth and the development of productivity. The impact of a pandemic is a reduction of population growth, but what is the impact on productivity? Focussing on the long-term impact economists deployed the neoclassical Solow model that essentially explains how saving, investment, population growth and technology interact in the long run to determine productivity. A key building

block in this model is the process of capital accumulation where a larger capital-to-labour ratio (that is, the capital goods per worker) positively influences labour productivity (that determines per capita income). A pandemic reduces population and thereby increases the capital-to-labour ratio and consequently leads to higher labour productivity. Such positive effects of pandemics have been estimated as we saw when we discussed the cases of the Spanish flu and HIV/AIDS, although it is unclear if this reflects an actual increase in trend growth of productivity or a return to trend only.[17] Moreover, other authors have established insignificant or negative impacts of pandemics using alternative versions of the Solow growth model or studying different periods. It is also important to note that the impact on macroeconomic growth does not need to be positive if productivity increases, because the underlying mechanism is the reduction of labour growth, that is, the other component of macroeconomic growth. If the reduction in the labour force is stronger than the productivity increase, then GDP will decrease.

Growth models are important to understand the long-run impact of pandemics and the academic community clearly has had an increasing interest for growth modelling since the turn of the century especially in the context of endogenous growth theories that focus on the impact of reduced life expectancy on schooling (Young, 2005, Boucekkine et al., 2008; Azomahou et al., 2016), but since they actually abstract from the short run they cannot be used to say something about the adjustment costs due to a pandemic shock.

2.3 THE FORGOTTEN COSTS OF SOCIAL DISTANCING

While looking at different aspects of the economy and using different methodologies, the available studies seem to agree on the stylized economic impact of an influenza pandemic. Firstly, the studies agree that a mild influenza epidemic (that is, with a case fatality rate of about 0.1) would not have a major impact and would probably not be distinguishable against the background of the normal pattern of business cycles.[18] Secondly, a severe influenza pandemic would hurt, but probably not exceed the depth of an average post Second World War recession. Moreover, the long run impact of a typical influenza attack on the supply side would be limited given the age profile of mortality that predominantly is concentrated in people that are (almost) retired. From this perspective pandemics would seem to be quite manageable for economic policy makers who after all have at their disposal a wide range of tools to fight short-term fluctuations with fiscal and monetary policies.

Somehow the economic analysis of pandemics, however, missed the turn that medical policy makers had taken. The epidemiological profession embraced social distancing as the tool to fight pandemics some ten years ago.[19]

Economics missed that change possibly due to the fact that the proposed return to social distancing met strong resistance as it was viewed as impractical, unnecessary and politically infeasible by many (Lipton and Steinhauer, 2020; Eubank et al., 2020, pp. 4–5). The new policy – labelled non-pharmaceutical interventions or NPIs – was, of course, reviewed, updated and published.

> When a novel influenza A virus with pandemic potential emerges, nonpharmaceutical interventions (NPIs) often are the most readily available interventions to help slow transmission of the virus in communities, which is especially important before a pandemic vaccine becomes widely available. NPIs, also known as community mitigation measures, are actions that persons and communities can take to help slow the spread of respiratory virus infections, including seasonal and pandemic influenza viruses. (Qualls et al. 2017, p. 1).

The comprehensiveness of the NPI measures was, however, not well articulated, as illustrated by the following excerpt from the summary that accompanied the 2017 USA Guidelines (Qualls et al., 2017):

> NPIs can be phased in, or layered, on the basis of pandemic severity and local transmission patterns over time. Categories of NPIs include personal protective measures for everyday use (e.g., voluntary home isolation of ill persons, respiratory etiquette, and hand hygiene); personal protective measures reserved for influenza pandemics (e.g., voluntary home quarantine of exposed household members and use of face masks in community settings when ill); community measures aimed at increasing social distancing (e.g., school closures and dismissals, social distancing in workplaces, and postponing or cancelling mass gatherings); and environmental measures (e.g., routine cleaning of frequently touched surfaces).

The document itself, of course, goes into more detail and mentions *in passim* closing of public places and the role and impact of NPIs in non-health care workplace settings, but it is clear from the document that lockdowns are limited to the class of 'Very high severity (very severe to extreme pandemic)' as 'During a very severe or extreme pandemic (similar to the 1918 pandemic), CDC is likely to take an aggressive stance and recommend certain additional NPIs' (Qualls et al., 2017, Table 10). The 2017 US guidelines also incorporated a change from the Pandemic Severity Index towards the new Pandemic Severity Assessment Framework (PSAF); a change that for the first time brought attack and transmission rates at workplaces into the equation.

The change in thinking and the communication about considered policies in the US are exemplary of what happened elsewhere, for example, in the EU *Guide to public health measures to reduce the impact of influenza pandemics in Europe*:

During a pandemic with lesser severe disease and of fewer falling sick, such as those seen in 1957 and 1968, some possible community measures (proactive school closures, home working, etc.), though probably reducing transmission, can be more costly and disruptive than the effects of the pandemic itself. Hence such measures may only have a net benefit if implemented during a severe pandemic, for example one that results in high hospitalisation rates or has a case fatality rate comparable to that of the 1918–19 'Spanish flu'. For these reasons, early assessment of the clinical severity of a pandemic globally and in European settings will be crucial. Though early implementation of measures is logical, application of the more disruptive interventions too early will be costly and may make them hard to sustain. (European Centre for Disease Prevention and Control, 2009, p.2)

Noteworthy is that the evidence-base for the benefits of workplace restrictions and cancellation of public gatherings and international events was lacking (and this was transparently reported), while the estimated costs were judged to be massive. The only available detailed study of economic activity and the spread of viral diseases in an advanced economy (Adda, 2016) concluded that school closure and limitations on domestic transport reduced the speed of spreading influenza, gastroenteritis, chickenpox viruses in France in 1984–2010, but that the measures were not cost efficient (this conclusion, of course, depends on the mortality rates of the investigated viruses).[20] Sometimes Adda finds the interventions to be insignificant and sometimes these are significantly counterproductive. School closures, for example, are associated with *higher* incidence amongst the elderly.

Microeconomic research also aimed at filling the knowledge gap and focussed on costs per QALY (Quality Adjusted Life Year) or DALY (Disability Adjusted Life Year) and provided detailed analyses of pharmaceutical and non-pharmaceutical interventions, often concluding that social distancing was a cost-effective intervention.[21] Importantly, reductions of non-essential work did not support that general conclusion. For example, Milne et al. (2013, p.7) conclude

It is the presence of workforce reduction which causes this to be less cost effective than other strategies; it is costly in terms of productivity lost and not very effective in reducing the attack rate and subsequent mortality rate.

Microeconomic studies do, moreover, not add up to macroeconomic results, due to both the Fallacy of Composition and the lack of macroeconomic feedback loops that may take substantial time to emerge (see Kotsopoulos and Connolly, 2014 and for a different opinion Bloom et al., 2019). For example, a pandemic does not only cause a productivity loss that typically is included in microeconomic research but also reduces the tax base increasing the budget deficit and thereby public debt so that over time interest expenditures increase.

Even so, there was a dearth of empirical knowledge on the costs of non-pharmaceutical interventions. Velasco et al. (2012, p. 6) in their systematic review of the 2009 Asian Flu pandemic provide several explanations for this gap in our knowledge:

> This may be explained by the nature of non-pharmaceutical interventions, for which effectiveness and cost effectiveness are difficult to assess. For instance, it may be unethical to restrict travel or to introduce public communication and advisory measures for only specific population groups. There is a lack of standard protocols for non-pharmaceutical interventions resulting in a large variability of practice across settings. Also, most of the non-pharmaceutical interventions are complex, involving multidimensional aspects and difficulties to control confounding factors. Lastly, in the absence of a pandemic event, it is difficult to introduce radical public measures (e.g., travel restrictions, school closure, and quarantine), which hinder opportunities to generate robust and reliable evidence on effectiveness.

So, why *did* the advanced economies resort to the unprecedented use of non-pharmaceutical interventions. Eubank et al., (2020) note three key aspects of the COVID-19 pandemic that explain this health policy reaction:

- absence of both a vaccine and anti-viral treatments (which means that no pharmaceutical interventions exist so that NPIs are the only possible tool)
- newness of the disease which means that public perceptions create their own dynamic
- the availability of mobile internet access both for communicating, advocating and monitoring social distancing measures

And comparing the earlier controversy about the use of non-pharmaceutical interventions with the general adoption of the measures during the COVID-19 pandemic, they observe:

> A beneficial result of these differences is that social distancing measures whose practicality was suspect then have been widely adopted today even in the absence of—or sometimes in opposition to—official guidance. School closings, community programs to support vulnerable people, state and county policies to require social distancing, as well as business and government support for telecommuting are widespread around the world. (Eubank et al., 2020, pp. 5)

Such issues remained in the health policy and health economics domains and did not reach the macroeconomic debate on the impact of shocks.[22] In this sense economics was unprepared for the COVID-19 pandemic. Economics was not unprepared because pandemic's probability was underestimated or its raw 'policy-free' impact was not understood, but because economists had not realized that a new treatment was being designed and would be administered.

The idea behind social distancing is that the best way to deal with a pandemic is to put a break on the social networks that are the transmitter of contagious diseases (Veldkamp and Fogli, 2020). If we could manage to switch off those social networks for the duration of the period that the infected spread the disease, then the virus could be eliminated. Closing schools, halting non-essential activities (especially in the hospitality sector) and shelter-in-house orders break down the chains along which the virus spreads. In a theoretical world that is the perfect solution; in the real world the solution creates a lot of practical problems that make full implementation impossible so that the virus cannot be eliminated, but only slowed down. Vital activities in key sectors need to continue (for example, food production and retail, energy, public transportation, logistics, health care, emergency services, government). People will break the rules. Self-isolation is not an option for the homeless, in the informal sector and for low-income earners that do not have sufficient savings so that they have to work in order to survive; an issue of concern in developing economies with a large informal sector but also for the working poor in advanced economies. Still, even imperfect social distancing can slow down the speed of a pandemic to some extent.

The economic side effects of this medicine, however, were not transparent to society and policy makers, although elements of NPIs (or endogenous reactions with similar expected behavioural impact) were sometimes included in sensitivity analyses and alternative scenarios. The economic consequences of social distancing had been recognized in policy discussions amongst health care analysts (Lipton and Steinhauer, 2020), but unfortunately never entered the economic domain as an issue of concern. The consequences would become transparent soon after COVID-19 hit the Western market economies.

Key takeaways of Chapter 2

- The world's lacking pandemic preparedness was already identified prior to COVID-19 by international researchers and the WHO.
- Mainstream economics and economic policy makers did not pay (enough) attention to pandemics.
- Pandemics differ in economic and health impact.
- The Spanish Flu, Ebola, HIV/AIDS and SARS have been more threatening in terms of local mortality than COVID-19.
- Parameters from previous pandemics cannot be used to guestimate future pandemics but need to take changing conditions of time and place into account (especially the changing age structure).

- Economic studies have taken different approaches but, by and large, find that modest influenza pandemics have a limited global impact while severe pandemics result in a sharp V-shaped recession.
- The average annual costs of pandemics in the long run are comparable to the costs of Global Warming.
- In contrast, a pandemic event can be extremely costly in the short term.
- Policy papers on epidemiological interventions mentioned lock-downs, workplace closures and (domestic) travel bans as an instrument of last resort.
- Economic studies did not cover the massive use of non-pharmaceutical interventions.

ENDNOTES

[1] Cirillo and Taleb (2020, Table 1), for example, report 17 epidemics and pandemics in the 19th century, only 10 in the 20th century and already 11 in the first two decades of the 21st century.

[2] Sands et al. (2016) also investigate Standard & Poor's sovereign ratings but do not report transparently on what was exactly investigated and therefore S&P is not included in Figure 2.2.

[3] In a broader critique of capitalism Wallace et al. (2020) point out the monetization of health care and the related drive to reduce costs as one of the structural causes of a lack of preparedness.

[4] See Lederberg (1988) on these issues.

[5] The uncertainty of 'time to pandemic' together with time preferences (discount rates) makes traditional investment decisions extra complicated (Drake et al, 2013).

[6] See Oppenheim et al. (2019) for a discussion of the methodology and construction of the indicator and Semenza et al. (2019) for a Europe-focussed assessment of preparedness.

[7] *NRC Handelsblad*, April 17, 2020, p. E6. Jonung is co-author of the 2006 EU report on macroeconomic effects of a pandemic (Jonung and Roeger 2006).

[8] See, e.g., Suijkerbuijk (2018) on this.

[9] The distribution is $X \sim Bin(n,p)$ with $n=100$ because we want to know the occurrence of the phenomenon per century and p is the annual probability of a pandemic based on the data in Table 1.1.

[10] See also Barro et al. (2020) and Correia et al. (2020a,b) for recent reassessments.

[11] A handful of cases reached Spain, the United Kingdom and the United States.

[12]   The search strategy included all major search engines and scientific data bases as well as dedicated websites. Dixon et al. (2002) also contacted key researchers and did a secondary search of the bibliographies of all the identified studies. Their overview therefore probably was exhaustive.

[13]   Compare the extrapolation implicit in MacKellar (2007, p. 445) 'A mild pandemic, or one affecting only the very young and the very old, even if deadly, will attract relatively little attention. On the other hand, a repetition of the 1918–20 W-shaped pattern, even if overall pathogenicity is rather mild, will be a severe event' (an example of Simpson's paradox, see Textbox 5.2). Barro et al. (2020, p. 3) similarly argue that a reasonable upper bound can be derived from the Spanish Flu.

[14]   See Shinde et al. (2020) for an overview of forecasting models and the state of the art. Useful introductions to epidemiological models for economists are Avery et al. (2020) and Niepelt and Gonzalez-Eiras (2020).

[15]   Compare IMF (2020b, p. 5): 'The loss of working days is smaller than the number of days severe containment measures are in place given that essential businesses continue to operate during the shutdown. The duration of containment efforts will vary across countries based on the intensity of the measures.'

[16]   Note that the temporary GDP loss is the supply side effect of a perfect lockdown, since a perfect lockdown reduces mortality.

[17]   Positive impact on firm-level productivity has also been observed in the context of other natural disasters. See, for example, Brata et al. (2018).

[18]   MacKellar (2007, p. 442), for example, concludes that 'the view that the global economy would "shut down" in the event of pandemic influenza [is] speculative in the extreme, and indeed it overlooks the fact that in 1918 the global economy demonstrably did not skid to a halt'.

[19]   See, for example, Council of Economic Advisers (2019). Other study fields also missed the change in medical strategy Helsloot and Quinn (2009), for example, discuss the phases of a pandemic and the reactions of the public without any reference to non-pharmaceutical interventions.

[20]   Building on the standard epidemiological model, Adda (2016) investigates non-pharmaceutical interventions and intervention-like events such as school holidays and public transportation strikes that mimic closures and limitations of public transportation. These events show important heterogeneity with respect to location and timing. Formal closures, of course, have an additional signalling effect, because they are directly linked to an epidemic disease (Buchheim et al. 2020). Interestingly Adda's investigation also deals with the impact of reductions in travelling time due to the construction of high-speed train connections during the research period and the impact of intraregional trade. Both factors are associated with a higher speed of transmission.

[21]   See, however, Madhav et al. (2017, Figures 17.5 and 17.7) who identify the costs of death averted by means of school closure to be a multiple of pharmaceutical interventions and social distancing.

[22]   This is exacerbated by the fact that roughly three quarters of economic evaluation studies appear in the biomedical literature and only one fifth is published in health economics, systems and policy journals (Pitt et al., 2016).

3. The Outbreak of Pandonomics

It is probably true that the COVID-19 pandemic should not be seen as a Black Swan in view of the evidence discussed in the previous Chapter. Academics, policy analysts and policymakers all around the world had recognized the substantial (and increasing) risk of pandemics. Preparations – although still far from sufficient – were underway. Economists understood the risk and knew what to do. The following quote from the June 2018 issue of the IMF's quarterly *Finance & Development* probably gives a fair representation of the situation in the economic profession pre-COVID-19:

> Economic policymakers are accustomed to managing various forms of risk, such as trade imbalances, exchange rate movements, and changes in market interest rates. There are also risks that are not strictly economic in origin. (…) We can think about the economic disruption caused by outbreaks and epidemics along these same lines. As with other forms of risk, the economic risk of health shocks can be managed with policies that reduce their likelihood and that position countries to respond swiftly when they do occur (Bloom et al., 2018, p. 47).

The policy reactions to COVID-19, however, were truly a Black Swan. This is both the case for health policy and for economic policy. Indeed, a complex of unexpected policy activities comprising of initial neglect, followed by very strict lockdowns (sometimes up to the level of curfews) and unprecedented monetary and fiscal policies emerged when the pandemic hit the Western world. With hindsight one can and should question the rationality of these policies: was fear the driver of health authorities and economic policymakers?

I will use the term 'pandonomics' as a shorthand for this multifaceted cluster of policies. The 'onomics' part of this neologism reflects the impact of health policies on the economy as well as the response of economic policymakers to the health policy shock by means of fiscal and monetary policies. The 'pand' part is also chosen on purpose. Indeed, pandonomics spread quicker than COVID-19 to the capitals of developed and emerging economies and one of the theses of this book is that pandonomics enhanced the destruction of the COVID-19 pandemic.

It is therefore vital to understand the development of the pandonomics virus. This Chapter documents the outbreak of one of the costliest policy viruses humanity created in the past century.

World Health Organization

Emergencies preparedness, response

Pneumonia of unknown cause – China

Disease outbreak news
5 January 2020

On 31 December 2019, the WHO China Country Office was informed of cases of pneumonia of unknown etiology (unknown cause) detected in Wuhan City, Hubei Province of China. As of 3 January 2020, a total of 44 patients with pneumonia of unknown etiology have been reported to WHO by the national authorities in China. Of the 44 cases reported, 11 are severely ill, while the remaining 33 patients are in stable condition. According to media reports, the concerned market in Wuhan was closed on 1 January 2020 for environmental sanitation and disinfection.

The causal agent has not yet been identified or confirmed. On 1 January 2020, WHO requested further information from national authorities to assess the risk.

National authorities report that all patients are isolated and receiving treatment in Wuhan medical institutions. The clinical signs and symptoms are mainly fever, with a few patients having difficulty in breathing, and chest radiographs showing invasive lesions of both lungs.

According to the authorities, some patients were operating dealers or vendors in the Huanan Seafood market. Based on the preliminary information from the Chinese investigation team, no evidence of significant human-to-human transmission and no health care worker infections have been reported.

Figure 3.1   WHO Disease Outbreak News, January 5, 2020 (screenshot)

3.1 DEVELOPMENTS ON THE GROUND

The Corona virus was first detected towards the end of December 2019 when a cluster of some forty hospitalized patients with pneumonia of unknown cause was identified in Wuhan, China (a quarter of the patients were severely ill and one had died at that point in time). The World Health Organization reported this event January 5, 2020 (Figure 3.1).[1] To put this announcement further into perspective, it should be recognized that reports of suspected cases of clusters of patients regarding a disease with unknown cause are not often issued. Indeed, Disease Outbreak News items that contain the word 'unknown' occur with a low frequency (only some eight relevant cases since the year 2000 could be identified on the WHO website).[2]

The medical profession was not on uncharted territory. It had prepared for a pandemic for many years. WHO had listed 'disease X' in 2018 as a priority for research and development in emergency contexts: 'Disease X represents the knowledge that a serious international epidemic could be caused by a pathogen currently unknown to cause human disease'.[3] Epidemiological models were in place and running to assess the risks of spreading the disease both within and across borders. The profession was ready, as illustrated by a Global Viruses Network (January 7, 2020) statement:

> In light of the recent pandemics emerging from China including the 2003 outbreak of severe acute respiratory syndrome (SARS), a viral respiratory illness caused by a coronavirus, and the 2013 outbreak of H7N9, an influenza virus that jumped from birds to humans, the Global Viruses Network (GVN) will stand by China and the international organizations at stake. GVN will carefully follow up on the information from China, including the origin of the virus, diagnostic and therapeutic options, and disease progression, among other important findings. GVN's experts stand ready to contribute to the containment of this new, emerging virus through its international network of laboratories and collective knowledge.

Obviously, the models were not perfect and indicated, for example, low levels of risk for European countries that soon would be amongst the most significant victims of the first Quarter of 2020, but at the same time the models were quickly able to indicate the relatively high risk of this virus spreading to the United States.[4] As an economist, I was at the same time, on the one hand, impressed by the amount of modelling analyses that was produced in a short period of time by the epidemiological community, but, on the other hand – as a model builder and model user in my own discipline – also felt quite uncomfortable with the epidemiological models, because the uncertainty regarding the value of key parameters was so large and the impact of interventions was apparently *a priori* unknown. This unease was, moreover, fuelled by the need to re-estimate the models continuously as seems to be common practice (cf. Delamater et al., 2019).[5]

Governments and policy makers were less prepared, or so it seemed. Some observers argued that denial, cognitive dissonance, self-overestimation and incompetence formed a toxic combination. Indeed, policy interventions (if any) were too little and too late.[6] To those observers the Corona virus was especially harsh for countries with underlying political conditions. Others noted that Western policy makers were not on the alert and slow to respond because previous epidemics with pandemic potential had remained, by and large, confined to Africa and Asia and perhaps also (as we saw in the previous Chapter) because many (self) evaluations of preparedness were unrealistically optimistic. It may, however, also have been the case that the Corona virus played tricks with detection, as it was also spreading in the pre-symptomatic phase. Indeed, an initially unrecognized 'patient zero' in France suggests that the virus had already arrived in Europe in December 2019 (Deslandes et al., 2020) but remained unobserved probably due to a veil of seasonal influenza. It is thus very likely that the virus was spreading in many countries before the first cases were reported (the first WHO situation report on COVID-19 was published January 21, 2020 and reports cases in China, Taiwan, Japan, Thailand and South Korea).

For policy makers in February 2020 it probably looked as if the outbreak had been contained (Figure 3.2).[7] When the extent to which the Corona virus had advanced in the G7 countries became apparent in March and early April, policy makers implemented very strict measures at an increasingly large and eventually unprecedented scale.

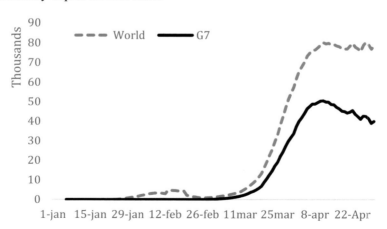

Source: Calculations based on Our world in data, Roser et al. (2020), accessed on May 19, 2020

Figure 3.2 Daily cases (7 day moving average)

These policy measures spread quicker than the virus. Figure 3.3 reports the legal stringency index (a composite index to measure the stringency of government responses to COVID-19) that is constructed by the Oxford COVID-19 Government Response Tracker group and covers measures related to school closure, workplace closure, limitations on public gatherings, closure of public transportation and domestic and international travel and stay-at-home requirements. While some countries, especially in Asia, responded early on, globally government measures only really took off by mid-March.

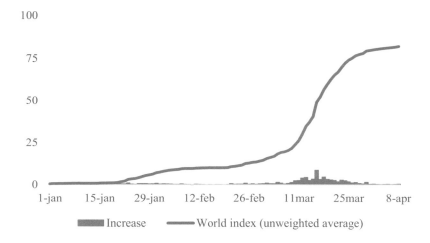

Figure 3.3 Worldwide Coronavirus Government Response

Figure 3.4 focusses on the spread of the three measures which have the strongest impact on economic activity: limitations to international travel, workplace closure and stay at home orders. Other measures such as school closures, cancellation of public events and limitations of gatherings have of course also an impact but are encapsulated by a stay-at-home order. Yet other measures do not have an economic impact (such as wearing masks, a ban on handshakes and intensive handwashing) or are less binary and influenced by cultural perspectives on the meaning and extent of social distancing (Textbox 3.1).

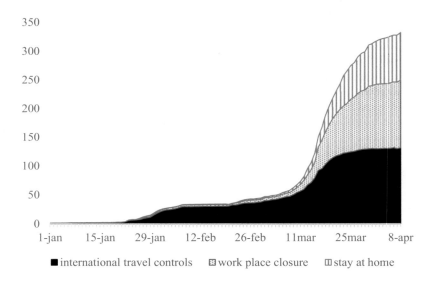

Note: Sum of (country score/maximum score per category)
Source: Calculations based on Hale et al. (2020), accessed May 9, 2020

Figure 3.4 Development of measures with the largest economic impact

These measures did not come out of the blue, of course, as these non-pharmaceutical interventions had been discussed and analysed for quite a long time.

What came as a surprise was the large-scale and almost universal application in the advanced economies for a new influenza virus that seemed to be characterized by a lower morbidity than, for example, Ebola or HIV/AIDS – a morbidity that, moreover, was concentrated in the older generations. It is still unclear what triggered the massive use of non-pharmaceutical interventions, especially in view of their apparent economic fallout: was it the example set by China, existential fear or a devoted belief in the medical profession, or the fact that people in the advanced economies can no longer accept adversary and misery?

Anyhow, the health policy reaction to the virus contaminated the economy. Once the general application and the expected duration of the lockdowns and social distancing measures became clear, a new – economic – virus emerged fuelling a break-out of pessimism and reductions for global growth forecasts.

Textbox 3.1
Social distancing meaning differs in different social settings

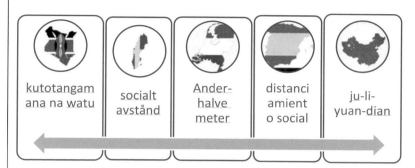

| kutotangam ana na watu | socialt avstånd | Ander-halve meter | distanci amient o social | ju-li-yuan-dian |

It is important to recognize that different forms of social distancing exist. China isolated the province of Wuhan and applied very strict rules, closing everything that was not essential. Even home isolation was not allowed as the infected were relocated to special facilities. In Italy, Spain, France and Belgium the lockdown was also very strict albeit using home isolation, but (economic) activity also came to an almost standstill here. In Sweden and the Netherlands, the authorities to different degrees imposed an 'intelligent lockdown'.[8] In Sweden fewer rules were imposed leaving behaviour more to the realm of personal responsibility. In developing countries often strict adherence to rules and regulations was impossible because isolation threatened livelihood and survival of the marginalized and the poor. The complete alternative to the social distancing model, namely 'no social distancing', although sometimes propagated, for example, by the Brazilian President Bolsonaro, was nowhere practised, with the exception of Antarctica as illustrated by the legal severity index by the end of April 2020.

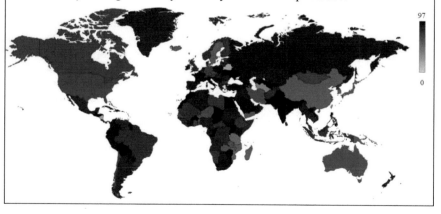

3.2 HOW DID ESTIMATES OF THE IMPACT OF THE COVID-19 PANDEMIC CHANGE?

Early predictions of the impact of the pandemic assumed that the medical problem would remain essentially local in nature. Containment policies in Wuhan, China, were strict and incidental outbreaks in the rest of the world would be limited and could be contained, so was the assumption. The major impact according to the modellers would be due to the closing of an important market both in terms of customers and in terms of suppliers and would propagate via international value chains.

Downward risks of economic projections were identified without specific numbers attached throughout February 2020. An example is the European Commission's *European Economic Forecasts* (winter 2020) that did not yet use the word pandemic, but discussed implications of both a longer lockdown in China as well as a spread of the virus to other parts of the world:

> The outbreak and spread of the '2019-nCoV' coronavirus and its impact on public health, human lives and economic activity has been a source of mounting concern. Questions about the duration and severity of the outbreak raises uncertainty over short-term economic prospects in China and abroad. The baseline assumption is that the outbreak peaks in the first quarter, with relatively limited global spillovers and with a recovery in the following quarters. As such, the duration of the outbreak, and of the containment measures enacted, are a key downside risk. The economic impact on other countries could also be larger and more lasting if infections spread more globally, or if there were spillovers related to global value chain disruptions which are difficult to anticipate. The longer it lasts, the higher the likelihood that the outbreak sparks knock-on effects on economic sentiment and global financing conditions more generally, which add to direct supply-side (e.g. number of work days lost) and demand disruptions (e.g. travel bans, mobility restrictions, shop closures) (European Commission, 2020, p. 12)

The first international organization to publish an estimate of the COVID-19 pandemic was the Organization for Economic Cooperation and Development (OECD) that on March 2, 2020 published an Interim report of the OECD Economic Outlook (OECD 2020a), its biannual flagship publication. The interim report *Coronavirus: The world economy at risk* presented two scenarios. In the base scenario 'contained outbreak' global annual economic growth was expected to reduce by 0.5 percentage points; in the 'domino scenario' that assumed broader contagion the reduction was about 1.4 percentage points.

The OECD was followed swiftly by the United Nations Conference on Trade and Development, with an update of its Trade and Development Report *The Coronavirus Shock: A Story of Another Global Crisis Foretold* that was only slightly more negative.

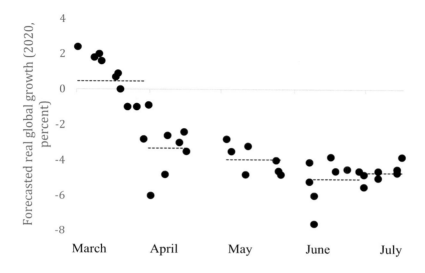

Notes: Base or most likely cases as identified by the forecaster

    - - - Monthly unweighted average

Source: Appendix A3.1

Figure 3.5   Development of forecasts for world GDP growth (March–July 15, 2020)

Global growth in these scenarios stayed in positive territory. By mid-March the expectations for global economic growth crossed the zero axis and from there forecasts started to show a contraction of a size that had not been experienced since the Second World War. This is illustrated in Figure 3.5 that summarizes the forecasts of the international institutions and leading commercial and academic/independent professional forecasters.[9] In April 2020 at the launch of its forecasts the IMF noted:

> Global growth is projected at –3.0 percent in 2020, an outcome far worse than during the 2009 global financial crisis. The growth forecast is marked down by more than 6 percentage points relative to the October 2019 WEO and January 2020 *WEO Update* projections—an extraordinary revision over such a short period of time (IMF, 2020a, p. 5)

Would it be possible to be more pessimistic than the IMF? The OECD June 2020 *Economic Outlook* did not provide one central forecast as usual but two 'equally likely' scenarios: a double-hit scenario of a second wave *cum* lockdown with a global GDP decline of 7.6% in 2020 and protracted stagnation afterwards and a 'single-hit' scenario, with world GDP projected to decline by 6% in a quick and sharp recession that would end 2021 at the pre-crisis level. Be that as it may, the OECD (2020b, p.12) noted that 'in many advanced economies, the equivalent of five years or more of per capita real income growth could be lost'.

Textbox 3.2 Dr Doom on world trade

The WTO's annual trade forecast published in April developed two scenarios: an 'optimistic scenario' in which the volume of world merchandise trade in 2020 would contract by 13%, and a 'pessimistic scenario' with a real contraction by 32%. In May the World Bank's *Global Economic Prospect* forecasted –13.4%. In June the OECD presented two scenarios (–9.5 and –11.4%) in its *OECD Economic Outlook*. The June IMF *World Economic Outlook* downgraded its April forecast to –12.9%.

Figure 3.6 summarizes these forecasts for 2020 world trade by means of the most optimistic and the most pessimistic forecast of the international economic organizations. To these forecasts the monthly World Trade Monitor estimates of the development of world trade have been added that suggest that world trade has been much more resilient than assumed in the flagship publications of the Bretton Woods institutions and the OECD.

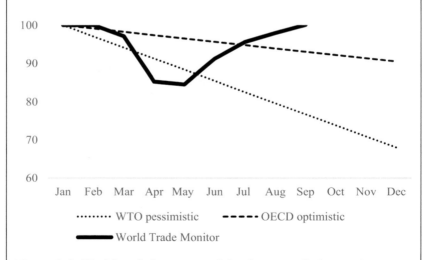

Figure 3.6   World trade forecasts and developments (index numbers, January 2020 =100)

The development of forecasts in the first half of 2020 illustrates very well the unpreparedness and the lack of awareness of the international economic institutions, commercial forecasters and academic institutes that seemed to struggle with the reality of the outburst of comprehensive non-pharmaceutical interventions. The ever increasingly depressing forecasts are a key characteristic of pandonomics and therefore the background against which economic policy makers reacted; at the end of the first half of 2020 pessimism amongst forecasters reached its apex.

3.3 ECONOMIC POLICY RESPONSE

The outbreak of the pandonomics virus contrasts sharply with the medical reaction to the emergence of COVID-19. Whereas the medical profession and health policy officials at least had playbooks and protocols, economists had not prepared for the fallout of an actual pandemic. According to the IMF's Economic Counsellor,

> [a] pandemic scenario had been raised as a possibility in previous economic policy discussions, but none of us had a meaningful sense of what it would look like on the ground and what it would mean for the economy (Gopinath, 2020, p. *v*)

So, in all advanced economies economic policy makers were confronted with a new kind of shock: a shutdown of the economy to different degrees. (The use of the term 'advanced economies' is intentional, because policy makers in Asia and Africa that had experienced epidemics before were, to a large extent, on common ground.) Clearly the spread and intensity of the lockdown at a global scale that we discussed in Section 3.1 is a shock of historic proportions that threatened the viability of firms and the economy at large. The Corona virus infected at first the people – and the medical profession had administered its medicine that would soon prove reasonably effective at containing the pandemic – and now reached their livelihoods, starting most visibly with an initial collapse of the stock exchanges but moving equally fast into the real economy. The non-pharmaceutical intervention forced monetary and fiscal authorities to do four things:

- Central Banks needed to provide liquidity in order to counter an expected credit crunch and to stabilize financial markets.
- Monetary authorities needed to show that they were in control in order to reduce loss-of-confidence effects.
- Governments needed to provide financial support to consumers in shelter and to firms that were closed during lockdown to ensure both

short term survival, to enhance medication compliance and to cushion the fall in effective demand.
- Fiscal authorities needed to show that they were in control in order to moderate loss-of-confidence effects.

Policy makers were not unprepared for this set of economic and financial 'non-pharmaceutical interventions'. Only a decade ago the Great Recession had asked them to react to an unexpected economic meltdown and that experience was still ingrained in their collective memory. It is unclear if the experience with policy making during the Great Recession was an advantage; economists may have been trying to win the previous war, but this is an issue that we will discuss in somewhat more depth in Chapter 5. The point here is that the monetary and fiscal authorities were not paralyzed by the 'Great Lockdown' but acted quickly and almost always in the same direction. The contagion of policies worldwide was a matter of days. In a sense, economic policy makers were thus prepared, but they were in a sense not equipped well because the room for manoeuvring was still limited since many interest rates in the advanced economies were close to zero.

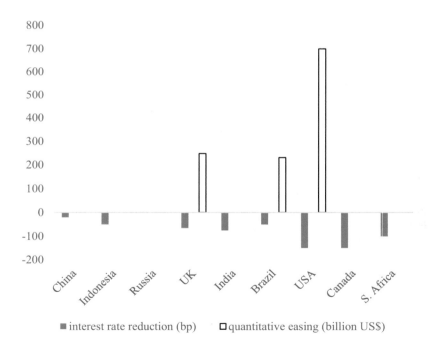

Figure 3.7 The monetary policy bazooka (measures in March 2020)

With that caveat in mind Figure 3.7 summarizes the immediate monetary policy measures announced by the G7 and the BRIICS countries.[10] (Japan and Russia do not appear because their announced policy responses did not relate to the policy interest rate or some form of quantitative easing in the period that we are discussing here, that is, March 2020.) In the Euro area interest rate reduction was not meaningful and therefore it resorted to quantitative easing. The headline figure for the US underestimates the potential size of the monetary response as the Federal Reserve Bank before the end of March switched to *open-ended* quantitative easing.[11] In addition to these highly visible actions Central Banks worked overtime ensuring that credit could be provided by and between financial institutions.[12] All in all, the monetary policy interventions were extraordinary providing a bazooka to main confidence in the financial sector and its institutions.

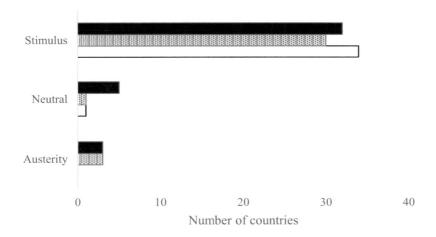

■ Low income   ▣ Emerging markets & middle income   ▢ Advanced economies

Sources: IMF 2020b, Figures 1.9 – 1.11

Figure 3.8 Synchronisation of fiscal policy stance by level of development

Fiscal policy also changed overnight, without precedent and in almost all countries. Figure 3.8 illustrates that in almost ninety percent of the countries the fiscal stance loosened in reaction to the Corona crisis. Income support was quickly provided along a broad spectrum of recipients to ensure survival of households and firms during the lockdown. Differences in the focus of tax relief and income support were relevant. In Europe support to the private sector, by and large, was a means to avoid mass unemployment, and thus one of the few conditions that was imposed by European countries was that firms under stress would not fire people. The United States attached no conditionality at all to private sector support. Difference also occurred regarding the speed of the rolldown and payout depending on the efficiency of the public services involved and the capability of their internet platforms to handle large numbers of new applicants.

It would be fair to also characterize the worldwide fiscal process as an emergency bazooka since it was unfocussed with respect to sectors and actual needs. In a sense the economy was frozen. Non-viable sectors were supported to prevent business failures due to an emergency that was perceived to be immediate and short-term in nature. While it is too early for a proper evaluation, it would also be possible to see the pandonomics approach as a bailout of firms with a business strategy that had relied on credit too much and had not generated sufficient capital to weather the storm of natural and/or manmade disasters. The fiscal bazooka provided breathing space but did not allow for the restructuring of businesses and sectors that had become unavoidable due to the pandemic. Again, the use of large-scale programmes in support of households and firms aimed at cushioning confidence effects and the reduction of effective demand. The fiscal (and monetary) policy bazookas therefore were generally seen as necessary and first best policy responses. Telling is the subtitle of the timely CEPR's e-book on mitigation of the COVID economic crisis: *Act Fast and Do Whatever It Takes* (Baldwin and Weder di Mauro, 2020c).

Spending more while at the same time receiving less taxes because of the lockdown means that the budget deficit increases. This deficit adds to government debt. Figure 3.9 illustrates the numerical consequences by means of the debt-to-GDP ratio, an indicator with proven merits to summarize the sustainability of government policies. This graph takes a longer-term perspective and starts after the Second World War. Reliable estimates for Gross Planetary Product are not available for that point of time and therefore the graph starts by showing the debt level for the G7 countries until around 1980. In the 1950s, 1960s and early 1970s the debt-to-GDP ratio decreases thanks especially to the strong growth record of the Golden Age of Capitalism, but the Oil Crisis of 1973 and the ensuing period of stagflation forced a turning point on that trend. The upward trend is illustrated for the advanced economies and – starting in the year 2000 – confirmed at the world level. Since the turn of the Millennium the Great Recession and the Corona crisis are associated with jumps in the debt-to-GDP ratio both via the nominator (higher deficits) and the denominator (slower growth).

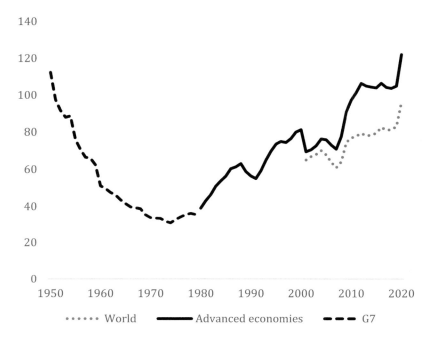

Sources: IMF 2018, data underlying Figure 1.13 and IMF 2020b, Table 1

Figure 3.9 Gross government debt in percent of regional GDP (1950–2020)

For the advanced economies Figure 3.9 clarifies that these countries are now as a group experiencing indebtedness in excess of the debt-to-GDP ratios that were reached because of the war efforts and the massive destruction during the Second World War. This is a worrisome level, also because it is not evident that economic growth can be restored soon. Moreover, quantitative easing may have created a monetary sword of Damocles, although many policy analysts argue that this is not a problem because deflationary risks are more relevant in the current economic environment. Rising unemployment and increasing inequality both within and across countries add to the burden of the COVID-19 pandemic, also health-wise.

Clearly then the room for manoeuvre (that from a historic perspective was limited to start with) has reduced further due to pandonomics. One of the unavoidable consequences is that we need to increase the policy space again. In the end interest rates need to return to normal levels and the debt-to-GDP ratio needs to be kept within reasonable limits. If not, an economic policy response to the next pandemic will be impossible.

3.4 CONTAGION OF THE GLOBAL SOUTH

While COVID-19 emerged in China, the outbreak of pandonomics started in the Global North and the international institutions. The massive use of non-pharmaceutical interventions in the OECD, both in health policy and in economic policy, did not consider the external effects on other countries. But the impact of non-pharmaceutical interventions crosses borders just as easily as the Corona virus and pandonomics impacts on the Global South. The economic risk of the pandemic is not concentrated where the death rate is highest, but in Sub-Saharan Africa and the Least Developed Countries in South Asia (Noy et al., 2020). The economic impact was felt by those countries before the disease reached developing countries and emerging markets, when the epicentre of the COVID-19 pandemic spread to the Americas by the end of May 2020. The transmission mechanisms are multiple[13]:

- **global tourism** stopped overnight (in 2019 the share of tourism in regional GDP had ranged from 6.5% in Sub-Saharan Africa to 13.9% in the Caribbean; see World Travel and Tourism Council, 2020)
- **exports** were under pressure from weaker activity, first in China and then in the advanced economies, with reductions occurring for both the quantities and prices of exported commodities. The price effect has been immediate: primary commodity prices decreased by 5% between March and April 2020; energy exporting countries experienced a peak-to-trough price decrease of 60%.[14] Due to the time that is required to import and export and because of the transportation time, changes in the quantities of international trade are observed with delays, but it is informative that the *CPB World Trade Monitor* (CPB Netherlands Bureau for Economic Analysis, 2020) reported a month-on-month decrease in the exports of developing countries and emerging economies of -6.9% for April 2020.
- **capital flows** went into reverse with some $30 billion in bond portfolios flowing out of emerging market economies while interest rates surged by about 100 basis points and exchange rates weakened substantially (Hördahl and Shim, 2020).
- **remittances** reduced, because most migrants work in urban areas that were in lockdown. World Bank, 2020a, estimates a drop of remittance flows to low- and middle-income countries by 20% or $109 billion in 2020.[15]
- **vaccination and health care programmes** for HIV/AIDS, tuberculosis and malaria and other infectious diseases derails with a catastrophic impact that may be higher than COVID-19's direct impact. A survey, covering 106 countries, found that approximately

three-quarters of current programs were impacted negatively –
threatening an additional indirect death toll of 1,440,000 in
developing countries (Global Fund, 2020).

The point of this incomplete overview is that external effects on the Global
South are directly relevant and that ignorance of the global effects is one of the
pitfalls of pandonomics.[16] The essentially national and sometimes nationalistic
lens through which pandonomic measures are being analysed is a huge
problem for preparations for the next pandemic as we will see in Chapter 7.
Essentially the external effects of the non-pharmaceutical interventions in the
Global South will have a negative economic – and thus health – impact in the
Global South. One of the areas of concern is global poverty. Sumner et al.
(2020a,b) estimate that a five percent reduction in the level of per capita
income would result in a turnaround in global poverty reduction that had been
on a stable downward trend since 1990.

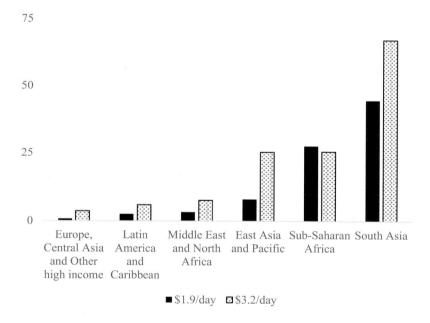

Source: Sumner et al. 2020a, Table A2, p.12

*Figure 3.10 Increase in global poverty (millions) due to a 5% reduction in
income*

Their assumed reduction of per capita income would exceed the World Bank (2020b) base line forecast of –3.6% but would be easily exceeded in the more serious World Bank scenario. Depending on the poverty line, this would amount to 85 to 124 million people falling back into poverty (for poverty lines of $1.9/day and $3.2/day, respectively). Figure 3.10 shows that Asia and Africa would see the largest increases. Poverty impacts on health both via the income effect and because the marginal poor simply do not have the option to practice social distancing as this would endanger their day-to-day survival (Blofield et al., 2020).

These external economic cross border effects of a lockdown in the Global North are often ignored but will have an impact on life expectancy in developing countries (Jetter et al., 2019). Such negative worldwide health effects are not reported on the information leaflet of evaluations of non-pharmaceutical interventions. Examples of studies that use national lenses to evaluate the impact of non-pharmaceutical interventions are Flaxman et al. (2020) who report that in 11 European countries 3.1 million deaths have been averted and Boissay et al. (2020), who in their assessment for the need for integrated epidemic-macroeconomic models as a means to produce a coherent framework for cost benefit analysis of non-pharmaceutical interventions, start from the global viewpoint ('the world has never been required to pay such a high price') but only analyse the issues from a national standpoint. For a global problem, evaluations at the national level miss a very important piece of the puzzle.

3.5 IS PANDONOMICS HERE TO STAY?

The key question at the end of this Chapter is whether the pandonomics virus, just like COVID-19, will be amongst us for the foreseeable future, that it will flare up time and again or that we will have to learn how to live with it. Or would it be possible to create a vaccine? Or even better, could we become immune?

I remain optimistic. Country experiences are sufficiently diverse to learn what works and what does not work to contain the Corona virus and how measures can be taken efficiently, both in terms of reducing suffering of patients and from a socio-economic perspective. When the next wave occurs, we will be prepared *and* better equipped. Non-pharmaceutical interventions will therefore in all likelihood be less draconian and, moreover, it will be possible to keep the interventions geographically limited.

I am also realistic. The national orientation of policy making during a health crisis is very much ingrained in our DNA: like the *Homo neanderthalensis* we want to protect our tribe. I am not sure that humanity's evolution will enable us to focus on the survival of our species rather than that of our countrymen. However, the realization that global problems need global solutions will break through as an unavoidable truth. This is an issue to which economists can make a major contribution: a global cooperative coordinated equilibrium is optimal to all considered alternatives as will also become clear in Chapter 6 when we analyse alternative settings for societal organization.

The macroeconomic policy decisions of the past cannot be undone, and we will have to live with that while trying to crawl back to the monetary and fiscal conditions before the outbreak of pandonomics. In the meantime, we cannot afford to continue with unfocussed support. We need to design future economic non-pharmaceutical interventions more intelligently, helping the economy to restructure so that we can make the transition from a basically ignorant to a pandemic-aware society and from a national to a truly global governance of pandemic outbreaks. Only dynamism and adjustment can help us out of this crisis. Supporting old non-pandemic resistant sectors with outdated business models is a waste of energy and money. So, pandonomics will disappear. The journey towards a pandemic-resistant economy will be taken up in Part III which discusses the future. Now let's leave the past and move to the present.

Key takeaways of Chapter 3

- The health policy and economic policy reactions ('pandonomics') have been the 'Black Swan' of the Corona crisis.
- The development of forecasts for global real economic growth in 2020 from 2% in early March to on average –5% shows the unpreparedness and the lack of awareness of the economic community.
- Monetary and fiscal policies (bazookas) by advanced economies have been massive and unprecedented by any standard and with no apparent exit strategies.
- Important differences in support programs and tax relief between the US and Europe reflect different views on the need to avoid mass unemployment.
- Advanced economies have reached a higher debt-to-GDP ratio than at the end of the Second World War.
- The room for manoeuvre for economic policy has become very limited and finding an economic answer to further lockdowns or other forms of economic fallout from the pandemic will be very difficult.

> - The impact of pandonomics on developing countries and emerging markets has not been considered when policies were implemented.
> - The health impact of pandonomics on the Global South may exceed that of the virus.

ENDNOTES

[1]   This event directly drew global attention from the scientific community. For example, *Science* covered the new emerging disease inter alia voicing the need for transparency: 'Although the city is being praised for quickly sharing information, infectious disease specialists around the world are eager to get more details on the mysterious pathogen and the disease it produces in patients. In today's report, Wuhan officials ruled out influenza, avian flu, and adenovirus; they call the disease a 'viral pneumonia of unknown cause.' (Science, 'Novel human virus? Pneumonia cases linked to seafood market in China stir concern', *Science*, January 3, 2020.

[2]   I have checked the WHO website on the word 'unknown' and after elimination of irrelevant hits, I have found 7 other cases since 2000, namely Afghanistan 2000, Angola and Congo 2007 (possibly related), South Africa and Zambia 2008, Cambodia 2012 and Bangladesh 2017.

[3]   https://www.who.int/activities/prioritizing-diseases-for-research-and-development-in-emergency-contexts, accessed May 10, 2020. It is noteworthy that WHO uses the term 'international epidemic' rather than pandemic.

[4]   See, for example, Boldog et al. (2020), Gardner (2020), Pullano et al. (2020) and Robert Koch Institute (2020).

[5]   One of the unknowns that complicates this process is the actual impact of the estimates on individual behaviour.

[6]   See, for example, Pei et al. (2020).

[7]   For example, during its February 18-19, 2020 meeting in Stockholm, the ECDC Advisory Forum observed that the 'transmission of COVID-19 at the present time in Europe … was low for the next few (2-4) weeks, and this was based on the fact that [normal] influenza would reach its peak in the next few weeks and that COVID-19 transmission would begin sometime afterwards'. Minutes of the Sixtieth meeting of the ECDC Advisory Forum, available at https://www.ecdc.europa.eu/sites/default/files/documents/AF60-Sixtieth-meeting-ECDC-Advisory-Forum-18-19-February-2020.pdf.

[8]   See Jonung (2020) and von Gaudecker et al. (2020) for a discussion.

[9]   Occasional forecasts presented as research output are not included. Examples are the CGE exercise by Maliszewska et al. (2020) and the VAR analysis by Caggiano et al. (2020) that predicts a 14% decline in world output. The major

academic modelling study on the impact of COVID-19 (McKibbin and Fernando, 2020) already appeared in February 2020 and, while not providing a number for the world as a whole, forecasts for countries and regions. One of the scenarios forecasts a median deviation from the baseline by -6.7 percentage points and a global GDP loss of 9.2 billion US dollars.

[10]   The BRIICS are Brazil, Russia, India, Indonesia, China and South Africa.

[11]   Cavallino and De Fiore (2020) estimate that the balance sheets of the Bank of Canada, the Bank of England, the Bank of Japan, the ECB and the US Fed will grow on average by 15–23% of GDP before the end of 2020.

[12]   The IMF maintains a regularly updated overview of these activities at its policy tracker website, see https://www.imf.org/en/Topics/imf-and-covid19/Policy-Responses-to-COVID-19.

[13]   See Djankov and Panizza (2020) for an overview.

[14]   IMF Primary Commodity Prices, available at: https://www.imf.org/en/Research/commodity-prices and accessed June 11, 2020.

[15]   See Murakami, et al. (2020) for a case study on the Philippines, and Berlotta, and Giunti (2019) on the link with health capital investment in Peru.

[16]   See also Noy et al. (2020) who estimate that Sub-Saharan Africa and South and South-East Asia are most at risk of economic losses from the COVID-19 pandemic.

Appendix A3.1 Overview of Forecasts for Global Growth in 2020

Table 3.A.1 lists 39 publicly available forecasts for global growth in 2020 of 19 forecasters (institutions, not individuals). The criteria for inclusion were that the forecaster has a track record of forecasts for the world economy. The forecasters are in the private sector (44%), academic/independent (26%) and international organizations (31%). The trigger for monitoring and collecting this set of forecast data was a blog contribution by Suyker (2020).

Table 3.A.1 Forecast of global growth in percent for the year 2020 (base case or most likely case as indicated by the forecaster (real, annual, percent)

Forecaster	Sector	Global GDP growth	Dated
OECD	IO	2.4	March 2, 2020
UNCTAD	IO	1.8	March 9, 2020
Kiel Institute	A	2.0	March 11, 2020
RaBo Bank	C	1.6	March 12, 2020
IHS Markit	C	0.7	March 18, 2020
RaBo Bank	C	0.9	March 19, 2020
Oxford Economics	A	0.0	March 20, 2020
Goldman Sachs	C	-1.0	March 23, 2020
NIESR	A	-1.0	March 27, 2020
IHS Markit	C	-2.8	March 30, 2020
UNDESA	IO	-0.9	April 1, 2020
Unicredit	C	-6.0	April 2, 2020
WTO	IO	-4.8	April 8, 2020
RaBo Bank	C	-2.6	April 9, 2020
IMF	IO	-3.0	April 14, 2020
S&P Global	C	-2.4	April 16, 2020
NIESR	A	-3.5	April 17, 2020
Oxford Economics	A	-2.8	May 4, 2020
EU	IO	-3.5	May 6, 2020

(continues)

(continued)

Forecaster	Sector	Global GDP growth	Dated
HSBC	C	-4.8	May 12, 2020
UN	IO	-3.2	May 13, 2020
Kiel Institute	A	-4.0	May 25, 2020
Fitch ratings	C	-4.6	May 26, 2020
Oxford Economics	A	-4.8	May 27, 2020
RaBo Bank	C	-4.1	June 8, 2020
World Bank	IO	-5.2	June 8, 2020
OECD	IO	2.4	March 2, 2020
UNCTAD	IO	1.8	March 9, 2020
Kiel Institute	A	2.0	March 11, 2020
RaBo Bank	C	1.6	March 12, 2020
IHS Markit	C	0.7	March 18, 2020
RaBo Bank	C	0.9	March 19, 2020
Oxford Economics	A	0.0	March 20, 2020
Goldman Sachs	C	-1.0	March 23, 2020
NIESR	A	-1.0	March 27, 2020
IHS Markit	C	-2.8	March 30, 2020
UNDESA	IO	-0.9	April 1, 2020
Unicredit	C	-6.0	April 2, 2020
WTO	IO	-4.8	April 8, 2020
RaBo Bank	C	-2.6	April 9, 2020
IMF	IO	-3.0	April 14, 2020
S&P Global	C	-2.4	April 16, 2020
NIESR	A	-3.5	April 17, 2020
Oxford Economics	A	-2.8	May 4, 2020
EU	IO	-3.5	May 6, 2020
HSBC	C	-4.8	May 12, 2020
UN	IO	-3.2	May 13, 2020
Kiel Institute	A	-4.0	May 25, 2020
Fitch ratings	C	-4.6	May 26, 2020
Oxford Economics	A	-4.8	May 27, 2020

(continues)

(*continued*)

Forecaster	Sector	Global GDP growth	Dated
RaBo Bank	C	-4.1	June 8, 2020
World Bank	IO	-5.2	June 8, 2020
OECD	IO	-6.0	June 10, 2020
OECD	IO	-7.6	June 10, 2020
Kiel Institute	A	-3.8	June 17, 2020
Oxford Economics	A	-4.6	June 19, 2020
IMF	IO	-4.9	June 24, 2020
Fitch ratings	C	-4.6	June 29, 2020
Capital Economics	C	-5.5	July 1, 2020
Ifo Institute	A	-4.8	July 1, 2020
EU	IO	-4.6	July 7, 2020
Oxford Economics	A	-5.0	July 7, 2020
Capital Economics	C	-4.7	July 15, 2020
Oxford Economics	A	-4.5	July 15, 2020
S&P Global	C	-3.8	July 15, 2020

Note: A Academic; C Commercial; IO International Organization

PART II

THE PRESENT

4. Flying Blind

The best description of the 'present' that I came across during the COVID-19 pandemic is that of 'data fog'. Reality is always difficult to gauge, but during the early phase of the Corona crisis this was especially difficult. We learned the hard way that the only certainty during a pandemic is uncertainty. Since the virus is new, its characteristics – in particular the speed by which it spreads and its severity and mortality – are unknown (and while we are on a steep learning curve much remains unclear). Therefore, epidemiological modelling is an art rather than a science, and that is true even though its approach is scientific, evidence-based and contains a lot of mathematics. Learning about reality is indeed a very essential part of any attempt at managing an outbreak of a new contagious disease. We start with zero knowledge about the parameters of the epidemiological models although we perfectly understand the mechanisms. These parameters are basic and reflect:

- the ease with which a virus jumps from one person to another;
- the duration of the time between receiving and sending an infection;
- the age profile of the severity of symptoms and health impact and the age profile of the population (and similarly for other potentially relevant demographic characteristics);
- the development of the disease (including the time spent at hospitals in general and Intensive Care units in particular), and eventually
- mortality (and its relationship to patient characteristics).

Of all these parameters only one is known beforehand, that is the age/demographic profile of the population. Of the unknowns, death is the clearest concept and it would seem to be easy to measure, since it can be directly observed and the collection of data on deaths and their medical analysis has a history of several centuries (Sheynin, 1982). Key variables in epidemiology and the social sciences cannot be observed directly. In epidemiology the number of infected persons and 'R naught' or R_0 (the reproduction number that indicates the contagion of an infectious disease) are not observed. These concepts are estimates and often very inaccurate especially when they are recent.

Although it is not generally recognized, key macroeconomic variables, such as the general price level or world production, are essentially unobserved concepts that are estimated with significant margins of error. As with epidemiology new data lead to different assessments for the value of a specific variable but in economics this can happen even for values reported a decade ago. Similarly to the epidemiologic key concepts, the estimates of the rates of economic growth fluctuate significantly, but in contrast historical economic growth rates do not always converge (van Bergeijk, 2017). Measurement in social sciences is further complicated in comparison to the field of medicine because, as argued in a forgotten but still highly relevant classic in economic thinking, 'Nature may hold back information, is always difficult to understand, but it is believed that she does not lie deliberately' (Morgenstern, 1963, p. 17).[1] Pandemic economics has to deal with a double whammy of inaccurate measurement in the development of the disease and the changes in the economy. Let's first look at a very basic pandemic number to uncover what kind of measurement issues are at stake

4.1 DEATH RATES

I want to focus first on the death rate, not because of a negative attitude – I do think that reporting during a pandemic should be much more balanced and provide much more information about recovery – but because death does not give much discussion.[2] For example, for non-symptomatic cases and recovery at home infection is difficult to establish and count, so this is a very complex concept from the perspective of measurement. Since death is such a clear and observable concept, it is easier to see what goes wrong with measurement in general. All the errors that we encounter with death will be relevant for other aspects of the pandemic as well and our findings will act as a warning on the inaccuracy of those medical and social science indicators.

The concept that we want to measure is the number of people that have died due to the disease during a time interval. We want to know both the daily number (because it gives an indication of the speed and spread of the pandemic) and the total number of deaths (because it helps us to establish the deadliness of the disease).

Measurement error per se
Even in normal circumstances and for countries with a well-developed statistical apparatus, the registration of deaths in relation to diseases is inaccurate (Hernandez and Kim, 2019). An example is the registration of European road deaths or, more precisely, as the official definition runs, casualties who, in or after a crash on a public road in which at least one moving

vehicle is involved, die within thirty days from the consequences of that crash, with the exception of suicides. Measurement is strengthened because deadly crashes occur in public space and are reported by the news media on a regular basis. Road deaths are investigated by the legal system (because a road accident is an 'unnatural death' and the body has to be cleared for funeral) and by insurance companies (that have a strong financial incentive to investigate the accidents from the perspective of liability) in addition to the hospital accounts. These statistics are often incomplete with significant underreporting even after the national statistical offices combine different registration systems of hospitals, police and insurers (Derriks and Mak, 2007).[3] The point is that, even for well-defined observable causes of death for which a tested registration system has been in place for more than a decade, measurement error in initially reported fatalities can easily exceed ten percent. During pandemics we can expect the measurement of the death rate to be even less accurate.

Validity

Before we further investigate measurement, it is important to pause and think about the validity of the number of deaths, that is, the degree to which deaths measure what they are supposed to measure. This may seem an odd thing to do for such a clearly defined and observable concept but we need the number of deaths as data from an applied theoretical perspective. We may be like a drunk man who is searching under a streetlight and is asked by a policewoman what he is doing and he answers that he is looking for his keys. When asked where he lost the keys, he answers: 'in the alley'. So, she asks 'why are you looking here?' and he replies 'Because it is dark over there and I can't see anything'. Many scientists look in the light (where there is data) but they need to also look in the dark. So, we need to ask ourselves first why we need the data (this can be based on a theory or policy need) and then see if the death rate is a valid indicator from that theoretical or practical viewpoint.

Crude death rates from a medical and economic perspective do not provide the necessary information. It makes a lot of difference to the medical and economic profession in which age cohort death occurs – even if one values each life lost as equally bad from a philosophical perspective – since a disease that kills the young rather than the old (as the Spanish Flu of 1918 did) has a stronger impact on reproduction and the labour force than the normal flu age pattern (Hsieh et al., 2006).

Death rates are a poor indication for implementing and lifting non-pharmaceutical interventions, because it takes time to die and therefore the death rate does not describe the actual conditions on the ground. The death rate is late to report that the disease is speeding up and it is late to signal that the pandemic is on its return. From a health policy perspective, the false negative that the disease is advancing is more problematic than the false positive that misses the point where the pandemic passes its apex.

Bias

Several forms of bias influence the measurement of death. Bias occurs due to perceptions. A disease that kills the older generation rather than the young (like the 'normal' flu) will be more difficult to observe because of the inherent bias of our expectation that old people die. Indeed, a disease that (also) kills the young, such as HIV/AIDS and Ebola, will be more accurately identified and measured because it is unexpected and because younger age patients have lower rates of underlying diseases that could lead to misclassification. Other forms of bias occur due to non-reporting of cases of illegal immigrants, the homeless and the marginally poor that cannot avoid going to work if they are sick because isolation would threaten their livelihood and that of their families. Religion and anti-vaxxing is associated with a lower willingness to test and the belief systems of religious people and anti-vaxxers may prohibit self-recognition of a disease. During pandemics these non-reported and non-reporting groups are vital because the risk of spreading the disease is great in marginal groups with poor housing conditions and lack of health care access and in faith communities especially if they organize mass gatherings.

Classification errors

Counting the specifics of deaths is thus not easy, but classification is even more difficult. During the COVID-19 pandemic it became increasingly evident that the determination of the cause of death is difficult for those that die untested outside a hospital. One solution has been to look at total mortality of a population against expected mortality based on historical data and patterns. The key assumption that the difference between expectation and realization can be attributed to the virus is reasonable. There are, however, two issues that mean that the total mortality statistics are not a panacea, especially in the early weeks of an outbreak. First, data arrive at the bureau of statistics with a delay and procedures typically are not in place to report the data quicker. Second, the death rate is influenced by behaviour as people may avoid seeking medical help because of fear of infection or an inability to get access to overstressed health care providers. During a lockdown some forms of death may be reduced, such as those related to heavy traffic and polluted air. These deaths are obviously highly relevant, but do not provide (and may even distort) information necessary for establishing the key parameter values of the epidemiological model.

The mobility of people is another complicating factor. People tend to flee from disaster areas, especially during contagious national disasters. This distorts the statistics both for their original location and their new destination.[4]

In the same vein geographical mobility plays havoc for tourism because it does not assign disease and death to the place where the infection occurred – the data is, so to say, exported to the home country of the tourist (see the case of Ischgl that is discussed in more detail in Textbox 7.9). Running away from the disease is likely to give rise to policy relevant distortions in destinations because the incoming flow may be large in relation to the original population; returning home from a holiday distorts the numbers for the source location as the disease on the basis of local data seems to spread slower than it actually did.

Textbox 4.1 Severity and deaths

At the start of the pandemic a popular representation of the severity of diagnosed COVID-19 cases was a pyramid that illustrated that about 80 percent of the cases were mild, 15 percent were severe and 5 percent critical. The death rate in the population was put at between two and three percent. The problem with this diagram is that it suggests that the undiagnosed and unidentified cases were mild and thus that mortality must have logically been lower than reported – the pyramid model, however, is a submarine.

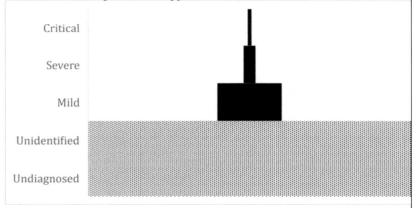

Figure 4.1 Severity of diagnosed cases (submarine model)

It takes a randomly sampled survey for the submarine to submerge. The June 2020 phase two antibody testing survey of New York State showed that 15 percent of the state's population (about 3 million people) had antibodies whereas the confirmed cases amounted to less than 500 thousand.

Sources: https://coronavirus.health.ny.gov/covid-19-testing and
https://www.worldometers.info/coronavirus/country/us/
accessed June 16, 2020

The number of deaths is an important input to both epidemiological and economic evaluations that investigate the spread of the disease, its consequences and the instruments that are used to counter the impact of the pandemic. Obviously, the problems discussed in this section are relevant and cause part of the fog. The first conclusion is that early analyses suffer even more of these problems than later studies that clear at least part of the data fog.[5] The second conclusion is that the measurement problems for other concepts must be even larger because they are influenced by human behaviour. People hide and lie. Infected people that do not test cannot be counted. People avoid, innovate and move on with their daily lives in ways that may not be recognized by traditional statistics. Let's see how this translates into the very basic uncertainty of pandemics.

4.2 EPIDEMIOLOGICAL UNCERTAINTIES

An important variable in the epidemiological models is the basic reproduction number a.k.a. R_0 or 'R naught'. This is the number of new infections that an infected person will generate – new cases per case. The reproduction number has been adopted from population studies where it is the number of offspring; in epidemiology it describes the multiplication of a virus.[6] For growth to occur, R_0 needs to be larger than 1. In population studies reproduction continues in principle ad infinitum; in epidemiology, reproduction comes to a halt when a sufficiently large part of the population has been infected. Neither in population studies nor in epidemiology is R_0 fixed for ever. It will be influenced by conditions of time and place including the probability of meeting relevant persons (a fertile woman and fertile man; an infected and a non-infected person) and average characteristics of the individuals in a population and the environment in which they are living. In epidemiology the characteristics of the virus are also important, in particular the duration of the disease and the period of contamination.

The most important point to note is that this is all unknown during the outbreak of a new disease. Indeed, 'the demographics of the illness, such as variations in the severity of illness, from asymptomatic to those requiring ventilator support, are almost unknown' (Eubank, 2020, p.5). So, finding the value of R_0 is the initial focal point of research. By mid-March a structured review and meta-analysis (Alimohamadi et al., 2020) identified 62 primary studies on the basic reproduction number of which only 23 could be used. The primary studies all related to China and provided midpoint estimates ranging from 1.9 to 6.5. Each and every number in the previous sentences is meaningful.[7] The '62' of the identified studies gives an idea of the information overflow, the '23' of the included primary studies gives an indication of the statistical noise that is produced by the majority of studies and the range '1.9 to 6.5' gives an idea of the imprecision (the meta regression reduced the inexactness to some extent but it was not resolved as the basic reproduction number was estimated to be between 2.8 and 3.8 with a midpoint of 3.4). Model users do not have the luxury of waiting for an empirical evaluation of a sufficiently well-developed body of literature. The leading publication by the Imperial College (Ferguson et al., 2020) used the value that was estimated in Wuhan (2.4) and thus significantly underestimated the speed of contagion.

Why do we see so much disagreement about the basic reproduction number? Think about R_0 as a multiple of the number of days during which an average person can spread the disease and the number of contacts a person has per day with non-infected persons. The former can be observed on the basis of case histories, although this was possibly complicated for COVID by the fact that the incubation period and the infectious period partially overlap (so-called pre-symptomatic transmission).[8] But observing the number of contacts per person per day is impossible and therefore needs to be estimated with models. Those models need to be fed with the share of infected (or proxies such as the hospitalized) in the population over time. These shares are observed inaccurately due to all measurement issues discussed in section 4.1 for the case of deaths but, to a larger extent, because of identification problems and behavioural reactions. Lack of testing capacity, priorities for high-risk categories, self (non) selection of the non-symptomatic infected in combination with the false positives and negatives of testing procedures are more than technicalities.

> While increasing testing capacity increases data quantity, there is no guarantee for increased data quality. ... [A]ggressive pushes for ramped up testing capacity that are tied to decreases in data quality may have a mitigated impact in our ability to estimate quantities of interest such as prevalence and effective reproduction number. (Dempsey, 2020, p. 2)

These measurement errors and biases make epidemiological modelling too optimistic before the apex and too pesimistic after the apex even if testing protocols and procedures are kept constant (Dempsey, 2020). So, monitoring of the developments during a pandemic has technical built-in biases that coincide with (and probably strengthen) human nature and cognitive biases (Baldwin and Weber di Mauro, 2020b; Rajaonah and Zio, 2020) and further complicate the usual measurement errors such as coding errors, inaccuracies, and procedural errors (van Smeden et al., 2020) and data reporting delays (Gutierrez et al., 2020).

At the start of the pandemic measurement and prediction are extra complicated, because only a few data points are available for the calibration of the epidemiologic models.

> Although R_0 is a biological reality, this value is usually estimated with complex mathematical models developed using various sets of assumptions. The interpretation of R_0 estimates derived from different models requires an understanding of the models' structures, inputs, and interactions. Because many researchers using R_0 have not been trained in sophisticated mathematical techniques, R_0 is easily subject to misrepresentation, misinterpretation, and misapplication. (Delamater et al., 2019, p.1)

This uncertainty, of course, neither influences R_0 nor the course of the disease; it only influences the estimates of the speed of transmission and the understanding of future trajectories by the epidemiologists. If a disease spreads quicker than anticipated by a model that is calibrated with too low a value for the basic reproduction number then the modeler is tempted to conclude that a pool of undetected infected 'must' have existed before the arrival of a pandemic and/or that transmission 'must' have been pre-symptomatic. This is how the data fog creates perceptions and influences analytical conclusions that have a bearing on health policy.

Now, R_0 can only be observed in the very beginning of the pandemic. Once the disease spreads the number of infected persons increases and that reduces the probability for a virus to find an uninfected person. So, the actual or effective reproduction number R_t decreases over time first approaching 1 in the expansion phase of the epidemiological cycle and then approaching 0 when the pandemic dies out naturally. Moreover, once an outbreak is recognized it will change behaviour, initially endogenously as people will start to use face covering and avoid public places, public transportation, public gatherings, restaurants, hospitals and so on.[9] Mouth covering occurs spontaneously although not always by many in public both to protect oneself and to protect the society. Some behaviour increases the spread of the disease. For example, people flee from disaster areas bringing the disease from urban hotspots to the rural areas and they become more religious during natural disasters (Bentzen, 2019) while churches became super-spreading locations (Shim et al., 2020).

Later in the pandemic, authorities will try to influence the reproduction number with a broad range of measures including social distancing, travel limitations and stay-at-home orders. We know that these changes in the virus' environment are effective in reducing epidemic spread in general – we know the sign of the impact of the intervention – but we do not know the specific effects of the government interventions – that is, the size and significance. This is both because non-pharmaceutical interventions have never been applied at this level and scale and because they are applied at the same time and on top of the behavioural changes that were happening anyway. Moreover, the Corona virus was a new pathogen and measures that make a lot of sense for one pathogen may make lesser (or no) sense for another one. School closures, for example, would not seem to have helped much in reducing the spread of COVID-19, because children play only a minor role in the spread of the novel Corona virus. Indeed, attempts to predict the impact of the non-pharmaceutical policy interventions will logically fail. Incidentally, this is a lesson that economists have learned the hard way as their belief in large scale macroeconomic modelling was torpedoed in the mid-1970s by the so-called Lucas Critique (Lucas, 1976): policy interventions change the coefficients that drive the models and thus the impact of a policy intervention, according to Lucas, cannot be predicted with a model (see also Chang and Velasco, 2020). This does not mean that diagnosis is not possible – the implication is that the size of the policy impact is unknown.[10]

This uncertainty makes the application of non-pharmaceutical interventions look like trying to steer an oil tanker under fast-changing weather conditions. Steering an oil tanker is always difficult because the ship only reacts very slowly to the steering wheel and the throttle pedal. But under fast-changing conditions steering a steady course requires experience and piloting skills as well as patience and a cool head. Since the pandemic seemed to roll on (although the oil tanker was already reacting to the steering wheel), interventions in European countries were stacked and perhaps maintained for too long in the sense that the marginal contribution of the policy instruments decreased significantly. A smaller less intrusive application would have been possible in a world with perfect knowledge. The knowledge was not available of course, and many would argue that the interventions were optimal in a second-best world.

4.3 ECONOMIC UNCERTAINTIES

Not only the epidemiologists are flying blind in the first phase of the pandemic. Economists have similar problems. They perfectly understand the mechanisms but also have limited knowledge about the parameters of the models when the economy is in the uncharted territory of pandonomics. These parameters are basic and reflect:

- the reaction of labour supply to the risk of contagion
- the reaction of firms to a pandemic crisis
- the reaction of stock markets to a combination of negative news and monetary stimulus
- the reaction of consumers and firms to an increase in government spending and the significant build-up of public debt
- the reaction of prices when transactions come to a halt

- the extent to which perceptions of future development are influenced by panic

Economists are from the start aware of many of the dimensions of policy making during a pandemic. They know, for example, the 'oil tanker on the sea of behavioural change and perceptions' problem by experience (Woodford, 2005) and are used to policy optimization in a second-best world (Bhagwati and Srinivasan, 1969). Economists do, however, have a flawed understanding of what happens during pandemics with non-pharmaceutical interventions. Understanding the psychological impact and the short-term massive application of restrictions on economic activity would seem to be relatively straight forward and unlike pandemics global economic crises have a sufficiently high frequency so that for several parameters historical estimates can be used. Economists know that the multiplier works in reverse during a recession where people stop spending thereby reducing income that further shrinks expenditure and also that perceptions can be self-fulfilling prophesies, for example, when firms reduce investment because they expect that the economy will slow down. The consensus is that such vicious spirals need to be countered by countercyclical fiscal and monetary policies. While economists are thus quite prepared for the problem at hand, they are less aware of the uncertainty and inaccuracy of their measurement tool in the wake of a pandemic. Global downturns are general and hit all sectors of the economy although to different degrees, but the impact of a pandemic is sector specific.

Why is this important? The reason is that economists and society thus do not see that a half empty glass is half full. In the media King Doom reigns also because those hit by the crisis feel the need to express that they are in trouble to mobilize government funds. In contrast those gaining are too busy to talk to the press and may want to hide successful business strategies to competitors. Traditional indicators, moreover, may need reinterpretation.

Old numbers and new realities
Economics is a numbers science: economists are addicted to numbers and calculus and so is the public in general because economic statistics make the headlines all the time. Economic numbers are also in normal circumstances ridden with significant inaccuracies (although this is not generally acknowledged), but during a shock the measurement problems increase manifold. During a lockdown the statistical problems multiply:

> Face to face surveys are being suspended, the in-store collection of prices is no longer possible and surveying businesses is becoming problematic as they temporarily shut down or simply are not able to respond to government questionnaires. On top of these operational [issues] there are abrupt changes in economic behaviour that call for much more timely and frequent

indicators (Committee for the Coordination of Statistical Activities, 2020, p. 82).

It is important to recognize these problems because economic reasoning and advice is so much data driven. So where are the numbers no longer reliable indicators during the outbreak of the pandemic?

First, some variables which had shown high correlations with consumer spending before the pandemic were used to nowcast. Their values during the pandemic, however, did not only decrease due to lower spending but also due to changing spending patterns.[11] If people, for example, reduce the amount of times they visit the supermarket per week (as they are asked to do by the authorities) then big data such as the number of debit card transactions or the number of shop visitors show decreases while we know from direct observation that spending per visit increased, especially during the hoarding episodes at the start of social distancing.[12] Moreover, a lot of shopping was redirected to e-commerce channels, implying significant growth of e-commerce and delivery services that was overlooked by those that looked at traditional indicators for bricks and mortar consumer spending.

Second, a lot of economic activity continued because working from home over the internet became the standard overnight. It is not generally recognized, but in this sense the world economy had effectively become much better prepared for a pandemic over the last decades.[13]

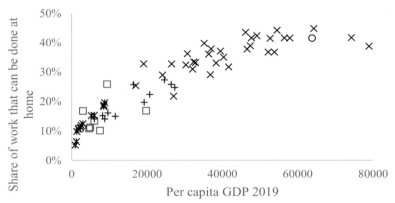

Note: The figure excludes Luxembourg (share 53%; per capita income of $116.000)
Source: Dingel and Neiman, 2020

Figure 4.2 Share of work that can be done at home (2014–18) and income level (2019)

Had the Corona outbreak occurred in 1990 when teleworking, e-learning and e-commerce did not exist, the crunch of economic activity would have been a manifold of what happened in 2020. Figure 4.2 is based on research by Dingel and Neiman (2020) and does not cover all countries (especially the coverage in Asia is not good because China[14] and Japan[15] are not included), but is still informative as it illustrates the range and the association of the teleworking potential and the level of development.[16] The figure suggests for lower middle income countries a median share of teleworking of ten percent that increases to sixteen percent for upper middle income countries. The median for high income countries is a third, with 12 countries having a share in excess of 40%. Note that these are shares in jobs – e-working typically is associated with higher paying jobs so the share in GDP can be expected to be larger.

So, the reality of empty roads, empty shopping malls, empty cinemas, empty lecture halls and empty offices during the COVID-19 pandemic was different from what would have happened had the disease hit us only a quarter of a century ago. Yes, we lived in a ghost town, but we were teleworking, Netflixing, studying, ordering home delivery and visiting web shops. Indeed, very large parts of the economy continued and some even expanded thanks to the Internet revolution, an improvement of economic resilience against pandemic disturbance that was not generally acknowledged.

Third, and relatedly, household production increased significantly during the pandemic.[17] In the European countries that were not in complete lockdown queues emerged at the gates of consumer construction centres and garden centres signalling not only spending thrift but also an imminent increase in household production. Supermarkets did not only serve hoarders of toilet papers but also the higher food segments for those that wanted to make the best of home cooking. Importantly, the value added of household production needs to be imputed because it is not traded in the market, and thus neither generates observable revenue nor commands a price. The registration of home production for the National Accounts uses surveys to find out how much time people are working unpaid to provide the services in their household and the information typically only becomes available after some time.[18] Typically, household production is some twenty percent of GDP in advanced economies (although substantially lower in Asia) and that share is larger for developing countries and emerging markets (Abraham, 2005, Bridgman et al., 2018; see also Figure 4.3). Historically, market services and home production have been close substitutes with a significant structural impact on the economy (Moro et al., 2017) and the directly observed contraction for market services thus would seem to have enforced an increase of home production that is only observed with delay. That increase would, moreover, have been facilitated by the permeability of the (household) working time restriction during lockdown.

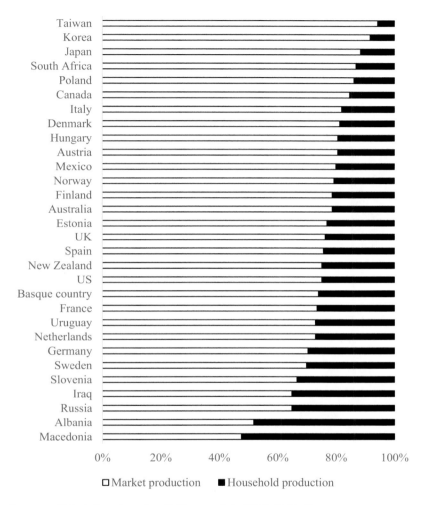

Source: Calculations based on Bridgman et al., 2018, Table 5

Figure 4.3 Share of market versus household value added

Substitution will not have been perfect due to lower levels of productivity in the household sector and for some activities a ready alternative does not exist. Also, household transportation and travel, which is an item of household production, came to a halt so that the movement for this component is in the same direction as market production. The point is that a sizeable part of GDP is not reported in the early estimates of the indicator. Under normal conditions this is not problematic but during lockdowns the fact that we get the information on the substitute with delay means that initial estimates of activity will be biased.

Fourth and at an even more fundamental level, the universal National Accounting model is biased by its natural focus as a regular economic statistic, that is, a focus on what can be readily observed in monetary terms, on what generates income (Bos, 2003). Some activities destroy value during a pandemic, but they get a plus in National Accounting. Superspreading events have been tied to live music performances, Zumba, cruises, meatpacking plants, ski resorts and restaurants (Kupferschmidt, 2020). While seeding and spreading death and disease, in the traditional National Accounting approach they have generated wages and profits and thus created value added. The reason is that the external health effects of the activity are not reflected in market prices. For example, the cruise ship Diamond Princess had 13 deaths and when we use cost of human life estimates that are common in cost benefit analyses (see, for example, Thunström et al., 2020) this would amount to a loss (value destruction) of some 50 to 100 million for this cruise. This loss is not counted in National Accounts that only report the sales minus economic costs, but there is a loss for society. Closing down such activities that destroy value does increase welfare, but this is not reflected in the traditional numbers. From a long-term perspective, the traditional way of observing economic activity missed an essential part of the puzzle and the price tag of that ignorance has only now become crystal clear. Indeed, as observed a decade ago by Daszak (2012, p. 1884):

> [p]andemics are a product of our economic development — they emerge when we domesticate new species, open up new trade routes, build roads into forests, or expand air travel networks. Perhaps these industries should insure themselves against the rare but devastating pandemics their activities can sometimes cause. Additionally, health-impact assessments, already used in many large development projects, could calculate and assess the pandemic risk of a project. The ultimate public health programme would work with, and be funded by, high-risk development projects to develop better clinics, pathogen discovery, and surveillance programmes that prevent pandemics at their source.

The bottom line is that the core of the necessary knowledge is inaccurately measured and highly uncertain both in epidemiology and in pandemic economics. The royal road is to acknowledge this uncertainty and to accept that we make errors. Making errors is not bad; it is the best and possibly the only way we learn.

4.4 LEARNING DURING AN EMERGENCY

At this point it is good to pause and rethink the extraordinary events since January 2020 and to analyse how we form our opinion on what is happening and what we must do. Rethinking how we form these opinions is relevant because disagreement is already developing even with respect to what would seem to be basic and empirical facts. The public debate is hampered by an epidemic spread of wrong or sometimes deliberately false information and the algorithms of social media seem to magnify the problem (Cinelli et al., 2020). An important issue is what role the scientific process of discovery can play in this battlefield of opinions. So, how does science respond, and does it help?

One thing that has become obvious is that the Ivory Towers of academia are not a place to self-isolate from the Corona virus. Research has exploded. Pezzani (2020) reports on the increase in medical articles in the early phase of the COVID-19 pandemic that amounted to an 'unmanageable' 470 articles per month.[19]

> At this point, an obvious question comes to mind: how much can we rely on this literature? Is it really the product of an evidence-based medicine? The first impression is that this pandemic has led to a sort of 'gold rush' where the gold is the publication at the expense of the quality of the paper contents. The final result of this hectic publication rhythm is to increase uncertainties rather than decreasing them as on any given day there is an 'evidence' for a treatment which is likely to be contradicted the day after (Pezzani, 2020, p.2).

This assessment is the more relevant since scientific journals speeded up the publication process without paying due attention to the necessary vetting during peer review (turnaround times halved) and because authors massively resorted to so-called preprint articles to avoid the publication delay associated with peer review (Horbach, 2020). On the one hand, one is, of course, happy with all the energy and enthusiasm but at another level one sees a pandemic of COVID-19 related articles that threaten a breakdown of the scientific publishing process. For example, at the end of July 2020, *Retraction Watch* reported 30 retractions, 3 temporary retractions and 1 expression of concern.[20] Retractions are different from the normal discussion that scientific findings generate – they occur for substandard, blatantly wrong or falsified research output.

In economics the situation was different: the number of analyses started as a ripple in the final week of March, and then increased steeply, but did not become a tsunami. It took economists longer to start working on the economic impact of the COVID-19 pandemic probably because it was not recognized as a significant problem early on but also because economic data collection takes more time. The number of outlets for real time research typically is also more limited in economics – it should, however, be noted that a great many blogs appeared on the topic. So, while there was a steep increase in studies and a big flow of opinions and assessments, the process stayed manageable. Figure 4.4 illustrates the development for economic publications on COVID-19 by means of the working papers of the Centre for Economic Policy Research and the National Bureau of Economic Research (there is some overlap as studies sometimes appear in both series). Focussing on the working papers of the CEPR and NBER is helpful because of the quality checks of these organizations. Early circulation of vetted papers improved significantly with the start of the CEPR's *Covid Economics* series. Quality is, however, not a recipe for agreement and the discourse on the implications of COVID widened considerably over time.

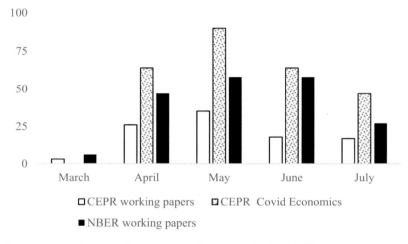

Sources: www.nber.org and www.cepr.org Date accessed July 31, 2020

Figure 4.4 Published studies related to COVID-19 by leading economic research institutes (cumulative)

The response by the economic profession in itself is, of course, encouraging, but also carries a risk. In the publish-or-perish culture of academic economic research, assessments of policy issues emerged that could essentially only cover short-term effects and use preliminary data.[21] Moreover, these early assessments can be problematic in a scientific field that unlike medicine does not have a strong tradition of replication. This could tend to further strengthen the short-term nature of policy making during pandemics, but it may also hinder discovering the correct relationships when more and better data become available later.

To understand why disagreement is a common feature of high-impact low-frequency events, such as the COVID-19 pandemic and the ensuing lockdowns and also to help you to see the uncertainty and weakness of the arguments in the debate on the economics of the pandemic (including my own!), it is helpful to think a bit about how we learn about the real world during a pandemic.[22]

a) Empirical cycle

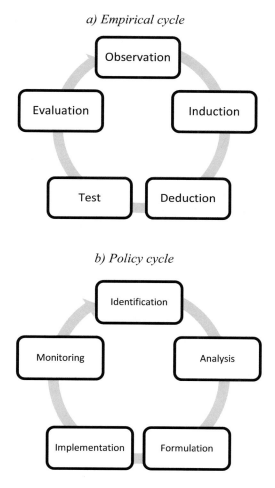

b) Policy cycle

Diagram 4.1 Cycles in the production of knowledge

The process of scientific discovery and the practice of policy development are both generally seen as heuristic and iterative: typically, theory and policy are described as empirical cycles of observation, analysis, proposal, implementation or testing and evaluation (Diagram 4.1).

The idea is that people (even policy makers and scientists) learn from their mistakes (Duffey and Zio, 2020). These iterative cycles are not only relevant when we want to understand how a literature on a specific subject develops over time (the empirical cycle) and how this may differ from the views held by policy makers (the policy cycle), but also to better understand our own position. Like the theories and policies of the past that we may want to challenge from our current perspective, we should be aware that this is most likely to also occur in the future when others evaluate our own thinking.

While these cycles are already relevant in general, they are even more so during periods of crisis, especially if no consensus exists yet on the characteristics of a phenomenon, its causes and its impact. Typically, the development of theory and policy during 'Black Swans', such as a lockdown-induced recession is characterized by uncertainty of developments and outcomes and by constant learning about the actual real-world conditions. Therefore, many hypotheses are formulated by different people about possible 'states of the world'. Contradictions are likely because human nature is such that many people suffer from disaster myopia ('do not see or believe that the event is coming') or cognitive dissonance ('do not understand or are unable to combine the available sets of information') and also because people are willing to accept different levels of certainty in their judgements. As more evidence/information becomes available, probabilities of the different possible states of the world are re-evaluated: the weight of evidence determines perceived probabilities.

Four important characteristics of phases following low-frequency-high-impact socio-economic events should be recognized: the waning policy relevance of knowledge after the fact, the impact of prior beliefs, the possibility of interdependent errors and the circumstance that empirical cycles cannot be run repeatedly.

Diminishing policy relevance after the fact
Firstly, policymaking and scientific discovery take place in an evolving context. After the event policy making will no longer be concerned with the original problem, but the scientific discourse can run on for several decades. An example is the timing of the imposition of the lockdown which is an important issue for policy makers. Epidemiologists do not want to impose measures too early because they want to avoid unnecessary disturbances of daily life and costs and because support for non-pharmaceutical interventions will decrease unless the benefits are clear. Policy making during the period before the lockdown can be enormously helped by applied research.[23] The point is that this was a policy problem only until the economy went into lockdown. The academic debate, however, has only started with a first evaluation for the United States by Pei et al. (2020).[24] Academic debates can

actually rage on centuries after the fact – the new interest in the Black Death is an example (Alfani, 2015; Jedwab et al., 2019, McKinley, 2020; Álvarez Nogal et al., 2020).

The impact of prior beliefs
Secondly, considerable hysteresis exists with respect to the priors, in particular if a well-established theoretical framework and a coherent policy recipe existed before the event or if these priors are formulated strongly by intellectual and political leaders or leading institutions. One of the clearest examples is the idea of asymptomatic spread, documented in much detail by Apuzzo et al., 2020:

> Interviews with doctors and public health officials in more than a dozen countries show that for two crucial months — and in the face of mounting genetic evidence — Western health officials and political leaders played down or denied the risk of symptomless spreading. Leading health agencies including the World Health Organization and the European Center for Disease Prevention and Control provided contradictory and sometimes misleading advice. A crucial public health discussion devolved into a semantic debate over what to call infected people without clear symptoms.

The point is not about whether asymptomatic spread is a relevant reality, but that priors and theoretical beliefs and egos are an important barrier for new ideas. Economics is not safe from this problem as we have seen before. The experiences during the Great Recession have shaped the reactions by policy makers as well as the analytical approach when they opted to provide financial stimulus to all sectors. That approach is appropriate during a global financial crisis where every sector is hit and there is no apparent reason to discriminate. During a pandemic, however, some sectors are necessary, some sectors grow, and some sectors have no real prospects in the world after the first wave unless they adjust. Financial support should thus be focussed on the activities that are necessary, have potential during and after the pandemic and where adjustment on short notice is costly. Adjustment is not only unstoppable and necessary; structural change is also beneficial and necessary (Krueger et al., 2020; Snower, 2020). This implies that governments should rely more on resilience and adjustment, that is, the strength of a market economy. The recent experience of the Great Recession thus may have hindered and biased a clear view on the pandemic economy. Rather than seeing and stressing the positive and hopeful achievement that an economy in lockdown can still produce more than eighty percent of the pre-pandemic level, the view that the worst recession of our lifetime was threatening our livelihood dominated media and economic discussions. The framing of the pandemic was that of the Great Recession ('what did we lose'). It should have been that of the Corona challenge ('what can we still do?').

Endogeneity and causality
Thirdly, scientific advice and policy actions exert impact on the socio-economic system, and this creates a channel by which errors in science and policy are no longer independent. A key example is that the forecasts for the epidemiological curve have a strong impact on individual and aggregate behaviour. The model prediction bites the model assumptions in the tail. During a lockdown individual behaviour will on average be stricter than anticipated by model builders yielding over-prediction; during the opening up phase people will become more relaxed because 'the numbers are good' and thus the model could underpredict.[25]

In economics the impact of sentiment, expectations and self-fulfilling prophesies is well understood; bad news makes the economy worse (Petropoulos Petalas et al., 2017; Algaba et al., 2020). Policy makers, for example, have to steer between the Scylla of announcing a pessimistic forecast transparently to get preparation going and the Charybdis of announcement effects that may impact on consumer and business confidence. Perceptions may be completely different than expected by the policy community. The pre-emptive use of a monetary policy bazooka may be understood by the public at large as if non-reported underlying problems have urged the massive use of quantitative easing making the intervention, to a large extent, counterproductive.

Interrupted empirical cycle
The problems of interruption and abandonment of the empirical cycle that plague the truly 'Black Swan' events at first sight would seem to be less relevant for a pandemic that after all comes in waves. Prediction is an important, influential and often used tool of epidemiology and this in principle opens the possibility to evaluate the errors of the models and theories. It is, however, unlikely that full-scale lockdowns can be applied repeatedly because the economic burden is too large. In the same vein a repetition of the monetary and fiscal bazookas is unlikely. Hence a second wave of pandonomics is unlikely and if it were to occur it would take place in a different context. From a medical perspective the second wave's context is different, because people are prepared and know what to do, testing is expanded if not up to standards, part of the population is immune and the volume of vulnerable people has been reduced by the first wave. From an economic perspective the vulnerability of the system has increased significantly with higher indebtedness, public finance deterioration and monetary policy in unknown territory. In sum, significant hysteresis exists: the first wave of pandonomics persists, so to say, into the future, even after the number of infections has been stonewalled, and a second wave in this sense also constitutes a unique event. This compromises

prediction (one of the key elements of an empirical cycle) and implies a high risk that errors and impressions of initial assessments may not be corrected.

Perhaps imperfections of the empirical and policy cycles can to some extent be remedied by relying on the use of a disaggregated approach. Indeed, performing an analysis that is in principle based on individual country experiences could offer much needed detail, prevent distortions of aggregation and also allow for the analysis of differences in national policies. Indeed, learning from other places is not a bad thing at all and would seem to be also quite possible because the pandemic develops in staggered phases where the heat moves from continent to continent.[26]

In as far as national experiences inform and inspire theoretical analyses this can help to explain why differences of opinion develop and persist. Typically, one expects that perspectives on the pandemic (on characteristics, causes and consequences) depend on the actual geographical, political and socio-economic 'location' of the observer and this may be a reason for the apparent heterogeneity of the interpretations of stylized facts.

4.5 HOW TO LAND SAFELY?

I am not a pilot and I have never flown myself without vision and with inaccurate instruments, but I am a life-long sailor and I know by experience what it means to sail open waters in a quickly emerging dense fog. It is a somewhat frightening experience. You feel lost and have no idea of your whereabouts and the location of other ships. All your senses give blunted information. There are basically two rational solutions for the captain of a ship in murky waters. Firstly, to cast anchor and wait for the fog to clear. Secondly, to change course to the nearest coastline and from there try to reach your destination. Neither solution avoids the risk of collusion (unless every ship drops anchor and waits). Both solutions cause considerable delay. There is thus no recipe for a safe arrival, but anchoring is only possible if the winds and the currents allow and do not deteriorate when you shelter. Likewise, continuing under sail is only possible with an experienced, energetic and alert crew. Mixing strategies does not work and once you have the coastal line in sight you should not try to shortcut and lose visual contact again. You are the captain of the ship – what would you do?

Firstly, it is best practice to acknowledge that the measuring instruments are imprecise. The imprecision needs to be communicated transparently in order to manage expectations, but also to stimulate people looking for alternative perspectives on the same phenomenon. It is best practice to use multiple sources and alternative indicators for the same imprecisely measured phenomenon, to announce beforehand that discrepancies and even contradictions may occur and to provide an interpretation. We knew that total death rates that became available later in time would show bigger numbers than the deaths in hospitals which were reported early on, and we should have prepared data users for the underreporting based on hospital data and the excess mortality that would become apparent when the bureaus of statistics reported based on nationwide death certificates. We should triangulate the data not to arrive at a single truth, but to learn why the data are different (Patton, 2014, p. 316–17). We should also see (emerging) discrepancies as an important indicator of what pandemic problems we are possibly overlooking.

We know that information is lacking and admitting that one does not know is better than pretending that we know exactly where we are during a pandemic. This fundamental uncertainty needs to be communicated transparently in order to manage expectations. There is perhaps some merit in signalling confidence and showing leadership during a crisis but not when this comes at the cost of falsified unrealistic presumptions. Calling COVID-19 a bad flu is bad leadership: it may provide hope but not for the best because it will later turn out to be false. To be ruthlessly honest is the only possible way to avoid losing credibility later and it also incentivizes focused research to fill in the blank spots. The best practice is to work with scenarios and to run multiple forecasts under slightly different assumptions so that intervals rather than point estimates are reported.

Do we need single point estimates?

It is often argued that policy makers prefer a point-estimate and under normal conditions that may provide an explanation for both their dominant use when ranges are more appropriate and the absence of the reporting of measurement errors in official statistics (Manski, 2019). Pandemics are, however, in no way normal. Thus, policymakers need to confront their fundamental uncertainty. What would their world look like? How would they make decisions?

Table 4.1   Hypothetical payoff matrix for a non-pharmaceutical intervention

	Additional death toll	Economic loss	Total monetized loss[*]
NPI is not needed	0	0	0
NPI is insufficient	100	200,000	10,200,000
NPI is adequate	10	400,000	1,400,000
NPI is too large	0	1,000,000	1,000,000

Note: * valued at 100,000 per life

NPI: Non-pharmaceutical intervention

Table 4.1 by way of example offers a hypothetical payoff matrix for a considered non-pharmaceutical intervention. The numbers are made up and they only serve to clarify by example. The story behind the payoff matrix, rather than the numbers in the table, is a representation of reality of decision making under uncertainty. We know that the intervention will work, but it may not be needed; it may be too weak, about right or overachieving. First, if the measure is insufficient an additional death toll occurs. Second, the intervention can be more or less adequate – it does not reduce the death toll to zero, but the outcome is deemed acceptable. Finally, the intervention may be too large from an economic viewpoint. It reduces the death toll to zero (but that result could also have been achieved with a smaller intervention).

If you are only interested in avoiding death then the solution to the problem is equally simple as the case for a policy maker who is only interested in money, but with opposite choices, of course. The economically blind chooses maximum NPI and the money-only man chooses minimum NPI. Policy makers, of course, consider both aspects of the outcome if only because an economic disaster puts pressure on the health care budget and death carries an economic cost as well. Therefore, policy making in Table 4.1 will be based on total monetized loss. There are three rules to solve the problem:

- *Maximax*: this is the decision rule that chooses the maximum of the best possible outcomes, that is, reduces the total monetized loss. It is, so to say, a pure optimist who assumes that the best will happen and decides not to implement the NPI.
- *Maximin*: this is the decision rule that chooses the best one of the worst outcomes. The rule implies that the NPI will be implemented (the worst outcome when an NPI is needed but not applied is 10,200,000 and the worst outcome if an NPI is not needed but applied is 1,400,000). Given the choice between possibly too little or possibly too much intervention, the rule stipulates the choice of an NPI that may be too large
- *Minimax regret*: this is the decision rule that minimizes the maximum regret of choosing the option that is wrong with hindsight. Choosing no intervention while strict intervention is necessary yields a loss of 10,200,000; choosing an intervention that is too large while no intervention is necessary yields a loss of 1,000,000 and is therefore the outcome of minimax regret decision making.

Of course, this is an enormous simplification – if only because in reality all numbers are uncertain, but it helps to see how we decide when we do not have estimates of the probabilities of the imprecisely assessed potential outcomes. Indeed, it explains in an accessible way how the same information set can lead to different decisions depending on personal traits of the decision maker, helping us to understand both some of the basic principles and to see how risk preferences relate to heterogeneity of preferred policies. It is also important to note to what extent different economic valuations of life matter. In the numerical example of Diagram 4.1 the outcome is not influenced by higher valuations of life, for example. Lower values can lead to different outcomes evidently with the already discussed moneyman that implicitly gives life no economic value as the extreme. The point is that in this example it does not matter if we have an exact understanding of that valuation and that the order of magnitude may be a sufficient beacon. This is a more general point. Policy makers and the population at large can handle situations of extreme uncertainty, especially if they understand the underlying processes. It is a comfort that we understand the pandemic processes as that helps us to work on mitigation even if we do not know the exact size of the impact of interventions. Likewise, economists can relate to a well-tested body of knowledge. Their mainstream theories provide a compass that works even under the extreme conditions of COVID-19 as we will see in the next Chapter.

Key takeaways of Chapter 4

- Measurement is difficult during a pandemic, even for 'easy' concepts such as the number of deaths.
- Monitoring of the developments during a pandemic has technical built-in biases that coincide with (and most likely strengthen) human behaviour and cognitive biases.
- Epidemiological models and the basic reproduction number (R_0) are susceptible to measurement error and may provide wrong policy conclusions.
- Economic data are collected with lags that distort the analysis of the impact of the pandemic missing activities that are observed via surveys.
- Framing matters: do not focus on what is lost but on what is achieved.
- Adjustment and substitution reduce the economic impact.
- Strong prior beliefs hinder learning.
- Sentiment, expectations and self-fulfilling prophesies create over and underprediction.
- National experiences inform and inspire theoretical analyses, and this explains why differences of opinion develop and persist.
- It is best practice to acknowledge that the measuring instruments are imprecise.

ENDNOTES

[1] Moreover, 'economic constructs are social constructs. Economic statistics are products or by-products of changing social institutions and relate to changing historical reality. Errors in such data are, therefore, complex and largely unique historical phenomena' (Kuznets, 1950 , p. 577).

[2] Not using a light-hearted subject for a discussion on how statistics are produced runs counter to the advice of Hendricks (2019). I came across his plea in the midst of a pandemic, when fatality rate junkies could choose between the eight o'clock news, talk shows, our world in data and the new worldometer.

[3] Even if registration was exhaustive (as many authorities in the survey by Derriks and Mak, 2007, erroneously reported), some grey areas exist such as the determination of suicide and murder by car or undetected causes of death or unconsciousness just before the traffic accident. The thirty-day limitation is practical but not logical.

[4] About 5% of New Yorkers left the city following the closure of schools. Among top income earners the rate was 30%: 'The Richest Neighborhoods Emptied Out Most as Coronavirus Hit New York City', *New York Times*, May 15, 2020.

[5] It may take decades to revise pandemic data, see, for example, Johnson and Mueller (2002) on the Spanish Flu and the jury is still out.

[6] The approach has also applications in other fields. Cinelli et al. (2020), for example, estimate R_0 for reliable and unreliable COVID-19 information on social media (Twitter, Instagram, YouTube, Reddit and Gab).

[7] Also, the fact that all studies pertain to China and cannot *a priori* be generalized to other societies, climate zones and demographics is relevant.

[8] Compare Eubank (2020, p. 5): 'To be sure, calibration has been hampered by the lack of testing, especially our poor understanding of the prevalence of asymptomatic infection'.

[9] An example is the 30% reduction of outpatient hospital visits during the SARS outbreak in Taiwan (Bennett et al., 2015).

[10] See also van Bergeijk and Berk (2001) for a critical discussion of the Lucas Critique and an example that it is possible to estimate meaningful econometric models that continued to work during significant changes in regimes (*in casu* EMU). So, econometric analysis per se is not inappropriate, even regarding seemingly unique events such as the COVID-19 pandemic.

[11] See Castle et al. (2009) for a discussion of nowcasting problems and solutions in the wake of the Great Recession. Nowcasting problems due to sharp behavioural changes may also be relevant for often used indicators such as electricity use (Cicala, 2020) and prices and transaction data because consumer baskets change significantly (Seiler, 2020).

[12] See Baker et al. (2020) on consumption patterns before and during lockdowns.

13   See also Wei (2020) for a similar conclusion. However, Noy et al. (2020, p. 11) argue that 'the advent of social media, and loss of trust in traditional sources of information (especially the "old" media and government) are all likely to have amplified the economic losses, by creating additional vulnerabilities, and amplifying behavioural responses.'

14   China was very effective in moving workers to teleworking with half the respondents working from home (Belot et al., 2020).

15   Okubo (2020) estimates that teleworking in Japan reached a share of 17% during the COVID-19 pandemic – that is less than half the EU average.

16   See Saltiel (2020) for an assessment for ten developing countries and emerging markets who finds ranges from 6% in Ghana to 23% in Junnan (China).

17   Production was also influenced by activities that blur the role of consumer and producer via platforms such as Airbnb and Uber, but these activities are properly registered as business activity and reported via the platforms themselves so that this is not a source of observational disturbance.

18   Moreover, surveys may be more biased during pandemics with lower response rates, self-selection and stronger expressions of sentiment (Pohlman and Reynolds, 2020).

19   The situation is probably worse. The World Health Organization reportedly has to review 500 new papers a day, 'W.H.O. to Review Evidence of Airborne Transmission of Coronavirus', *New York Times*, July 7, 2020.

20   http://retractiondatabase.org date accessed July 31, 2020.

21   Of course there is also a lot of repackaging going on where pre-COVID findings are – with a little twist – made to bear on the pandemic. This is more than marketing: while no new knowledge is produced, it provides a new application for existing knowledge and is thus rightly recognized as novel.

22   A key question for empirical researchers is, of course, whether anything can be said at all. It may be the case that structural change presently is so far-reaching that econometric analysis (based as it is on past experiences) cannot be used to analyse and/or predict the impact of key economic events. This is especially true for the significant changes in economic relationships and policies during and after lockdown.

23   See, for example, Eichenbaum et al. (2020), Ng (2020) and Wells et al. (2020).

24   See for similar 'what-if the authorities had acted earlier or differently' studies Chernozhukov et al. (2020), Cho (2020) and Berlemann and Haustein (2020).

25   It is seldomly observed during a pandemic: the only 'good number' is zero.

26   Importantly, while the disaggregated approach clearly has merit, an important logical problem with this approach should be recognized: it may be vulnerable to the Fallacy of Composition. Perhaps the best example is the (non) representation of Western Europe in reports of COVID-19 cases and fatalities. Reporting typically focused on individual countries which would not seem to make sense for a borderless and strongly interlinked continent.

5. Reliable Tools

The Corona crisis increased social cohesion in many countries: an external and invisible threat and the shared misery created a feeling of togetherness. Unexpectedly, the tribe of economists also showed a lot of unity, especially regarding the macroeconomic diagnosis and the policy advice. There were, of course, differing views at the time, but, by and large, Dr Doom reigned over economic analysis in the first two Quarters of 2020: the pandemic was a significant negative shock of a size not seen since the era of death and destruction of the World Wars and the Spanish Flu. Accommodating and supportive government responses were necessary, both regarding fiscal policy and monetary policy, in order to both cushion the fallout of the lockdown measures and to prevent short-term damage from becoming permanent. If ever a mainstream existed in economics, it was during the first half of 2020. (Neo and Post) Keynesians, (Neo) Marxists, Evolutionary economists, Monetarists and (Neo) Classical economists at least temporarily seemed to have buried differences because the short-term advice did not depend on the school of economic thought. Of course, some of the usual 'greatly exaggerated reports' on the Death of Capitalism appeared, but it was difficult to find the kind of disagreement that is common amongst economists in times of crisis. The reason for the apparent agreement may have been that economists were in shock, but more likely is that the tools being used to analyse the Corona crisis all belong to Economics 101.

This Chapter provides an overview of how the core economic apparatus could be and actually has been used to shed light on the economy during the first phase of the pandemic. The message is that we do not need new theories to understand pandemic economics – we need to know which theories are useful. The Chapter is organized a bit differently in that we will start with the supply side and the long-run before we move towards the demand side of the economy and the policy responses that are typically the starting point for Economics 101. The reason for the detour is that a pandemic is essentially a supply shock. Demand aspects only become relevant because of policy and confidence reactions to that shock – hence the analytical precedence of the supply side. Next, we take a look at international economics.

Although the analytical tools are thus basic, logical flaws could be observed in applications. I have added text boxes in this Chapter with short discussions on the faulty arguments. These digressions are the icing on the cake; they should not distract from the fact that economists, by and large, agree on what – in economic terms – happened when the Corona crisis emerged and unfolded. If economic theories are not your cup of tea, I recommend a shortcut via the textboxes and the key takeaways at the end of the Chapter.

5.1 THE SUPPLY SIDE AND THE LONG-RUN

Let's first recap the basics of macroeconomic supply before applying these basics to a pandemic. Supply of goods and services involves combining labour and capital. People work with tools, machines and infrastructures. They can use combinations of production factors: machines can replace workers to some extent; more employees can sometimes achieve similar production as could be produced with more capital. In the long-run, the quality and quantity of production factors determine maximum supply. Firms decide on the best mix of production factors based on their prices and their contributions to production. For instance, if wages increase, firms will invest in labour-saving technologies reducing the amount of labour and increasing the amount of capital used in production. Typically, substitution implies reallocation of factors of production and that requires time. So often in the short term the possibilities for substitution are limited. This means that we do not only need to consider the long-run maximum but also short-run supply.

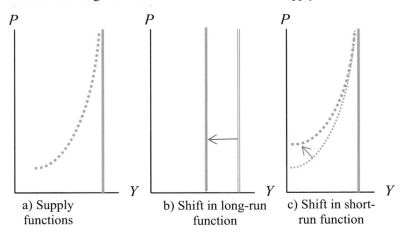

Diagram 5.1 Long-run and short-run macroeconomic supply functions

Panel (a) of Diagram 5.1 illustrates short-run and long-run supply. On the vertical axis is the general price level *P* and horizontally production *Y*. Under normal conditions the short-run macro-economic supply curve (the dotted line in Diagram 5.1) slopes upward, because at lower prices production will be reduced, while higher prices will induce firms to hire more labour and stretch production and move towards long-run supply. It is, however, difficult to maintain such high levels of production so the price level increases more steeply when production gets closer to its maximum, that is, the vertical line in Diagram 5.1 that represents long-run supply.

Textbox 5.1 It's not a war economy

Economists have used the metaphor of war a lot during the Corona crisis. They described the lockdown as a war-like shock, they spoke about pandemic war and they used the analogy of a war economy to discuss the economics of lockdown. It is easy to see why they use the butter or guns metaphor because a command-and-control economy in the traditionally market-oriented economies of modern capitalism only occurs during wartime.

    The comparison, however, is missing the point that during wartime the national effort aims at maximal production with a limited labour force. Consumption restraint during the war reflects both scarcity and a deliberate policy to free resources for the war. So, reducing consumption is a goal. Consumption restraint during a pandemic is due to both a prohibition to produce and confidence effect that reduce demand.

    We can express this in the mathematical equation that economists love so much, the national income identity: $Y = C + I + G$ where Y = national product, C is consumption, I is investment and G is government spending. The war effort requires maximizing G and I and all policies (debt, credit, money, labour market, rationing of consumer goods) are aligned to that goal, because a war is ultimately won that way. Therefore, the composition of Y changes with smaller C/Y and larger G/Y and I/Y. During a pandemic C and I reduce endogenously (so now I/Y also decreases) and the government share G/Y increases even if no fiscal stimulus is applied.

The pandemic does not bite into the capital stock.[1] It is not like a war, a hurricane, an earthquake or a flood that destroy infrastructure, machinery and buildings (see Textbox 5.1). The impact of the pandemic works through (future) labour supply.

    Two forces are at play for the working population. First, people get sick and cannot go to work or if they go to work their productivity will be lower. People may also want to avoid working as they self-isolate, because of the risk of getting infected. In both cases a return to work is to occur after some time: the sick after recovery and the sheltering after the pandemic has passed its apex. This is a temporary shock to labour supply. Because it is temporary, the economy can technically bounce back to the *status quo ante*. This is one of the basic reasons why economists expect the economy that is hit by a pandemic to develop a V-shaped recession.

The sick can also die and then the shock is permanent. In the long-run everybody dies, but for the foreseeable future labour supply will be lower than would have been the case without the pandemic. The strength of the permanent impact depends on the mortality by age. If fatalities occur in younger generations, as with HIV/AIDS, then labour supply is reduced both in the long-run and the short-run, but there is no impact if death predominantly occurs in older generations as with COVID-19. The mortality by age group and the distribution of various age groups in a population are important determinants that may differ by country (see Textbox 5.2).[2]

Textbox 5.2 Simpson's Paradox

When we want to understand the fact that Italy or Spain did so much worse than China during the outbreak of Corona or why Africa seems to have been spared to a large extent, we encounter the power of Simpson's Paradox. This is a statistical phenomenon by which a trend or relationship that appears in each different group of data does not occur in the aggregate – the pattern disappears or goes into reverse when these groups are combined. Von Kügelgen et al. (2020) point out that Case Fatality Rates in Italy for all age groups are lower than in Wuhan, China, but not for the total population. The same paradox occurs in Africa where health care is vulnerable. The explanation is the different age structure. Italy has an aged population (in Europe it has the largest percentage of elderly population with a fifth above 65 years); Africa is literally the young continent (some 60% is aged below 25) and China is in between. So, what we see for all subpopulations is not always true for the whole. Simpson reversals occur if structures are different and/or change over time and also play havoc in economic analyses, for example, because the shares of the Corona growth sectors (supermarkets, ecommerce, ICT, logistics, drive throughs and home delivery) increase sharply during a pandemic.

These reactions and their impact on macroeconomic supply are endogenous in an epidemiological-economic model and they occur independent of policy interventions. The COVID-19 pandemic reduces short run macroeconomic supply which shifts down and to the left in panel (c) of Diagram 5.1. Capital goods remain in place, but a restaurant without personnel and customers no longer produces and if the lockdown is lifted but social distancing is maintained then the restaurant will serve fewer customers (so capital costs per meal will increase). Some substitution is possible: for example, when new distribution channels are developed (for example, home delivery). This capital is, however, not obsolete; it is merely not used. It will be used later, however, when the restaurant goes belly-up because the building remains in place. (It is important to see that these economic aspects of a pandemic are unavoidable and would occur also in a hypothetical world without government interventions; see Textbox 5.4).

The lockdown measures add a third and fundamentally different element. First, because the non-pharmaceutical interventions are exogenous (it is not endogenous behaviour but government policy, although one might want to construct a model that endogenizes the government decision on the predictions of the health impact of the pandemic). Secondly, because the intervention either prohibits certain activities that the market in principle would like to provide or makes certain activities impossible due to shelter-at-home orders that technically restrict labour supply for non-essential activities that require proximity of provider and customer.[3] Thirdly, because the measures reduce the death toll and thereby actually support long run supply, an element often overlooked in the discussions on these measures. This is also the case for a pandemic like COVID-19, because a breakdown of the health care sector also has a direct impact on younger generations. Infant mortality increases and hospitalization of young people that could easily have been saved pre-COVID-19 becomes problematic thereby reducing the (future) working population.

The difference between the short-term costs and the long-term benefits of non-pharmaceutical interventions is often overlooked in discussions because people observe the concrete short-term disturbance but find it difficult to see the long-term benefits. Even more puzzling perhaps is that the direction of change of long-run supply is not clear beforehand without further research. In order to see this, we need a model for long-term growth.

The standard long-term growth model is the so-called Solow model. This neoclassical model essentially explains how saving, investment, population growth and technology interact in the long run to determine labour productivity. The neoclassical growth model is illustrated in Diagram 5.2. On the vertical axis we have production Q divided by the amount of labour L, that is, labour productivity Q/L denoted as q. On the horizontal axis we have the capital K divided by L, that is, the amount of capital per worker or the capital labour ratio K/L denoted by k. The relation between k and q is described by the production function $f(k)$. An increase in k gives a movement on the curve; the curve flattens because of the declining marginal productivity of capital for a given technology (an improvement in technology would shift the curve up). Typically, economists think about net investment (that is, an increase in the capital stock) as the driving force of k, but in the Solow model a decrease in L works in the same direction.

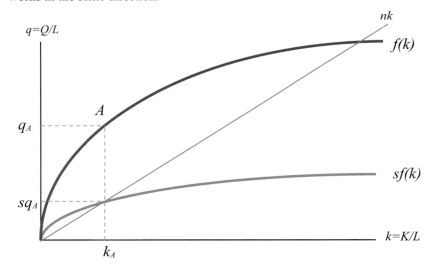

Diagram 5.2 Solow model

The relationship between labour productivity q and the capital-labour ratio k in Diagram 5.2 is an important stepping stone for understanding what factors drive long term growth.[4] The key issue is that productivity increases through the process of capital deepening that occurs when the amount of capital per worker increases. Capital accumulation enters the model via saving S that creates investment K. We write saving per worker as sq or $sf(k)$. The other determinant of the capital labour ratio changes over time as population grows at a rate of n and we use a ray through the origin to represent the condition nk. Indeed, in point A we have the equality $sq = nk$, that is: saving sq_A provides the capital that is needed to provide the new workers with the same amount of capital that an existing worker has to his or her disposal (k_A) so that the new workers can achieve the same level of labour productivity q_A. In a point to the left of A we would have that sq exceeds nk so there $\Delta k > 0$ and we would see capital deepening increasing the capital-labour ratio leading to a movement along the production function towards point A. The opposite (capital shallowing) happens in points to the right of A, so A is a stable equilibrium. In order to get development, that is, higher q, we need an increase in k. This relationship is also known as the fundamental equation of capital accumulation and we can write it as $\Delta k = sq - nk$.

A pandemic reduces n, and this shifts the nk-curve to nk^*, so that the new equilibrium becomes A^* in Diagram 5.3. Basically, this explains the counterintuitive results of the growth studies on HIV/AIDS (the pandemic increases productivity and capital accumulation) that we discussed in Section 2.2. Diagram 5.3 illustrates this case of capital deepening.

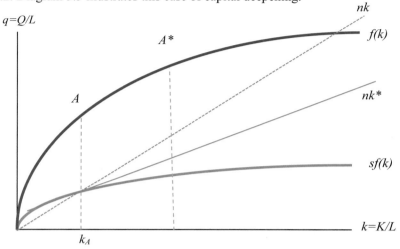

Diagram 5.3 Reduction of population growth in the Solow model

The introduction of non-pharmaceutical interventions, however, changes this straightforward story because we now have two changes occurring at the same time. Population growth is reduced as before (but possibly to a lesser extent due to the health policy).

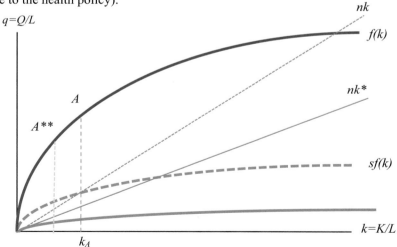

Diagram 5.4 Reduction of both population growth and saving rate

The new element in Diagram 5.4 is that the lockdown reduces the saving rate because (partial) firm closure and (partial) unemployment imply dissaving for parts of the population. The reduction of *s* means that saving *sq* is lower and this has a negative impact on capital accumulation Δk. The question then is: what happens on balance? Diagram 5.4 illustrates the case of capital shallowing (the new equilibrium A^{**} is to the left of A, the equilibrium before the pandemic). This possibility suggests that developing countries could get stuck into an 'epidemiological trap' with 'involution': a vicious circle of reduced saving, reduced (human) capital and reduced productivity (Drouhin et al., 2003; Goenka and Liu, 2019).

We need empirical flesh on the bones, because Diagram 5.4 is just one of many cases and depending on how the curves shift exactly capital deepening is still a possibility. The flesh is always a bit of a problem in economics as the debate on empirical relations can rage for quite some time, even for historic events. A clear example is the impact of the Spanish Flu pandemic that starts with Garrett (2009) finding mortality being associated with higher productivity and higher wages and has led to a debate focussing on the economic impact of non-pharmaceutical interventions (Correia et al. 2020a,b; Lilley et al., 2020).[5] That empirical disagreement should not blur the fact that a lot of agreement exists about the bones, that is, about the underlying mechanism.

Textbox 5.3 Paradoxes of productivity

Is COVID-19 bad for productivity? We know that existing traditional production facilities become less productive, both because more labour and more capital is needed. There are more cleaning and security personnel around to ensure that distancing is possible. The same restaurant can seat fewer customers, so the capital costs per guest increase. Human capital may decay in firms that are closed and if they follow a fire and re-hire strategy this will reduce labour productivity. We also know that in the Corona-growth sectors productivity must have increased tremendously. Web shops and delivery services have seen very significant increases in turnover, tracking and tracing must have become much more effective due to learning effects and the effectiveness and efficiency of the medical treatment of COVID-19 has increased sharply. So, productivity must have increased in these sectors.

On balance the impact of productivity depends on the shares of the sectors where we need more capital and labour per unit of output. We know that the share of the other sectors (the Corona-growth sectors) increases significantly. Evaluations of productivity will thus depend on which sector structure is being used. The old pre-COVID-19 structure or the new (post) COVID-19 structure.

The long-run effects of a pandemic are important to keep in mind, but for policy the short term is often the determining factor during crises. It is nice to know that an economy moves from one equilibrium to the next and it is good to have an idea of the endpoint, but the roadmap for that journey matters a lot. For a disease without treatment, the expectation is that (group) immunity will be built at some point in time so that the virus gets contained and this could be considered as the new stable equilibrium (it is not necessarily a return to the pre-pandemic health situation). But it is clear that we need to consider *how* one moves from the pre-pandemic to the post-pandemic situation. Comparative statics is a poor guide. A policy that would not aim at containment of the Corona virus but would let it rage uncontrolled will generate a high and immediate death toll and an overload of the health care system, but the ultimate impact on the economy might be relatively low (Robalino, 2020). A policy that aims at containment will slow down the spread, but at the cost of arriving at the new equilibrium only after considerable time and with significant economic costs.

The first point is that these two policies describe alternative realities and that the isolated analysis of either 'no containment' or 'containment' is not helpful. Information on both policy trajectories is needed for accessing the opportunity costs for the choice that is to be made. In each case the counterfactual is important, that is, the situation that would have occurred if the other choice was made (Textbox 5.4). The second point is that the trajectory matters and therefore we move from the long run and the supply side to the short-term issues that dominate the policy agenda and the public debate in the pandemic's first phase.

5.2 THE SHORT RUN: DEMAND

Most governments around the world moved in the same direction as we saw in Section 3.3: taxes are being reduced, support is offered, spending is increased, and liquidity is provided. There are many reasons for these financial and monetary policy interventions. One obvious reason is that pandemics reduce production, consumption and investment endogenously – even if no non-pharmaceutical interventions are implemented (Brahmbhatt and Dutta, 2008; Eichenbaum et al., 2020, Chen et al., 2020; see also Textbox 5.5). Moods and expectations may deepen the economic problems. If consumers and firms perceive this shock as long-run stagnation rather than a temporary shock, then consumption and investment would be further reduced, and the economy can end in an L-shaped depression. In this sense the activities of the government can be seen as countercyclical.

It is, however, important to note that the Corona crisis is not a business-as-usual recession that could be met with Keynesian demand management (an indication is that consumer prices *increased* during the lockdown; see Jaravel and O'Connell, 2020). This becomes clear once we take the non-pharmaceutical interventions into account.

Textbox 5.4 Missing or misperceived counterfactuals

One of the characteristics of pandonomics is that the counterfactual is often poorly understood. A very clear example is an argument that emerged quite generally after the apex had passed and death rates had come down from hundreds to tens or even less per day. The argument is that the health gain of the non-pharmaceutical interventions ('only a few deaths') is decreasing, while the costs of social distancing are increasing fast. The temptation is to conclude that the measures are too strong or at least getting too large in relation to the small gains in health that can be achieved.

The key problem with this argument that has been invoked by proponents of early lifting of measures is the improper definition of the counterfactual. The measures aim at reducing the risk of a second wave. The health benefit is not the reduction of an already low death toll, but the avoidance of the return of the apex. Counterfactuals are useful because they show the opportunity costs of no intervention: a good example is given by Avery et al. (2020, p. 34): 'the loss of learning when schools move online will be smaller if the alternative was to have teachers calling in sick and leaving classes in the hands of substitutes.'

More difficult to spot, however, are the equally important but missing counterfactuals. The costs of non-intervention could be much larger than the costs of intervention, especially if a pandemic spirals out of control and creates panic so that consumer and producer confidence reduce more sharply and take much longer to recover than during lockdown. Forecasts by the international organizations would be much more useful if they also kept the counterfactual of an uncontrolled pandemic in the picture by providing the base case of no intervention so that the costs *and* the benefits of measures can be part of the policy debate.

The government intervention is a rescue package: it provides income support for consumers in lockdown, it buys, so to say, time for those cash and credit-constrained firms that are obliged to reduce if not completely halt their business activities (De Vito and Gomez, 2020) and it tries to avoid massive unemployment. In many economies the rescue money is also necessary to enable workers and small business owners to adhere to the lockdown measures – without financial backup public support for the measures would erode quickly because the livelihoods of these people are directly threatened. The conclusion is that the fiscal and monetary bazookas that we have encountered in Chapter 3 should not be seen as a form of demand management of the type that would be encountered during normal recessions.

Textbox 5.5 Intervention or fear?

The non-pharmaceutical interventions (lockdowns, business closures) are drastic and dramatic, but the additional effect of interventions is often overrated. Without the interventions, behavioural reactions by large groups of people – even for diseases that ultimately generate little illness and/or death – have a strong impact on the economy.

- During the 1918 Spanish Flu 25% to 50% worker absenteeism rates that reduced output by 10% to 20% occurred despite government pushing to maintain production for the US war effort.
- The 1957 Asian Flu in Latin America was considered to be mild and without many complications, but school and industrial absenteeism were still in the range of 20% to 45%.
- During the 1994 outbreak of the Plague in Surat, India, half the civil work force reported sick and 400,000 to 500,000 people fled the city.
- During the outbreak of SARS in 2003 tourist attractions, exhibitions and hotels in Beijing reported a loss of around 80 percent.

The economic hardship (and also the health benefit) that is attributed to non-pharmaceutical interventions thus needs to be corrected for endogenous reactions to an infectious disease that spreads fast and is perceived to be life threatening. During COVID-19 these reactions could be observed because adjustments in mobility and restaurant visits already started to decrease before formal measures were taken.

Sources: Dunn (1958); Mavalankar (1995); Hai et al. (2004); Bodenhorn (2020)

The difference between traditional demand management and the fiscal and monetary policies during the Corona crisis can be illustrated with the hobby horse of macroeconomics, the ISLM model. The ISLM model essentially explains how interest rates and production are influenced by shocks and, moreover, what policy can and cannot do. The model has two components: the IS curve that describes equilibrium in the market for goods and services and the LM curve that describes equilibrium in the money market. The pandemic does not bite on the money market; it is a real shock.

In Diagram 5.5, the LM curve is upward sloping: at higher levels of income (on the horizontal axis of the ISLM diagram) people need more transaction money and that drives up the price of money, that is, the interest rate (on the vertical axis of the ISLM diagram). The IS curve is the downward sloping line that illustrates a negative relationship between interest rate and national income, because investment and consumption are stimulated by lower interest rates. The pandemic shifts the IS curve down due to the sobering perspectives consumers reduce their consumption and businesses scale down their investment plans, but it also truncates the IS curve in particular due to the lockdown that makes part of production impossible.

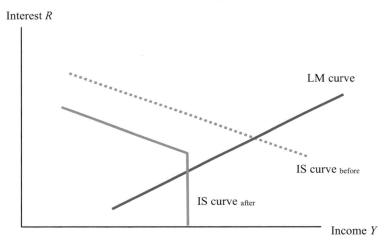

Diagram 5.5 ISLM diagram before and after the outbreak of a pandemic

Stimulating effective demand will not work in this situation– it will shift the IS curve upwards, but it does not change the truncated vertical part of the curve (compare Snower, 2020). Likewise, monetary policy (an outward shift of the LM) cannot increase national income Y, because income is at its technical maximum given the non-pharmaceutical interventions. Given these constraints it is not surprising that Coibion et al. (2020) find that US households do not change economic behaviour because they do not believe that the bazookas will be effective.[6] For fiscal policy this is a form of the 'Ricardian Equivalence' that holds that consumers understand that government spending today increases taxes tomorrow. Monetary policy can still be relevant, for example, if money hoarding occurs because people want to hold real balances for precautionary motives (as happened in the US, the Euro Area, Brazil and

Russia; see Goodhart and Ashworth, 2020). Money hoarding would shift the LM curve upwards to the left reducing income even below the constrained lockdown production maximum. Increasing the money supply can thus help to avoid negative repercussions of money hoarding but cannot provide a solution for the reduction of the production maximum (the truncation of the IS curve).

The monetary and fiscal bazookas lead to what economists call 'overhang': frustratingly we do not know when it will materialize. The massive fiscal rescue programmes that lead to very significant budget deficits create debt overhang as debt ratios jump to the levels of the Second World War.[7] We may want to be optimistic and note that interest rates are historically low but can be expected to decrease even further as happened endogenously during earlier pandemics (Jordà et al., 2020). If so, public debt is not a problem, because governments can afford the interest payments and wait until the economy grows out of the debt problem. In the same vein enormous liquidity injections bring so much money into the economy that they induce monetary overhang, that is, a risk of high future inflation. Again, we may want to be optimistic and note that inflation is still very low so that monetary overhang is not a problem.

Textbox 5.6 Risk versus uncertainty

Risk is like throwing a dice or a coin. With a dice you know that it will be either 1,2,3,4,5 or 6; with a coin it will be a head or a tail. So, the chance of an outcome is known beforehand – you know the probabilities ($1/6$ and $1/2$ respectively). Uncertainty is like throwing a dice, but now you do not know how many sides the dice has (it may also suddenly turn into a coin). In a situation of risk, we can calculate expected values and do cost-benefit analyses or compute risk mark-ups, but when uncertainty governs much standard economic approaches break down. Will a vaccine be developed – and if so when and how fast and will it work for all? Will the virus mutate? Will fiscal debt become unsustainable? Will hyperinflation occur? Will the economy follow a U-shaped or V-shaped recession (or an L-shape or a W-shape)? Often in common language we use the word 'risk', but it is important to recognize that these are all fundamental uncertainties. The most fundamental economic uncertainty is 'problem X', a problem that is not yet recognized. It is not unlikely that problem X will emerge, because we are in uncharted territory due to the unprecedented pandonomic reactions to COVID-19.

The COVID-19 pandemic, however, hit the advanced economies in the liquidity trap, that is, a situation where monetary policy is impotent because interest rates are already at historic lows.[8] In the liquidity trap we have a perfectly interest elastic LM curve (it would be a horizontal line in Diagram

5.5). Thus, increasing the money supply can no longer reduce the interest rate that is already at the zero-floor level. The reason why we see the major Central Banks providing more liquidity by means of a new round of quantitative easing (a form of money creation) is to enable banks to provide more loans to firms, so that they can survive in difficult times and to ensure financial stability (Reinders, Schoenmaker and van Dijk, 2020 estimate potential losses for European banks amounting up to 43% of available capital and reserves). So, liquidity matters to keep firms and banks afloat. Providing an overdose of liquidity in a physically constrained economy is, however, a bit like stepping on the gas while applying the parking brake.

Quantitative easing in times of a lockdown provides liquidity in a system that is contracting, not so much because of lacking demand but mainly due to health policy restrictions. Fisher's quantity theory of money ($MV = PT$) sheds some light on the monetary processes. In the equation M stands for the stock of money that will increase due to quantitative easing. V stands for the velocity with which this amount of money circulates. During a pandemic V decreases due to money hoarding but it increases due to the fact that people reduce the frequency of shopping while buying more per visit – as a practical solution and to keep the exposition simple we can assume that velocity remains about the same. T represents the number of transactions and if we multiply it with the general price level P then we have national income Y. Under normal conditions the quantity theory provides a handy summary of the Monetarist view. During a pandemic T contracts sharply due to both endogenous behaviour by consumers and firms as well as government regulations. Pushing money into the system will only have one way out: an increase in P, that is, inflation. So, does the money equation break down now that we do not see significant inflation emerging?

In order to find a solution to that puzzle we must decompose the equation from a truly macro equality into a multi-sector equation. We can keep the left-hand side of Fisher's equation (the MV part) as it stands because we use money for all transactions alike, but on the righthand side we have to acknowledge that economic activities take place at many markets and with many prices that often do not move in the same direction, but do form a system of interconnected vessels. Let's for simplicity introduce two markets only, the real economy sub-indexed g and the market for financial assets sub-indexed f. The disaggregated Fisher equation becomes:

$$MV = P_g T_g + P_f T_f$$

Increase the money stock M while the real economy is in the clamp of Corona and money has only one way to go: financial assets. Rising stock markets in the context of the Corona crisis are thus not a symptom of unrealistic expectations of traders but rather a symptom of the injection of an overdose of liquidity into the system. This may actually be the policy purpose of the exercise since stock market developments have a strong impact on consumer confidence and financial stability. The point is that we do have inflation in this system, but its manifestation is often ignored: it is asset inflation. The risk is that the money at some point in time will flow back to the real economy and then will appear as the headline inflation that economists traditionally put at the centre of the economic analysis.

An important conclusion from our discussion is that the COVID-19 virus is especially harmful if there are underlying conditions. The economic impact of a pandemic is like a pair of scissors with one blade representing health impact and containment measures and the other representing underlying economic conditions. Inflexible economic structures, high debts, significant unemployment, unsustainable public finances, monetary overhang and/or a liquidity trap before an outbreak imply that the cut that the pandemic takes out of the economy is larger. Indeed, these underlying economic conditions, to a large extent, determine what policy makers can do (Benmelech and Tzur-Ilan, 2020) and how sick the economy gets when it is visited by a pandemic.

Textbox 5.7 Hangover, coma or amputation?

The state of the economy during the COVID-19 pandemic has drawn many metaphors. The economy has been likened to a hangover (suggesting that the problems would go quickly after the toxins had left the body), to a coma (still with us but not functioning and waiting in the post-anaesthesia care unit) and even an amputation (lost forever, possibly with some phantom pain). The metaphors, of course, have some aspects that we recognize from reality, otherwise these figures of speech would not have been used. Still, they miss two of the major points of the lockdown. First, the closed sectors did not carry a disease before the outbreak. Second, due to the state of inactivity these sectors became seriously ill and sometimes the disease became life-threatening.

5.3 TRADE SHOCKS

So far, our discussion seems to have been focussed on the single economy only. That apparent neglect is appropriate, because the discussion thus also relates to the planet as a whole. From an Earth Economic, rather than macroeconomic, perspective it also matters that all governments applied pandonomic recipes in an uncoordinated but still highly synchronized manner as we have seen earlier in Section 3.3. So, it is actually a hidden benefit that we have discussed the long-term and the short-term as if we had only one economy. A pandemic is global, and the policy response should be global, so the perspective should principally be on the autarkic economy of our planet (van Bergeijk, 2013).

Studying international trade (which at the truly planetary level is immaterial because it cancels out) is, however, relevant in view of the fact that decision-making still predominantly takes place at the national level and because trade flows spread the economic impact of non-pharmaceutical interventions to other countries. It is noteworthy that the previous pandemic (the Mexican Flu) coincided with a global financial crisis and that the two crises were linked by observers and policy makers at the time (Peckham, 2013). Interconnectedness and globalization have been identified as essential elements of the anatomy of pandemics (Daszak, 2012). It is likely that policy makers, business men and the public at large will conclude that they have underestimated the costs of globalization, both in terms of disruption of international value chains (Udovički, 2020) and in terms of the contribution of global interconnectedness to the speed with which the disease has spread. Diagram 5.6 illustrates the marginal costs and benefits of globalization (van Bergeijk, 2019). On the one hand, the marginal gains of globalization decrease when a country gets more and more integrated in the world economy. In the initial phase large benefits can be reaped in terms of efficiency gains, consumer welfare, product variety and product quality, but moving from large openness to larger openness does not bring much more new opportunities for international specialization.

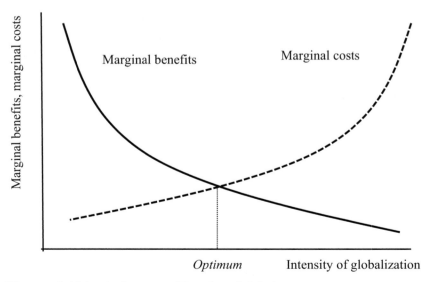

Diagram 5.6 Marginal costs and benefits of globalization

On the other hand, the marginal costs of adjustment and redistribution increase due to the distortive impact of high marginal taxes.[9] So the winners are winning less, and it is more costly to compensate the losers of openness. Where marginal benefits equal marginal costs the contribution of globalization is at its maximum.

The pandemic shifts the marginal costs curve up because private and public decisionmakers realize the pandemic costs of interconnectedness and the risk of value chain disruption. That risk has not increased due to the pandemic, of course, but the perceptions are adjusted. As a consequence, the optimal level of globalization is reduced fuelling a change towards deglobalization.

The staggered development of the disease and the lockdowns moving from Asia to Europe to the Americas and back and forth also means that economic front and aftershocks via trade flows complicate the picture. How does this trade uncertainty influence the development of the economy?

The least complicated and most transparent way to introduce trade uncertainty in the neoclassical trade model is to assume that two states of the world exist: a free trade environment where all trade is possible and a no-trade environment where all trade collapses (van Marrewijk and van Bergeijk, 1990). This abstraction can be taken literally but it can also be interpreted as describing the views of the economic subjects (firms, consumers, government) on the future state of the economy. This perception can be expressed in terms of a weighted average of these two extreme states of the world. Next it is also important to realise that an economy or its agents decide on the pattern of domestic specialization before the state of the world is known (that is, whether a no-trade or a free trade situation occurs). Once the decision about the optimal pattern of specialization has been taken, either by a social planner or decentralized through the market mechanism, the allocation of the factors of production cannot be changed overnight because of the costs of reallocation or, alternatively, the time needed to make adjustments.

Diagram 5.7 illustrates the standard model for a small open economy that trades two goods. We want to study the international transmission mechanism, and this is why we assume that the country itself is not in lockdown. The effects that we find in the model thus by construction relate to the impact that a lockdown in another country exerts via trade. The production structure is represented by a transformation curve *II* (all efficient combinations of good 1 and good 2 that the economy can produce). The preferences of the consumers are represented by indifference curves with utility levels U_F (of free trade) and U_A (of autarky), respectively. The economy trades at the international price ratio t, that shows the relative price of good 1 and good 2 in the international market. The economy is small and thus cannot influence this price ratio by its supply and demand. Three points in Diagram 5.7 are of special interest:

- the autarky point *A* (where the economy consumes what it domestically produces),
- the free trade consumption point *F* and
- the free trade production point *D* (the economy specializes in the production of good 1 which it exports).

Note that utility in *F* exceeds utility in *A* which in its turn exceeds utility in *D*. In the free trade situation, the economy consumes in point *F* and achieves the maximum level of utility attainable U_F. But if the no-trade situation emerges while the economy is fully specialized, production is at *D* because the factors of production have been used in specific combinations and reallocation will take time and be at high costs. By necessity consumption drops to *D*, the production combination that is actually being produced. Since this production combination is the result of decisions that assumed that international trade would be possible, the resulting consumption combination logically cannot be optimal if trade is impossible.

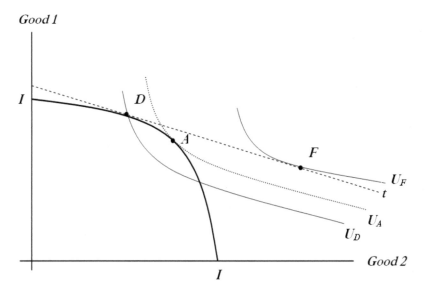

Diagram 5.7 Trade disruption in the neo-classical model

The extent of international specialization is thus suboptimal if the originally expected volume of international trade does not materialize and this situation will yield a lower utility level (actually, even *less than in autarky*). Consequently, the next step in the model is that the economy will start to de-specialize in the no-trade environment. The optimal point in the no-trade situation is autarky *A* but the economy will not reach that point promptly, because the reallocation of the factors of production will take some time.

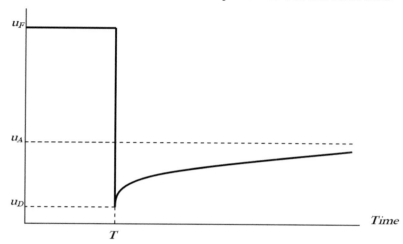

Diagram 5.8 Time path of utility from free trade to autarky

From this story we can derive the time path of utility which is directly related to the consumption possibilities in the economy and shows the abrupt drop at point *T* derived from the fall from point *F* to point *D* and then the more gradual movement towards point *A*. The time path of utility is illustrated in Diagram 5.8. This example, incidentally, reveals again the often-deceitful nature of an analysis based on comparative statics. Comparing the two equilibria (free trade and autarky) hides the journey from *F* to *A* that provides a highly relevant detour.

Text box 5.8 Green shoots and recovery

The first positive economic growth rate after the onset of recession is always greeted with joy. The party is, however, often premature. The neoclassical analysis of a trade shock clarifies that 'green shoots' are not necessarily a sign of improvement. After all, utility in this model starts to increase again after time *T*, but the trade shock continues, and the *status quo ante* is never restored. In other words, green shoots indicate the start of an adjustment process, but they do not necessarily indicate that the economy is improving and actually on a long-term track towards a better situation than before the trade shock occurred.

Consumers and producers will consider the expected utility of their consumption and production decisions and will *a priori* prefer a pattern of international specialization between autarky and free and undisturbed trade. Trade uncertainty thus yields less specialization in accordance with (and perhaps even against) comparative advantage and hence pandemic-related trade uncertainty induces a reduction of international trading opportunities and global welfare (van Marrewijk and van Bergeijk, 1993). That is to say that consumers and producers would prefer a point between *D* and *A* in Diagram 5.7 depending on their (implicit and/or subjective) probabilities attached to the respective states of the world. If they are certain that a trade shock will occur in the next period they will specialize in point *A* and if they are certain that undisturbed international trade will take place they will specialize in point *D*. Setting these limiting cases aside they will prefer a position in between and would like to be more located towards *A* if they think that trade is more uncertain. The expectation mechanism has a powerful impact on trade indeed. Even if trade continues to be free and undisturbed ex post, we expect to measure a reduction of trade once perceived uncertainty increases ex ante because the specialization in production will shift towards point *A*. This is again an illustration of theory helping to understand how the pandemic influences economic activity before we have the data to show how behaviour actually changes. Of course the model, as it focusses on exports and imports, does not deal with other channels of economic contagion, such as bank lending and foreign direct investment that require different models, but also here the basic result is that a reduction in cross border economic interaction can be expected. [10]

5.4 WHY PANDEMIC ECONOMICS?

On a final note, this Chapter is economic in focus and did not delve deeply into specific medical, social, psychological and (international) political aspects of pandemics. This is acceptable as a first step, but too strong a limitation for useful and effective analysis and policy advice. Looking at the future, *Pandemic Economics* therefore implicitly establishes the need for a comprehensive and multidisciplinary analysis that takes epidemiology, political economy and institutional design simultaneously into account. This finding suggests the need for fundamental change of the organization of (applied) science in the context of pandemic preparedness.

The upshot of this Chapter is that we do not need rocket science to understand the impact of the COVID-19 pandemic and the non-pharmaceutical interventions on the economy and the response of economic policy in reaction to that shock. I have read many very good and advanced analyses, but I have not seen anything that could not be understood in terms of the basic economic curriculum. From this perspective there would seem to be no need for pandemic economics – we have a set of reliable tools.

There is, however, one area where the economics of pandemics fundamentally needs to depart in two ways from mainstream economics and that is with respect to the assumption of rational behaviour and what is taken as given by economists.

Rationality

Psychological coping mechanisms (ignoring, denial), cognitive dissonance, fear and even panic can be strong driving forces during a pandemic that deviate from rational behaviour. Behavioural economists started monitoring behaviour early in the outbreak, but this is predominantly done from the perspective of providing analysis for pandemic response (Betsch, 2020). The context in which this research implicitly places itself is that of the evidence-based rational bureaucrat who has to deal with an irrational population. The behaviour, however, of decision makers during the pandemic does not fit this framework.

Quite a few populist leaders have visibly acted 'irrationally' – encouraging short-distance encounters, continuing to shake hands and organizing political mass gatherings are examples of activities that cannot be considered rational. These populist leaders have urged their franchises to follow suit and with a significant impact on the immediate death toll of the pandemic (see Mariani et al., 2020, on President Bolsonaro of Brazil). Indeed, populism is associated with high fatality rates as illustrated in Figure 5.1. Figure 5.1 illustrates a very basic pattern: countries with an older population (that is, a higher life expectancy at birth) are more vulnerable and thus will experience more deaths per million population. The figure shows that COVID-19 bites especially in countries with a high life expectancy at birth although some, such as Japan, Taiwan, New Zealand, Germany, and Scandinavia (with the exception of Sweden) managed to keep the death toll comparatively low. The figure distinguishes three groups of countries: countries with populist leaders and democracies and autocracies (both without populist leaders). In general, the pattern supports the idea that autocracies are associated with lower death rates than democracies (a notion that we will further investigate in the next Chapter). The second stylized fact that emerges from the data is that populist leaders appear to be salesmen of death. Not having a populist leader is, of course, not a defence against the vagaries of a pandemic. The easily identified outliers for non-populist democracies and autocracies in Figure 5.1 are Belgium, Peru and Iran, respectively. Neither is having a populist leader always associated with a high death rate. Israel is an example of a country with a high life expectancy at birth and a populist leader that, at least in the first instance, broke away from

the expected pattern. Still, the finding that irresponsible populism is a risk
factor in a pandemic is supported both by common sense and by the numbers
in Figure 5.1. A key challenge is thus how to manage the political managers
themselves and how to change their behaviour towards the desired direction.

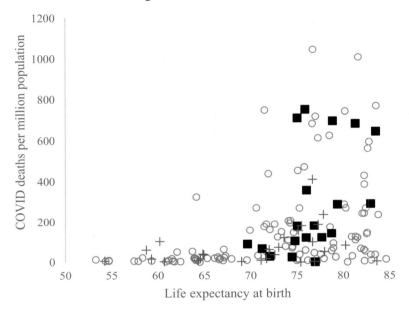

Note: ■ populist leader
           + autocracy; non-populist leader
           ○ democracy; non-populist leader

Sources: Kyle and Meyer (2020) and Norris (2020, p. 2) for the identification of
           populist leaders at the start of the pandemic. Autocracies have a negative
           Polity2 score in Polity IV for the year 2018 (Marshall et al., 2011). *World in
           data* for death count, collected end of October 10, 2020.

*Figure 5.1 Populism, autocracy and democracy: COVID-19 deaths per
           million population versus life expectation*

The policy preferences and political demands are exogenous parameters that
mainstream economists see as given by policy makers and these items are no
longer investigated. Since Jan Tinbergen published his *On the Theory of
Economic Policy* in 1952, it has become the standard approach to see the role
of goal setting as the exclusive domain of the politicians and policy makers
with economists acting as the experts that provide the analysis of how to
achieve those given goals using the available policy tools in the most efficient

way. There are at least two reasons why pandemic economics needs to take a different perspective. First, the value of saving the lives of COVID patients has been the dominant and almost undisputed goal of the policy response with an unwarranted neglect of both the short-term impact on non-COVID patients and the mid-term impact of that policy on the health situation due to rising poverty, lower levels of health care funding and reduced finance for Sustainable Development Goals. Second, we need to move – again in the words and spirit of Tinbergen – from a focus on quantitative policies to the analysis of structural change, that is, to consider how we can best organize society to meet a future pandemic. This is a task that forces us to think about the future. Let's therefore turn to the next Part.

Key takeaways of Chapter 5

- Economists, by and large, agree on the diagnosis of the economic problems created by the pandemic and non-pharmaceutical interventions.
- Without interventions the pandemic works through (future) labour supply and endogenous social distancing. The recession follows a sharp V-shape.
- Lockdowns are exogenous and reduce production; the long-term impact depends on avoided mortality, the impact on saving and productivity and the effectiveness of economic policy interventions.
- Negative perceptions and expectations reduce future production leading to a U-shaped recession or L-shaped depression.
- Effective demand management cannot be used to increase output during a pandemic.
- Monetary policy bazookas increase liquidity that finds an outlet in higher stock exchanges.
- Positive economic growth rates do not imply a return to the *status quo ante*.
- Underlying economic problems (such as the liquidity trap) magnify the economic impact of a pandemic.
- Pandemics, the associated uncertainty of recurring waves and the risk of future pandemics are important incentives to reduce cross border economic interactions (trade, lending, investment).
- Top decision makers do not always act rationally during a pandemic; populism is associated with a higher death toll.
- Economists can no longer take the national targets of politicians as given and should be actively involved in the formulation of those targets.

ENDNOTES

1   A pandemic, however, destroys human capital. The analysis can be extended to include human capital formation (see, for example, Young, 2005) and social capital (see, for example, Bonnel, 2000).

2   See Levin et al. (2020). In the case of COVID-19 it may be relevant to also consider the 'age-gender pyramid', because gender is also an important determinant of mortality.

3   One element in the discussion is the extent to which perceptions and beliefs of consumers and firms about their ability to return to pre-pandemic consumption and production patterns influence long-run supply. If this 'scarring effect' is strong and persistent recovery would not be sharp (a V-shaped recession) and could follow an L-shape or U-shape pattern (Kozlowski et al., 2020).

4   The focus on the long run means that we do not consider reduced labour productivity due to illness and fatigue although these effects probably influence the transitory stage (Drouhin et al., 2003).

5   See also Young (2005) and Jordà et al. (2020) for empirical studies that confirm the Solow-type increase of productivity effect for other epidemics and pandemics.

6   Binder (2020) in a separate survey at about the same time reports that only a third of her respondents had heard about the measures. Keane and Neal (2020) in a panel for 54 countries find that monetary and fiscal stimulus announcements also did not impact on consumer panic.

7   One of the problems is that countries that are already heavily indebted show less resilience (see, for example, Delatte and Guillaume, 2020, on sovereign bond spreads in the EMU countries).

8   In the emerging economies the possibilities for liquidity provision are more relevant as illustrated by Hartley and Rebucci (2020) who report a smaller impact than during the Great Recession for developed markets, but significantly larger impacts in emerging markets.

9   The often-followed policy to reduce the adjustment costs by means of inflation (Ruggie, 1982) is not available in the economic context of the 1930s and 2000s with actual deflation and strong deflationary pressures, respectively.

10   Note, however, that reshoring (bringing parts of the value chain back in the domestic economy) does not isolate the economy from the impact of the lockdowns (Bonadio et al., 2020).

PART III

THE FUTURE

6. Many Futures

It is important that we start to think about the future. Not about the immediate future and the fallout and hardship that the COVID-19 crisis will bring, but the future that starts after humanity has found a way to cope with the Corona virus. We need to think about the world post-COVID-19, because we cannot afford to react in the same manner as we did to COVID-19. And we need to start thinking now.

It is difficult to foresee what the future post-COVID-19 world will look like. It is quite common to say that the world will fundamentally change due to the pandemic. This cliché, however, may or may not be true. Trade patterns after significant and historic crises can recover quickly (van Bergeijk et al., 2017), strategic bombing of cities only has a temporary effect on city growth (Brakman et al., 2004), the microlevel reactions to natural disasters are much more resilient than one would expect (Stevenson et al., 2016) and people tend to return both by necessity and because the economic geographic location has benefits that continue to act as pull factors (Brake, 2019) – to give a few examples of situations where society returns to the *status quo ante* after a significant 'once-in-a-lifetime' shock. It is also unclear in what direction transformation will take place. Will inequality increase (as it usually does after a negative economic shock) or will the appreciation for essential workers (that are often low-income earners, see Kearney and Muñana, 2020) translate into higher wages at the bottom of the wage pyramid? Will the threat of pandemics stimulate international cooperation – and if so, under the leadership of which country – or will the virus increase fragmentation and erode global governance? Will the Global North with much more capabilities to invest in health care recover first or will the Global South after initial suffering be in a much better position?

So, questions and uncertainties abound but with one clear and obvious constant: a new pandemic will hit us again. We thus need to think about ways to meet this challenge and organize accordingly. The fact is that the next pandemic is underway and is just as likely to strike in 2030 as it is next year. Hence the urgency of the endeavour: we need to act now or be unprepared and unprotected when Mother Earth sends the next disease. But how to do such an analysis with so many fundamental uncertainties?

6.1 SETTINGS RATHER THAN SCENARIOS

In this Chapter I want to develop an alternative to traditional scenario analysis. Let me start by making clear what one can do with scenarios before moving to the motivation to step outside the box of a well-established methodology. When they do not know what is going to happen economists are fond of scenario analysis. Indeed, the literature on COVID-19 is flooded with scenarios with different numbers of waves and forecasts on its impact making assumptions on the duration of the lockdown, the general use of masks and/or the speed of relaxing of social distancing measures.

Scenarios are useful tools if the future direction of the economy is very uncertain. Rather than providing predictions, the scenarios explore possible futures that can realistically be conceived given the available knowledge. In order for a scenario to be useful it must describe a possible, conceivable set of events and thereby a potential future. It is not sufficient that a possibility existed in the real world – the event must be considered to be a future possibility. In the context of pandemics scenario analysis would seem to be particularly relevant given the so far unique character of the non-pharmaceutical interventions and their enormous societal and economic costs – moreover, the theoretical and empirical perspectives on the size and duration of the impact of health and economic policies differ a lot. Often our knowledge depends on recent post-Second World War experiences and it is not clear whether these regularities will be applicable to the situation of significant uncertainty, stagnant economies, geopolitical shifts and deglobalization – especially uncertainty exists about the question of whether knowledge is durable and can be extended over longer periods than previously experienced.[1] Typically, in a scenario analysis each scenario can be used to combine coherent perspectives that each use different assumptions underlying the economic processes and the uncertain development of the parameters in which these developments take place.

Economists have also developed a technique of choice scenarios to measure preferences in surveys and experimental situations. Choice scenarios are a collection of simultaneously presented alternatives with a description of their relevant attributes. So, you are offered a choice between A, B, C and D and the information of each of these outcomes. Choice scenarios are shorthand descriptions and the purpose is to give the headlines of the determinants that according to the researcher determine the choice of the respondents. The methodology is customarily applied in many scientific fields, including psychology, economics and sociology, and has also helped to understand the choice of decision making under uncertainty.

So why would I need an alternative for such well-established analytical instruments?

The basic reason is that I want to investigate a *certainty*, namely the fact that a pandemic will occur in the foreseeable future. We do not know what disease will cross humanity's path or when, but we know for sure that this will happen. This is one of humanity's White Swans – a highly predictable, low frequency, high impact event of which only the exact size and timing are uncertain. So, I want to investigate a certainty and its impact in the future world, and this is where uncertainty enters because we cannot predict what the future world will look like. It is therefore necessary to investigate different forms of global, regional and national ways to organize human affairs. These different forms of organization are the outcome of decisions of the past, so to say, the unfolded choice scenarios that have led countries to be what they are at the start of the Covid-19 pandemic. Thus, enters the analysis of settings rather than the development of scenarios. My settings are fundamentally different from the available scenarios of pandemics, since the latter typically have been 'policy free' and investigate different severities of the event. In contrast, I want to investigate the same event under different assumptions of the determinants of policy response. That requires an open mind with respect to what countries can and will do in the future. Indeed, a key issue is that preference for a scenario may not be helpful, because the basic idea of scenario analysis is that the other scenarios are also probable and in principle just as likely. An additional benefit of working with settings is that the currently observed settings and the impact of COVID-19 do contain information that can be distilled and provide insights into possible future pandemic trajectories.

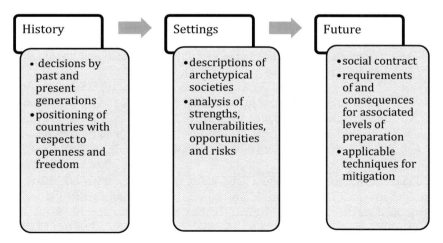

Diagram 6.1 Settings on the interface between history and future

Prediction – similar as in the case of scenarios – cannot be the goal of the present exercise. The purpose is to investigate the possible development of health policies and economic policies to combat a pandemic that is more serious than COVID-19 and thus has a significant impact on long-run labour supply, not because I am an alarmist or a fan of the 'World War Z' genre, but because this makes the societal choices and their consequences much clearer.[2] This is actually one of the most important purposes of the exercise: to help you form your own opinion about possible future states of the world in relation to the risk of pandemics. We need to rethink the organization of society, the extent to which we are willing to accept risks and to balance the costs and benefits before the next pandemic. The settings are corner solutions – archetypes of societies that make extreme choices with respect to (a) openness and internationalism and (b) freedom and individualism. They are, so to say, the corner flags of the pandemic playing field. So, the settings help you to form your own opinion about possible future states of the world in relation to the risk of pandemics. The settings do not offer you a choice – as with the choice scenarios – but rather a tool to think more clearly and comprehensively about what happens in the extreme. Settings are thus first of all a way to organize knowledge and a basis for discussion. I have four different settings in mind that provide corner solutions from which society may organize against pandemics:

- A Darwinian setting that basically accepts the health risk and sees a pandemic as a natural force that, via the survival of the fittest, forms an essential element of further human evolution.
- Deep deglobalization which is characterized by a significant reduction of the international movement of people and goods, and also includes a breakdown of global governance.
- A setting in which decision making (perhaps, especially) during pandemics is centralized and individual freedom is an important casualty on the pandemic battlefield.
- A world of autocratic autocracy that self-isolates in all dimensions before, during and after the outbreak of a pandemic.

To these corner solutions I add a fifth setting in which the trade-off between health, privacy and economics is investigated. This setting essentially deals with the three components of Article 3 of the Universal Declaration of Human Rights: 'Everyone has the right to life, liberty and security of person.' Life, liberty and security form a policy trilemma with health, freedom and the economy as the poles that require the balancing act that is at the centre of this setting (Phlippen, 2020). The location of this setting is less precisely defined in terms of its location in Diagram 6.2 and may wobble during a pandemic.

6.2 THE FOUR CORNERS

The settings will all be presented in similar format. We start with a narrative that describes the main characteristics of the setting. Next follows a discussion of the key 'building blocks'. This section is a form of colligation, as it brings together, on the one hand, scientific findings (both factual and empirical as well as speculative and theoretical) and, on the other hand, the social settings, philosophies and policy orientations that we want to investigate in this setting. This manner of colligation is an approach that dates back to Whewell (1847) who introduced this approach in the Natural Sciences but never really made it in economics possibly due to the fierce opposition against colligation by John Stuart Mill.[3] The innovation in the use of colligation in the settings is that the building blocks allow us to combine current scientific knowledge and different potential societies with a future development (the next pandemic) that certainly will occur but which timing is difficult to predict. Finally, each setting provides an overview of Strengths, Vulnerabilities, Opportunities, and Risks (SVOR) of the described societal attitude and response to future pandemics.

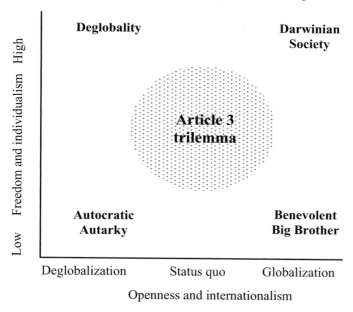

Diagram 6.2 Summary of the settings along two dimensions

The two axes
It is important to keep in mind that a lot of heterogeneity and nuance exist in the real world when we discuss the archetypical corner settings – typically,

countries will find themselves positioned (either by choice or because of historical developments) somewhere on the horizontal and vertical axes in between the corner settings. We use the archetypical corners as a tool to achieve clarity and not per se as real-world cases.

Openness and internationalism
The vertical dimension of Diagram 6.2 relates to the extent of cross border activities and can be thought of as having three aspects (Dreher et al., 2008). The economic aspect relates to interaction between the private sectors in different countries (or within multinational firms) and covers such items as foreign trade (exports and imports of goods and services), private capital flows (including bank lending, portfolio and foreign direct investment, mergers and acquisitions, remittances and official development assistance). The social aspect covers interactions between (groups of) individuals with different nationalities as being shaped by tourism, migration, cultural and personal exchanges. The political aspect relates to the interactions between States (both bilaterally and multilaterally) and can, for example, be observed by (changes in) their membership of international institutions, involvement in Treaties and participation in peace-keeping missions. Globalization, that represents an increase in, respectively a high level, of these aspects, has been associated with the spread of COVID-19 (Farzanegan et al., 2020) but at the same time globalized countries appear in principle to be better equipped to keep fatality rates low (Zimmermann et al., 2020).

Before COVID-19 countries were already repositioning across the globalization–deglobalization continuum towards lower levels of the economic and political aspects (examples include the Make America Great Again policies, the withdrawal from the Paris Protocol by the United States and Brexit). The lockdowns during COVID-19 added more impetus. The pandemic, however, created a real turnaround of the social aspect of globalization (especially global tourism) that before the outbreak was the only aspect of globalization that had returned towards the strong upward trend witnessed before the Great Recession (van Bergeijk, 2019). It is important to see that the settings that we will study do not use this manner of information to argue that pandemics by necessity drive societies towards deglobalization, but rather to argue that the possibility that the next pandemic could hit deglobalized societies is a relevant assumption. The assumption that the next pandemic hits a globalized world is equally relevant; so, we should study both.

Freedom and individualism
Successful containment has occurred in open market democracies such as Taiwan, New Zealand and South Korea and based on different degrees of lockdown. This is something to keep in mind in the two scenarios that focus

on autocracy, be it benign or *in extremis* harsh and autarkic. The reason to analyse autocratic structures is the greater ease with which such societies can intrude on privacy and individual liberty (Jenny, 2020) although the effectiveness in reducing, for example, domestic travel may be greater in democracies (Frey et al., 2020). Isolating villages and cities as well as obligatory quarantine of infected individuals in group facilities rather than at home are often seen as draconian measures in Western democracies. Also, and importantly, in autocracies the degree of lockdown measures differs. In Vietnam measures were quick, adequate and successful (Pollack et al., 2020). Russia initially appeared to be less vulnerable and was slow to implement lockdown measures. China's measures were much more comprehensive, and the virus was, by and large, contained to the province of Hubei where the outbreak of COVID-19 started.

The purpose of the exercise in the settings is not to investigate whether a pandemic stimulates a movement towards autocracy[4], but rather to investigate how a pandemic plays out in an autocracy versus a democracy. A striking difference between Asian autocracies and Western democracies during the COVID-19 pandemic is the difference in death toll that may reflect the fragmentation and lack of solidarity in modern democracies and individualistic societies, but note that democracy has also been defended because of the transparency and self-correcting mechanisms that over time are important to counter pandemics.[5]

Setting 1: The Darwinian Society
We start in the North-East corner of Diagram 6.2. The Darwinian Society can be characterized as a setting of prepared unpreparedness: the society does not invest in pandemic prevention, containment and mitigation. The setting is free from lockdowns, travel restrictions and other forms of interventions that we studied in Section 3.1.

At first sight the Darwinian Society is a prototype of the *laissez faire, laissez passer* attitude that many see as the key treat of neo-liberalism (for example, Ecks, 2020b) but there is more to this setting. The population and the authorities recognize both that pandemics are unavoidable for a globally connected and highly mobile species and the fact that natural selection and/or group immunity provide a medical 'non-intervention' to fatigue viruses. In this setting a clear priority is allotted to the economy. This may be motivated by a strong appreciation of material wellbeing, high social discount rates and/or risk-loving behaviour. The priority for the economy may also reflect an understanding that a sound economic basis is necessary both to avoid problems associated with deep poverty and for financing the health care sector and other essential collective goods. It may also be a negative and forced choice, because lockdowns are too costly for many developing countries (Robalino, 2020;

Fleurbaey, 2020). Lockdowns may also be too costly even in OECD economies, such as Chile with significant parts of the population living in the informal sector and on marginal incomes. In the advanced economies, the Darwinian Society accepts loss of human life and suffering as unavoidable collateral damage of a way of living that values the benefits of globalized production networks and freedom of travel. Social Darwinism can occur in any type of society, be it a multiparty democracy or a dictatorship, and economy, be it centrally planned or a market economy. The Darwinian Society is, however, more likely to occur in an open democratic market economy where the collective has in a sense typically less weight than the individual.[6]

Building blocks
References to the survival of the fittest are not uncommon in the literature on pandemics, but predominantly the topic is then the battle between the virus and the human population. It is common to read that viruses become more intelligent, find new cracks of our natural defence system and improve on their effectiveness (which are all similes out of phase with reality because viruses have neither a mind nor a will). Seldomly the medical literature considers pandemics as a natural selection tool that makes humanity stronger.

For many people, however, it is not illogical to see pandemics as something natural that needs to be accepted to a large extent and makes humanity stronger; after all we *are* what our grandparents (and their ancestors and so on) survived. Some may even see benefits of a reduced growth rate for the world population. This is not an alt-right ideology or a tenet of the anti-vaxxers as it pops up in many discussions and advocates have very diverse backgrounds – possibly resistance against the idea of natural selection is only strong amongst religious groups that oppose the concept of evolution.[7] The idea of the survival of the fittest is certainly not uncommon to economics and it is noteworthy that Malthus' (1798) *Essay on Population* actually was an important source of inspiration for Charles Darwin. Indeed, Claeys (2000) argues that key concepts of Social Darwinism were engrained in the Political Economy of the Nineteenth Century. In microeconomics competition and markets are assumed to weed out inefficient firms. Thus, at least among economists, the survival of the fittest is a commonly applied concept. The point is that the Darwinian Society is a relevant potential future world. Indeed, a long history exists in which non-intervention was the only course of action. Medical non-intervention may look strange in our world, but it is instructive to read a quote from the period in which large-scale vaccination was introduced.

> To physicians accustomed to the laissez-faire attitude toward influenza that has prevailed until now, the action taken must seem bewildering indeed. [… It …] has already been characterized as "a gamble," "risky," "unneeded," and a "political" machination (Kilbourne 1976, p. 15)

Undeniably, the second part of this quote could very well describe the initial reaction to, for example, the Swedish approach to COVID-19.

Strengths, Vulnerabilities, Opportunities and Risks
The pandemic shock will be sharp and relatively short compared to other settings. While no non-pharmaceutical interventions occur, economic activities will be reduced endogenously due to sickness and because of individual decisions to reduce the risk of contagion and avoid risky places, including the hospitality sector, the educational sector and crowded workplaces (Aum et al., 2020). Effective demand will also be reduced due to precautionary (money) hoarding, while labour supply in comparison to other settings reduces early on. Economic policies may thus be necessary to stabilize the economy that will enter a sharp recession, but due to the comparatively short period the costs associated with long-term unemployment can be avoided.

A dual health care system for the new *versus* the known diseases with strict and comprehensive triage needs to be in place in order to prevent contamination and breakdown of public health care provision. A risk with this strategy is that it may look acceptable on paper, but that popular support may wane in the reality of an outbreak with sharply increasing numbers of fatalities.

Since the approach to pandemics is transparent responsibilities are clear and these provide a strong incentive for individual preparedness by firms and consumers including a 'war chest' in the form of enough capital and savings.

	Pluses	*Minuses*
Internal	**Strengths** • Strong incentives for individual pandemic preparedness • No need for exit strategy	**Vulnerabilities** • Reduction of labour supply • Inequality in terms of access to private health care • Contamination of the health care system • Managing excess mortality • No trace and test approach
External	**Opportunities** • No need for international coordination	**Risks** • Not applicable to high mortality diseases • Insufficient protection of essential workers • More frequent pandemics

Diagram 6.3 SVOR for the Darwinian Society setting

The strong incentives at the microeconomic level are a strength of the setting and the same is true for the fact that no international coordination is necessary. Clearly cross border effects are relevant for a pandemic, but in this setting these effects are accepted if not ignored and therefore reliance on other countries is not necessary. In contrast with other settings the health policy strategy does not require a vaccine as the light at the end of the tunnel since the disease becomes endemic after some time (the point is not that a vaccine is not helpful, but that it is not a necessary condition for economic recovery). The biggest risk of this scenario is that it is a versatile breeding ground for pandemics with globalization increasing the transmission speed between countries and no interventions to contain the domestic spread. Therefore, this setting is characterized by a higher frequency of contagious diseases that are not stopped early on and become pandemics.

Setting 2: Deglobality
In the North-West corner of Diagram 6.2 the key distinguishing characteristic is that cross-border flows of people are strictly limited, but the movement of people is not limited within a country. Countries take the pandemic and its economic consequences more or less one by one.

The orientation of this scenario is towards the local community. The mood in this scenario is determined by shrinking social, economic and political cross-border linkages. We could label this state of mind as deglobality (van Bergeijk, 2019), juxtaposed with the mentality and expectations of ever-increasing international exchange during the era of globalization.[8] The multilateral and supranational organisations have lost both their authority and their support in this setting. Coordination of policies is thus difficult if not impossible.

Border controls in this setting have by assumption been reinstalled at the levels of the early 1960s, physical production has been localised and international travel is restricted and expensive (also timewise as mandatory quarantines are customarily applied in this setting). But while migration and travel flows (including tourism) are limited internationally, no restrictions are placed on domestic movements and activities.

The basic idea is that society is safe behind borders that stop foreigners from bringing contagious diseases. While human de-linkage can reduce the speed by which a pandemic unfolds, it cannot, however, avoid the occurrence of pandemics. Human trafficking, smuggling and exchange will occur and provide a pathway for infection, especially if borders are long. Moreover, it is not only humans that transmit diseases which increasingly are of a zoonotic nature: almost two-thirds of the roughly four hundred new infectious diseases that have been identified since the Second World War originated in animals (Karesh et al., 2012). Long-range transmission both on the ground and by our flying friends imply that contagious diseases, just like animals, cannot be stopped by borders. Finally, even the strictest border measures do, of course, not provide a defence against a pandemic that starts domestically.

Building blocks
It is important to see that in this exercise a setting always precedes the pandemic; deglobalization can be the consequence of a pandemic, but that is not the point here.[9]

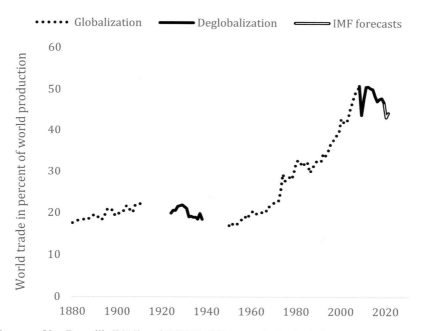

Sources: Van Bergeijk (2019) and IMF World Economic Outlook dataset April 2020

Figure 6.1 Openness of the world economy

Globalization and deglobalization are recurring phases of the global economic system, as illustrated in Figure 6.1, that also shows that current forecasts (that include the impact of the Corona crisis) do not foresee a return in world openness to the levels experienced in the 1960s (that we assume to have taken place in this setting). An important similarity of phases of deglobalization is the hollowing out of world leadership (hegemonism) leading to a reduction in the provision of global public goods, including global pandemic preparedness (that, as we discussed in Chapter 2, was insufficient). The breakdown of global cooperation reflects the second underlying mechanism of deglobalization. It is ironic, but sad, that the United States and the United Kingdom (the hegemons that helped to build a constellation in which trade, democracy and peace were reinforcing aspects of the world order) are spoiling global and European governance. Brexit is a dangerous mistake, but it is a disaster that the United States, in the midst of a pandemic, cut its support for the World Health Organization, in the same vein as it paralysed the World Trade Organization in early 2020. These attacks on global governance are dangerous, but this manner of international political behaviour can be expected from a declining hegemon in a period of deglobalization.[10] The international system also changes in other ways. An increase of border protection structures such as border walls and border fences is part of the deglobality setting (and this trend predates the outbreak of the Corona virus as illustrated in Figure 6.2).

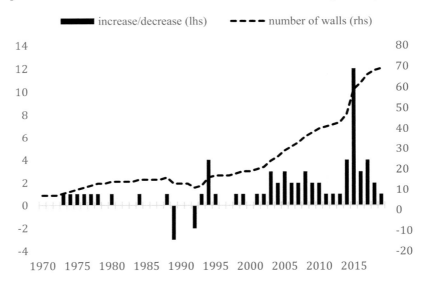

Sources: Kamwela and van Bergeijk (2020)

Figure 6.2 Border walls and fences before the COVID-19 pandemic

It is important to recognize that deglobality is not limited to Western democracies where populists have risen to power based on election platforms that 'put their nation first', oppose supra national governance and surf on the waves of the discontents of globalization (Stiglitz, 2018). The anti-globalist movement also has a basis in the Global South and the goal of these 'deglobalists' is to reduce the powers and roles of the Bretton Woods institutions that are perceived to be driven by the interests of transnational corporations and multinational financial institutions in the Global North (Bello, 2017). The international organizations in this philosophy are the engines of bad globalization. The movement's ambition is a radical transformation towards a form of decentralized, heterogeneous economic decision making that strengthens belonging and community. In a broader philosophical sense, deglobality can be grounded in non-Western economic approaches such as Buddhism. Buddhism offers an alternative for the Liberal Peace, that is, the idea that international trade strengthens democracy and reduces international conflicts. This idea that the benefits of international exchange offer a powerful antidote against initiation of international conflicts underpins much of the architecture of the international institutions. Buddhist economics provides a philosophical alternative by stressing that simplicity and low use in consumption allow for highly self-sufficient local communities that have no incentives to get involved in large-scale conflicts (Schumacher, 2011). The point again is that Deglobality is a conceivable and realistic future world for the next pandemic.

Strengths, Vulnerabilities, Opportunities and Risks
The international spread of pandemics in this setting does not follow the pattern of falling dominoes but rather a staggered repetition of national outbreaks. Economies are less vulnerable to economic contagion and the impact on the world economy will be smaller compared to a simultaneous outbreak and easier to manage. Healthwise the result, however, is the same as the disease arrives in all countries. The pandemic can be slowed down, but not stopped (Wells et al., 2020). Detection is more difficult because the global institutions required for sharing information are absent or impotent but it is not impossible because the internet is still an open global asset in this setting (indeed, social media activity has been used to assess the emergence and impact of COVID-19; see, for example, Kuchler et al., 2020).

	Pluses	*Minuses*
Internal	**Strengths** • Lower speed of transmission from abroad • Availability of tested border procedures	**Vulnerabilities** • Loss of economic efficiency reducing the capacity to finance health care • False sense of security may reduce preparedness
External	**Opportunities** • Reduction of the epidemiological footprint • Spread of the pandemic over a longer time period globally	**Risks** • Late detection of pandemics • Less incentives for international cooperation • No or difficult access to international supplies

Diagram 6.4 SVOR for the Deglobality setting

Arguably, lower levels of economic and social globalization, the associated lower levels of welfare and demand in this setting and the localization of food production could reduce the pressure on land in some countries and may limit the interfaces between human activity and wildlife and thereby the epidemiological footprint (Elbe, 2007), but this is by no means necessarily true.

International border procedures are in place and act as circuit breakers in a pandemic. Deglobality is thus associated with a lower speed of transmission for the planet, because countries have internationally distanced. But epidemic speed within countries is as high as in the other settings and especially in pandemic hotspots (Morse et al., 2012) that are concentrated in Western Europe, and in low-income and middle-income countries in Africa, Middle East, and South and East Asia deglobalization does not offer recourse. Deglobalization reduces welfare and thus the funds available for health care and also limits the possibilities of using foreign markets to source supplies of medication, medical machinery and protective gear should the need arise suddenly.

Setting 3: Autocratic Autarky
In the South-West corner of Diagram 6.2 the distinguishing characteristic is authoritarian rule. This setting would seem to bring together the most efficient policy mix since contact with the world at large is limited and the authorities have a battery of measures that can be applied in a much stricter way and on shorter notice than would seem to be possible in modern open democratic market economies. North Korea would currently be the prototype, with an alleged death penalty being applied for breaking quarantine. Efficiency may, however, be challenged if insufficient popular support can be mobilized or if the credibility of the regime is compromised. Lack of transparency may feed rumours and induce contra productive avoidance of health policy measures.

Building blocks
The first thing to observe is that isolationism *per se* offers no protection against a highly contagious virus. Indeed, probably the scariest thing about the Spanish Flu was its ability to reach even the most remote corners of our planet, in a world without mass tourism, global production networks and refugee flows. Social networks are extensive and provide transmission channels along which a disease can travel, as exemplified by the small world problem (Schnettler, 2009) that every earthling is only roughly six handshakes away from the Pope, Mr. Trump and Mr Jong-un. Moreover, diseases that originate domestically or are transmitted by migrating wildlife, birds and vectors (mosquitoes, ticks, fleas, and so on) cannot be stopped at the border.

It is relevant to distinguish between truly autocratic regimes, such as China and Vietnam, that appear to have been successful in keeping case fatality rates down (Sorci et al., 2020) and democratic countries with leaders that have autarkic autocratic sympathies, including to varying degrees the United States, Brazil, Hungary, India, the Philippines, Poland and the United Kingdom (Posen, 2020). In the latter case the mix of a democratic structure and a semi-autarkic autocratic leadership style has produced some of the world's worst outcomes for COVID-19 as we saw in Chapter 5. Autocratization as a trend has been observed over the last two decades (Lührmann, 2019) and could strengthen due to the Corona crisis, especially in view of the comparatively good performance of autocracies (Figure 6.3).

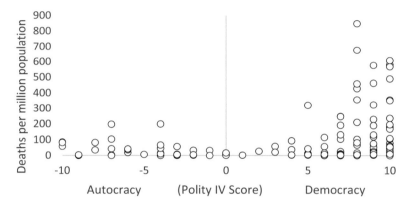

Sources: Polity IV for the year 2018 (Marshall et al., 2011) and *World in data* for
death count: July 31, 2020

*Figure 6.3 Registered COVID-19 deaths and autocracy – democracy
continuum*

A problem with the data reported in Figure 6.3 is, of course, that measuring health data during a pandemic is difficult as we discussed in Chapter 4, but also that data reporting is often influenced by politics (Davis, 2020) and that a long history exists of distorted data reporting by dictatorships and autocracies in particular (van Bergeijk, 1995; Carlitz and McLellan, 2020). Low numbers may thus reflect big lies.[11]

Strengths, Vulnerabilities, Opportunities and Risks
The combination of autarky and autocracy provides a strength with respect to the speed and rigour with which non-pharmaceutical interventions can be applied. This is a clear advantage and it may even be possible to isolate areas

where the disease is raging for a sufficiently long period (in relation to the incubation time and phase of contagion) to ensure that no cases will re-emerge. Monitoring, (digital) supervision, contact tracing and obligatory isolation in institutions rather than at home can be arranged with greater ease than in democracies. This comes, however, at a cost as legitimacy can be contested and popular support may not be forthcoming.

	Pluses	*Minuses*
Internal	**Strengths** • Quick and sharp health care policies that can be enforced offer the possibility to eradicate the disease	**Vulnerabilities** • Lack of transparency delays response • Lacking support • False sense of security may reduce preparedness • Health care access may be limited to the elite • Costs of autarky
External	**Opportunities** • Limitation of spread of diseases (also in pre-pandemic period)	**Risks** • Isolation makes it difficult to tap into new medical knowledge • No or difficult access to international supplies

Diagram 6.5 SVOR for the Autocratic Autarky setting

One important issue is the lack of transparency in autocracies where authorities may seek to muzzle medical professionals as they try to hide their own errors and mismanagement.[12] It is also not *a priori* clear that the health situation of the population is a policy goal in autocratic regimes, because typically the analysis of health indicators and the form of government find that democracy outperforms dictatorship (Okada, 2018). In other words, the observation that non-pharmaceutical interventions can be applied more efficiently in an autarkic autocracy does not imply that these tools will be used.

The costs of this setting occur both in the economy and in terms of a population's health situation. Economically, national self-isolation is damaging because the welfare level is significantly lower due to less opportunities for specialization. The opportunity costs are thus significant in this setting. An important lesson of the research on economic sanctions is that their impact also influences non-economic variables including health (van Bergeijk, 2021). An important issue is that the non-availability of foreign supply may reduce food security and increase vulnerability if famines occur.

Setting 4: Benevolent Big Brother
In the South-East corner of Diagram 6.2 individual liberties are offered for
containment and mitigation of the pandemic. Detection, registration,
surveillance and testing in this setting are massive, obligatory and invasive.
The population is required to use apps that can identify recent contacts of
identified new cases. Freedom and personal liberties are reduced. Mass
protests and religious group activities are, as all gatherings, forbidden. Social
pressure is strong and deviant behaviour is not tolerated. Big Brother, however,
is benign – the policy aim is, so to say, to maintain universal access to health
care by means of restricting the freedom to infect others. The mindset in this
setting is that the collective is more important than the individual.

Building blocks
Gourinchas (2020, p. 32), noting the swift and strict implementation of their
social distancing measures, singles out Taiwan, Singapore, and the Chinese
regions outside Hubei as examples that are 'unambiguously' applying 'the
right short-run public health policy'. Panizza (2020, p. 161) notes the success
of Singapore, Taiwan and Israel and also observes that South Korea (ibid.,
footnote 7) is successful without a complete lockdown. What these countries
have in common is a rigorous trace–test–treat approach that relies to a large
extent on invasive electronic surveillance and strict isolation of identified cases
and potentially infected (Calvo et al., 2020). The use of digital health
monitoring software can be by consent, but also obligatory and invasive – even
in democracies. Israel, for example, involved the secret service using a phone
tracking app originally designed as anti-terror software, that trails the location
histories of its whole population.[13] The app monitors and enforces obligatory
isolation of positively tested persons and allows citizens and authorities to
check for (accidental) meetings with infected persons and monitor and enforce
self-isolation of those potentially infected. The relative success of societies
with a non-Western model will be noted and influence views on governance.
Mahbubani (2020), for example, observes:

> The crisis highlights the contrast between the competent responses of East
> Asian governments (notably China, South Korea and Singapore) and the
> incompetent responses of Western governments (such as Italy, Spain,
> France, Britain and America). The far lower death rates suffered by East
> Asian countries is a lesson to all. They reflect not just medical capabilities,
> but also the quality of governance and the cultural confidence of their
> societies.

From this perspective, a striking difference between autocracies and
democracies is the difference in death toll of the virus (Figure 6.3), and this

may reflect not only differences in the quality of governance, but also the political division and lack of solidarity in some democracies.[14]

Strengths, Vulnerabilities, Opportunities and Risks
Speed of detection and action are the key factors that help to prevent and contain outbreaks and allow for nowcasting and crowd management. The economic benefit is that economic disruptions can be limited and that lockdowns, if necessary, can be complete and maintained sufficiently, limiting the risk of loosening measures too early.

	Pluses	*Minuses*
Internal	**Strengths** • A strong 'trace, test, treat' approach with short reporting time and actions • Monitoring and enforcement of self-isolation • Crowd management • Reduction of the speed by which the disease spreads • Potential for full elimination	**Vulnerabilities** • Avoidance and evasion • Lack of support in segments of the population • Bias towards smart phone owners excludes marginalized groups • Surveillance creep
External	**Opportunities** • Less need for international cooperation • Facilitates quarantine of international travellers	**Risks** • Cyber-crime (both cyber-attacks and hacking of private information) • Risk of developing towards deglobality

Diagram 6.6 SVOR for the Benevolent Big Brother setting

The two risks of this setting are the Orwellian potential of mass surveillance and the reliance on mobile phone ownership. Steps towards mass surveillance have been recognized as a dangerous move since Orwell's (1949) dystopian novel *Nineteen Eighty-Four* and 'surveillance creep' is a well-known concept that relates technologies that are introduced in the wake of a (public health) crisis but then used later to monitor behaviour from a national security perspective. Considerations about privacy and government control may undercut public support and stimulate evasion and avoidance of detection. Mobile phone ownership may look like a universally applicable instrument in view of mobile phone ownership of 108 phones per 100 population in 2018 (International Telecommunication Union, 2020), but is not a straightforward instrument to collect data. First, they need to be smart phones and ownership excludes groups, such as the poor and homeless and people living in areas without connection to the internet (the number of active mobile broadband subscriptions per 100 population in 2018 was 75 and 33 for developing countries and low-income countries, respectively). Second, high-income earners (both in developing and advanced economies) may own several mobile phones creating many possibilities for avoidance and evasion of digital monitoring. Third, in advanced economies the marginalized groups (low-income earners, homeless) are actually at the highest risk of getting infected and having to continue to work, but also less likely to possess an individual smart phone.

Important external risks for this setting are its vulnerability to cyber-attacks and cybercrime. Cyber risks in general increased during the COVID-19 pandemic also because of the greater reliance to the internet during lockdown, but this risk also relates to hijacking of websites and stealing of privacy sensitive information.

Central: Article 3 trilemmas

In the middle of Diagram 6.2 we find societies that try to balance individual freedom, the economy and health – issues that are central to Article 3 of the Universal Declaration of Human Rights 'Everyone has the right to life, liberty and security of person.' Life, liberty and security form the policy trilemma with health, freedom and the economy as the poles that require the balancing act that is at the centre of this setting. The fifth setting thus reflects societies that try to maintain the lifestyle, norms and values, including privacy, democracy and openness, at levels that are comparable to those reached before the Corona pandemic. When a pandemic occurs, this generates permanent puzzles and trade-offs along many dimensions. These trade-offs are summarized in a trilemma or impossibility theorem for pandemic responses, as argued by Phlippen (2020).[15]

The trilemma is that countries cannot achieve full respect of individual liberties, complete economic freedom and universal access to health care at the same time during a pandemic. It is possible to choose two out of three but impossible to have all three at the same time. It is, for example, possible (point *A* in Diagram 6.7) to maintain universal access to health care and avoid workplace closures and limitations on international activities, but only when deep monitoring, obligatory testing and group isolation are applied (this would bring us into the Benevolent Big Brother setting). Likewise point *B* that represents full economic and personal liberty is a possibility but that comes at the cost of strict triage and severe quantitative restrictions in the health care sector, as in the Darwinian Society setting. Point *C*, finally, shows that privacy and individual freedom could *in extremis* be aligned with access to the health care sector for all, but only when domestic and international economic activities are very much limited.

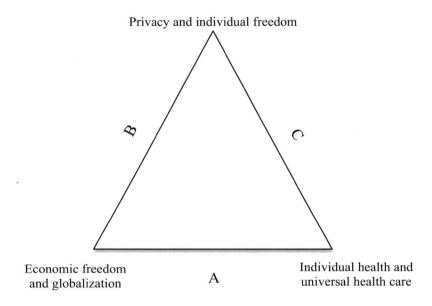

Diagram 6.7 Pandemic trilemma in the Article 3 setting

This trilemma is a powerful theoretically statement that makes the choices clear but should not be understood as if governments have no policy space. One can be somewhat critical about the binary nature of the trilemma. Policy choices seldom are as black and white as in the trilemma. Yes, if the choice is, for example, only between perfect economic freedom and very deep globalization or a total halt of all economic encounters, then the logical set up is the trilemma, but this is not a realistic picture of the world where we see countries positioning themselves on a continuum with more or less integration. Indeed, in this setting governments operate inside the triangle, balancing costs and benefits and evaluating their position in the light of new developments.

Building blocks
Policy trilemmas have a certain appeal to economists who are often blamed for their two-handedness because the economic policy advice typically is of the 'on the one hand,… on the other hand' type that is not much appreciated by policy makers and politicians. Trilemmas such the Mundell–Fleming monetary

policy trilemma (Obstfeld and Taylor, 1997) or Rodrik's (2011) trilemma of the world economy move beyond bilateral trade-offs that characterize much economic policy decisions on considered interventions and have helped politicians and policy makers to discover the boundaries of the policy space themselves. The binary solutions for the trilemma constitute the four corner solutions in Diagram 6.2.

The trilemma has become most apparent in the Western market democracies that assign high value to individual liberties and (data) privacy but implemented non-pharmaceutical interventions at an unprecedented scale. Some of the market economies have been relatively successful, including Norway, Denmark and Germany, but others did not perform well. Belgium, Italy and Spain are clear examples of a lack of success, probably due to a decentralized and delayed response and a lack of tracing and testing capacities.

Strengths, Vulnerabilities, Opportunities and Risks
The balancing act between the three poles of the trilemma may enable countries to avoid, to some extent, the pitfalls of the corner settings. Transparency and democratic accountability may help to generate broader support for non-pharmaceutical interventions. Adherence to the rules may initially be stricter if based on bottom-up own responsibility in comparison to top-down imposed regulations. But this comes at a cost, since the disease can hit an unprepared country that responds slowly and piecewise. Policy making may be overstretched and communication of a middle-of-the-road approach that may change course over time is complicated. Social distancing fatigue, opposition and lobbying activities may undercut adherence to the rules if they are sector specific. Resistance is expected to grow over time when the pandemic wave appears to wane leading to a push for early removal of lockdown measures even if the evidence base for relaxation is weak. Maintaining vigilance and social distancing is the main challenge in this setting. The economic developments are complicated, and recessions are likely to follow W-shaped patterns creating additional uncertainty when an economy climbs out of a trough while the sustainability of a recovery is problematic.

With respect to the external aspects of the SVOR in Diagram 6.8 two aspects are relevant. First, it may be difficult to achieve coordination between countries with positions that shift and may be incongruent at some points in time. Second, traditionally this group of countries have formed the best basis for building and strengthening supra-national governance. The trilemma thus also has a bearing on popular support for multilateral organizations, such as the World Health Organization, a point to which we will return in the next Chapter.

	Pluses	*Minuses*
Internal	**Strengths** • Avoid to some extent the pitfalls of the corner settings • Consensus and coherence • Broader support for the health policy strategy	**Vulnerabilities** • Overburdened and stretched decision making • Complicated communication of a strategy that is adjusted over time • Opposition and lobbying shifts policy possibly against the silent majority
External	**Opportunities** • This setting provides traditionally the best setting for policy coordination and cooperation • Adaptability of the strategy to other disease characteristics	**Risks** • The lack of a clear and stable (global) strategy • The necessary international policy coordination may be too difficult to achieve

Diagram 6.8 SVOR for the Article 3 trilemma setting

6.3 SEVERAL FUTURES: ONE CHOICE?

Our exploration of possible settings is not an exact science and therefore it is quite possible that the setting descriptions and/or specific knowledge that you now may have evoked different ideas of where you think the settings should be allocated in Diagram 6.2. To assist that manner of critical thinking, I allocated the names of the countries that we discussed in this Chapter in Diagram 6.9, not because that provides an exact truth about COVID-19, but as a starting point for discussion. A complicating factor is, of course, that countries will, in all likelihood, differ in their choices and that the world will consist of differently positioned countries with a complex interaction. Even for that fuzzy world the corner flags of the settings indicate the outskirts of the next pandemic's playing field. This is actually the most important purpose of the exercise: to help you form your own opinion about possible future states of the world in relation to the risk of pandemics.

We need to rethink the organization of society, the extent to which we are willing to accept risks and to balance the costs and benefits *before* the next pandemic. During an outbreak short term survival and fear are likely to dominate all considerations. For a rational discussion we need to take time and evaluate the pluses and minuses of the different approaches and we need to do that without the pressure of the day-to-day problems of the management of a pandemic and its economic fallout. In this sense the post-COVID-19 period essentially will be pre-pandemic again.

You may also use the discussion in this Chapter to identify a missing setting or a missing dimension that you think is predominantly relevant for the discussion on the response to the next pandemic. This would be logical because this book is written in the first half year of the pandemic and new information will become available after its publication and that will further shape the analysis of the best way to handle the next pandemic. We will learn a lot about the good and the bad of the way society has been organized (Wyplosz, 2020). Comprehensive evaluations of the economic and health policy responses to COVID-19 will only become available after the pandemic has run its full cycle that can be shortened by the invention, production and distribution of a vaccine (but note that a vaccine may not be possible for a next pandemic). The choice for the organization of society will, to a large extent, determine how we can prepare and is therefore an important input for the next Chapter.

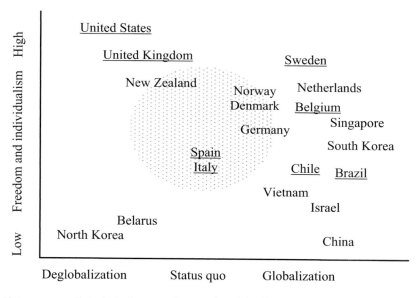

Notes: Only includes countries mentioned in this Chapter
            Underlined countries are in the top 10 of reported COVID deaths per
            million population (date accessed July 31, 2020)

Diagram 6.9 Indicative illustration of country positions

But before moving to Chapter 7, I invite you to consider the big moral dilemmas that we encountered in the present Chapter. The need for triage and the temporary halt of universal health access *versus* the economic performance that is necessary to fund a well-equipped health care sector. The loss of privacy and individual freedom *versus* the spread of the disease that endangers vulnerable people. The openness and international connectivity of the Global Village *versus* the increased use of border closures. The solution to these dilemmas is by no means easy and will need discussion before we can arrive at a new social contract that reflects the realities of recurring pandemics.

Key takeaways of Chapter 6

- It is important to investigate the societal context to understand the possibilities and costs of the mitigation of pandemics.
- Settings investigate the certainty of the next pandemic in different societal contexts to deal with the uncertainty of the future organization of nation states.
- Pandemic response involves trade-offs between the economy, lifestyle, norms and values, including privacy, democracy and openness.
- Globalization has been associated with the spread of COVID-19, but globalized countries are in principle better equipped to keep fatality rates low.
- International isolation can delay but not stop a pandemic.
- Autocratic societies can with greater ease intrude on privacy and individuals enforcing stricter adherence, but a number of democratic societies have also successfully contained COVID-19.
- A striking difference between Asia and Europe and the Americas is the difference in death toll that may reflect the fragmentation and lack of solidarity in democracies and individualistic societies.
- In a Darwinian Society suffering and the loss of human life are accepted as a force of nature; the economic shock will be sharp and relatively short compared to other settings.
- In a deglobalized world economies are less vulnerable for contagion (both health wise and economical). In the end the result, however, is the same: the disease arrives in all countries.
- Digital detection is a powerful instrument to contain outbreaks and for nowcasting and crowd management.
- The pandemic trilemma is key for societies that assign high value to individual liberties and (data) privacy but need to implement non-pharmaceutical interventions on a large scale.

- In all settings triage is an important tool to keep the health sector from collapse and to ensure care provision for diseases and conditions that are not related to the pandemic.

ENDNOTES

1   For example, while it could be argued that The Netherlands and Portugal were hegemons – world leaders – in their golden eras, that empirical real-world phenomenon cannot be the basis of a scenario for the next decades. While the historical experience that small open economies become world leaders exists, a future of small nations with hegemonistic status is not conceivable anymore (van Bergeijk, 2019).

2   I do see the COVID-19 pandemic as a useful warning for the Big One with a case mortality rate that is comparable to, for example, Ebola, but that is not point.

3   See Swedberg (2017) for a discussion in the context of social sciences, Pen (1985) for a more critical view on its use in economics and Forster (2011) on the debate between John Stuart Mill and Whewell.

4   See, for example, the Rockefeller Foundation's 2010 'lock step' scenario in which a global pandemic drives a move towards autocracy. Note that while much in the scenario has apocalyptic visionary quality, it also reflects the dominant perception before COVID-19 that the pandemic death toll would mainly be a problem of developing countries.

5   *A Call to Defend Democracy*, an open letter initiated by International Institute for Democracy and Electoral Assistance and the based National Endowment for Democracy June 20, 2020 and available at https://www.idea.int/news-media/multimedia-reports/call-defend-democracy.

6   Belarus is an example of an autocracy that followed the path of a Darwinian Society.

7   Interestingly religious solutions to the spread of COVID-19 were explored in Tanzania which organized a 3-day National Prayer and later claimed that this had effectively reduced the spread of the virus in the country, see: 'Magufuli says Tanzania has reduced Covid-19 patients' Voice of America: https://www.voaswahili.com/a/magufuli-asema-tanzania-imepunguza-wagonjwa-wa-covid-19-/5423549.html in Kiswahili, accessed June 9, 2020.

8   A recent example of globality is the OECD (2014, p. 4) foreseeing that 'global exports will continue to outpace GDP growth over the next half century'.

9   The pandemic that preceded the Great Depression did not cause it. Recovery of the recession triggered by the Spanish Flu was relatively quick and spontaneous. World trade did not collapse. A major difference between the context of the Spanish Flu and the economic background against which COVID-19 emerged is that our world was already in the downward phase of

Deglobalization 2.0. The Corona pandemic thus came on top of a Deglobalization wave.

[10] We can observe both in the Great Depression of the 1930s and in the Great Recession that the leading power of the time (the hegemon) deserted the rules of the game that underpinned globalization and were actually designed by its interest in an open trade and investment climate. An open stable and relatively peaceful system allows other countries to develop and grow faster capturing a larger share of the benefits of globalization. In the early phase of globalization a smaller share from a larger economic pie may still be an improvement. At some point the costs of being a hegemon, however, outweigh the benefits. This is where the emergence of China as the new hegemon comes into play.

[11] See, for example, *The Economist*, 'Russia's covid-19 outbreak is far worse than the Kremlin admits', May 21, 2020.

[12] The classic example is the case of Li Wenliang who tried to warn about the new disease that eventually became known as COVID-19. Reportedly the police compelled Dr Wenliang to sign a statement that his warning constituted 'illegal behavior' (*New York Times*, 'As New Coronavirus Spread, China's Old Habits Delayed Fight', February 1, 2020).

[13] See for a history and developing legislation: 'Intelligence Subcommittee grants government another 48 hours to submit a bill regulating the use of Shin Bet phone tracking to contain the spread of the coronavirus', Knesset News: https://main.knesset.gov.il/EN/News/PressReleases/Pages/press8620b.aspx, accessed June 8, 2020.

[14] This may to some extent also be a cultural treat: Confuciansim during the outbreak phase of COVID-19 has been associated with a significantly slower speed of the spread (Lin and Meissner, 2020).

[15] The trilemma is not unique for pandemics but would occur with all events with external effects of behavior that require a breach of personal freedom and privacy. From this perspective a pandemic is an example of an external effect that legitimizes government intervention. The extent of the breach is always a balancing act.

7. Five Ps for the Next Pandemic

Whether you want to be successful in life or want to beat the next pandemic, the key recipe will be the five Ps: prepare, prepare, prepare, prepare, prepare. COVID-19 reminded us that a virus cannot be stopped by border measures. Thus, Earth needs to prepare, prepare, prepare, prepare, prepare. We know that the next pandemic is coming, and that the frequency of pandemics is increasing. That is why the five Ps are vital.

Our point of departure is that we cannot rely on a medical miracle cure. Indeed, as argued by Elbe (2011, p. 849), we need to:

> reflect more deeply on one of the core elements of global health security: its aspiration to secure populations against pandemic threats through recourse to medical interventions. Indeed, scholars of medicalisation tend to display a much greater awareness about some of the limitations surrounding modern medical practice, and such limitations can also be shown to accompany our current pandemic preparedness efforts. Simply put, many of the medical countermeasures recently developed and stockpiled in the pursuit of health security are not nearly as effective as commonly thought (as well as having a number of unwelcome and potentially harmful side-effects).

Moreover, we cannot stockpile the two most important health care resources. Machines and equipment can be produced in advance, but there is a clear limit to the number of well-trained medical staff and space for quality care during pandemics. It would be unfair to suggest that the medical profession is unaware of the problems. Comparing modern pandemic preparedness with the state of affairs during the Spanish Flu, Morens and Fauci, (2007, p. 1025) conclude that 'Almost all "then-versus-now" comparisons are encouraging, in theory.' The 'in theory' is not an innocent addition, as the authors discuss antiviral and antibiotic resistance, medical capacity constraints and resource availability, the vulnerability of the just-in-time character of the medical supply chain as well as the fact that the burden of a pandemic would fall on the least privileged. Because of the obvious limits to medical solutions, we need to prepare and find ways to structurally mitigate the impact of a virus on the move. Our main efforts need to be non-pharmaceutical interventions, but we need to develop more intelligent solutions than lockdowns. Preparation should take place at the five relevant levels: individual (households and firms), local, national, international and global pandemic preparedness.

It is important to realize that the strength of the defence against the next pandemic will be determined by the weakest link and it cannot be stressed enough that all five levels of defence need to be active (Diagram 7.1).

Society's defence cannot and does not need to be perfect. It is not necessary that everybody adheres all the time. But we need at least a very substantial fraction of the population in order to slow down the spread of viruses and other contagious diseases. It is true that one of the lessons of the pandemic is that others cannot be trusted, because adherence to distancing and hygiene are determined by heterogeneous risk perceptions and risk preferences as well as economic and political motives. While adherence to the rules can be observed at some point in time, it cannot be observed all the time. A general rule is that those that break the rules have probably broken the rules before and are therefore at higher risk both of being infected as well as being a source of contagion. That means that one's individual preparedness is vital because it is the only line of defence of which one can ultimately be sure. Phrased more positively, it is the first line of defence for society and an individual can thus strengthen society's resilience (Rajaonah and Zio, 2020). Therefore, we will start with individual preparation in the next section.

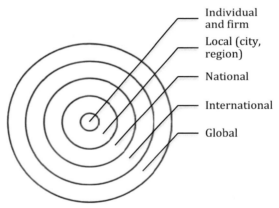

Diagram 7.1 Shields of pandemic preparedness

Collective action is, however, essential to prevent and contain pandemics. Good and safe societal and global environments support individual effectiveness in avoiding contagion. Individual effectiveness is obviously stronger if proper conduct at the other – higher – levels can be organized. Yes, we have learned (again) that authorities cannot always be trusted, that science is a social activity not free from delusion and that the politics and populism of pandemics hinder the rational fight against pandemics. At the same time, we know that government, politics and science urgently need to (re)organize, because only then can we mobilize the necessary resources to fight the next pandemic. And we have learned that governments, science and authorities cannot succeed unless individuals prepare and act accordingly.

7.1 BE PREPARED: INDIVIDUAL

The speed by which a pandemic spreads around the globe has always been underestimated and its impact has always surprised and puzzled medical professionals – COVID-19 in this sense is not an exception. Jackson (2009), for example, describing the arrival of the 1957 Asian Flu in the United Kingdom notes that while the media started reporting the potential for contamination early on in April, the World Health Organization advised that it was unlikely to strike until the winter – as it happened, the first cases were recorded in June. Moreover, authorities played down the severity of the emerging situation. So, individual preparation really starts with – critically – following media reports, especially if an epidemic becomes international and reaches a second continent. To be informed is thus the first step of individual preparedness. The next question is: what do you need to do when you recognize that the risk of a pandemic has increased?

One of the least intrusive and most effective measures against any contagious disease is washing your hands thoroughly. This is a daily routine that many people had lost. I remember that I was surprised to see my guide wash his hands for what felt like three minutes when I was on field work in Tanzania. My own handwashing typically would be done in ten seconds if I wanted to be thorough. After some thought it made sense to me. It was a lesson that I took to heart and I would do the same when I was in a developing country. Once back home, however, I would resort to the quick job…

Textbox 7.1 Wash your hands!

It is extremely important that handwashing is trained at home and at school and that this discipline is maintained. Global Hand-washing Day already exists (the event takes places every year on 15th of October, see www.globalhandwashing.org), but needs to be taken seriously also by adults and in the advanced economies. Family education and training is the best way to protect your loved ones. My respiratory hygiene training was intensive – there was a little nursery rhyme that urged me to turn my head away (correct) and cover my mouth with my hand (wrong; it should have been my elbow) – and washing hands was educated at home. With hindsight children and students should have been trained and required to wash hands when they enter the school. Family hygiene is an essential line of defence, because once in the house the risk of getting infected becomes almost a certainty.

Equally cheap but more intrusive is the habit of stopping with handshakes. Shaking hands is an important social tool to connect with people and show agreement, respect and friendship. Shaking hands, however, can be dangerous. Rational people will avoid shaking hands when they are aware of the risk of a contagious disease spreading. We should be prepared and willing to stop shaking hands when a pandemic occurs. Humanity should also become more tolerant towards religions where hand-shaking (touching of non-relatives) is a taboo.[1] As soon as we recognize that we are in the early phase of a potential pandemic – let's say when an epidemic becomes international – hand shaking should stop around the globe.

Textbox 7.2 No more medical handshakes

I stopped shaking hands early in the pandemic when the first cases were identified in my home country because that was what the development studies community did at international meetings during Ebola[2], but I was met by disbelief and annoyance when I told the doctor in my local hospital that I did not shake hands anymore because of COVID-19 (a week later this became mandatory in The Netherlands). I understood her reaction, also because I remembered how I myself was shocked when a doctor in New Zealand in 2016 simply refused to shake my hand telling me 'that is not the way we do this over here'. Rightly so, doctors should stop shaking hands everywhere and always when they are at work.

More expensive but less intrusive is wearing mouth caps or masks. These are one of the most cost-efficient interventions during pandemics (Madhav, 2017), but not a panacea – they can only work against respiratory diseases. COVID-19 offers the opportunity to capitalise on the fact that people have become accustomed to using a mask in public places. Maintaining that human and social capital requires that masks – like in Asia – return frequently in public space. The flu season would be the most obvious period of the year where masks could be worn. The point would be to maintain social acceptance of masks to contain the spread of viruses. There are important side benefits: a constant demand so that an industry with sufficient capacity can exist and innovation is stimulated (the best way to achieve general acceptance would be the invention of a good transparent mask). But these considerations are not relevant for the individual: it is likely that a mouth cap provides some protection, also against other infectious diseases, and it is thus on the to-do list.

The next items on the to-do list are not pandemic-specific. They are always important to meet other disasters (running from blizzards to general strikes) or simply to deal with bad luck. The pandemic has only made it clearer that emergency supplies are important, especially when hoarding occurs or when you have to self-isolate. Two weeks' supply of basic foodstuff would seem to be a good investment. Likewise, a financial buffer is helpful – a friend of mine recommends six months of 'f*ck you' money because that allows you to quit a job and find a new one.[3] It will also help you to get through the first tough period when a lockdown destroys your job opportunities. It would also make sense to rethink how you can use and organize your house for teleworking and to organize good and reliable internet facilities. You may not want to telework but even so, planning which room can be redesigned and used if need arises helps you to prepare.[4]

Textbox 7.3 Business and government

It is unlikely that governments can and/or want to provide similar massive rescue support as during COVID-19's pandonomic episode, if only because the bazookas stretched fiscal and monetary balances to the limits. Also, it is unlikely that support will be provided across the board and with no strings attached as happened during the pandonomics outbreak. Indeed, in many countries the second wave of support saw increasing conditionality and selectivity. Firms will thus have to fundamentally change their business strategies.

Individual level preparation is also necessary for businesses. Firstly, firms need to maintain higher financial reserves and achieve lower indebtedness in order to avoid the immediate threat of business failure. A better financial position avoids many problems and unnecessary dependence on banks. In the same way as we discussed for individuals this is helpful as an all-hazard strategy: the pandemic has only enforced a real-life stress test and we now know that all too many firms cannot survive a temporary disaster on their own.

Secondly, the use of physical space needs to be redesigned. We have learned valuable lessons: teleworking *is* possible and while the revolution in teleworking was enforced overnight and working from home has not been a success for everybody and everywhere, we can tailor-make working places and working conditions. Wherever teleworking is impossible workplaces need to be re-designed in such a way that social distancing is possible. In general firms need to reconsider how they can achieve protection for their employees, because that is the only way to reduce the risk of closure and, moreover, an obligation for industries that are seen as essential. Vulnerabilities in such industries have become apparent and the strongest example is meat and poultry processing where outbreaks were frequent and recurring. In addition to factory design, shops need to rediscover their blueprints. Counters and cash desks have been adapted providing shielding between customer and their handling has changed as the use of cards rather than cash has progressed at warp speed. Obviously, the best way deal with this is to make pandemic risk an item of workplace and shop design so as to allow for gradual adjustment and find cost efficient tailor-made solutions for individual firms.

Textbox 7.4 Telework is here to stay

Teleworking is a timesaver because it avoids the need to commute; the endemic disturbances of morning meetings due to traffic jams and delays in public transportation could be avoided for good. It is financially attractive because it allows firms to economize on office space and transportation costs. Teleworking will allow highly innovative solutions also in small businesses, for example, by facilitating the employment of workers in far-away locations across the globe. Teleworking meetings have different dynamics and can include and connect employees in an alternative way and are thus a useful new management tool. Successful management models will blend bricks and mortar working places and teleworking and by doing so make the firm (and thus the economy) more pandemic-resistant.

Thirdly, the organization of activities needs to be such that the disturbance of primary production processes and workflows due to contagious diseases is reduced. This implies that firms should diversify with respect to (international) suppliers and markets and balance the costs of maintaining stocks of intermediate inputs and raw materials against the risk of just-in-time logistics. It also requires rethinking distribution channels and options to diversify a customer base. The pandemic, for example, has forced traditional brick and mortar restaurants to develop home delivery and internet reservation and pre-ordering; it would be a waste if this would not remain an important activity because it would also be helpful during less severe disruptions of dining out. Customers were already increasingly using the internet, home delivery and e-commerce but internet savviness has made a big jump and also reached the older generations in a very short period of time. Once the pandemic is gone, that structural change in the business environment will not be undone and will become an even more important competitive edge requiring the further blending of traditional and digital ways to serve the customer base.

Entrepreneurs innovate and look for new products, new markets and new combinations of traditional and non-traditional products and thereby form the backbone of an economy's resilience and capacity to adjust. They are risk takers and that brings great benefits to all. But the risks should be known and therefore risk assessment should become better engrained in business plans.

7.2 BE PREPARED: LOCAL

One of the most important determinants of the speed of pandemic spread is population density. Mega-cities, well-connected with the global economy, crowded with offices, restaurants, theatres and sports arenas and relying on mass transportation offer a superb breeding ground for any disease that thrives on inter-human transmission. This is why Wuhan, London, Paris, Madrid, Rio de Janeiro and New York became such deadly hotspots. Half the world's population lives in urban areas. During the outbreak it became clear that social distancing was barely possible in these death traps. This is, of course, not a new phenomenon. Newton discovered the law of gravity at Woolsthorpe Manor where he was taking shelter from the Black Death that ravaged London and had reached Cambridge. De Montagne recognized that *philosopher c'est doubter* while he avoided Bordeaux where the Bubonic Plague had killed a third of the population. So, the problem of city hot spots during a pandemic is certainly not new: it has so far been largely ignored.[5] City design is, however, a promising area where much progress has been achieved over the longer term, as illustrated by the finding that epidemic mortality in the American cities in the 1920s used to be driven by dirtiness and crowding (Ager et al, 2020). City management and city design need to consider how transmission can be slowed down and how life under lockdown can be made more bearable and less distortive without fortifying our living space (Melone and Borgo, 2020).

Cities historically grew from two basic principles. First, the benefits from having many people living in proximity which creates a consumer market, a labour market and an environment that is conducive to the exchange of new ideas. Second, the need to protect these economically attractive hubs from attacks. Both principles will continue to be relevant, but rather than protecting against human invaders our mega-cities need to protect their inhabitants against microbes and viruses. City planning and the economics of cities tend to value compactness (for example, Harari, 2020), but compactness is at odds with social distancing. This is also an important matter, because mega-cities tend to be international travelling hubs (both for business travel and for mass tourism), making them very vulnerable to contamination during a pandemic and likely to seed the disease to their surroundings. There are benefits and costs of global connectivity and the economic dependency on an overstretched tourism sector also without pandemics, but COVID-19 has made these clear again to everyone. Pandemic resistance needs to get more weight in intelligent city design.[6]

It takes time to do this cost efficiently and to keep the required investments at a bearable level, but a sustainable approach to increased pandemic resistance is certainly possible. Intelligent mega-city design (Textbox 7.5) can enable that implementing and lifting of lockdowns can be organized at a local level reducing the costs of having to close down the complete mega-city. Given the long lead time and grabbing the momentum of the COVID-19 pandemic, mega-city restructuring should start as soon as possible and could be used as an important stimulus to restart economic activity.

Mega-cities also are excellent breeding grounds because of their internal connectiveness. Mass transportation is crowded and spreads diseases from one quarter of the city to another. Mass transportation is unsafe. First of all, for employees protection needs to become an integral part of vehicle design and training. Transportation authorities need to stock protective gear for those in direct contact with the public. Mass transportation is also dangerous for commuters and the first place where masks should be made obligatory during epidemic phases. Spreading transportation more evenly over the day would help to avoid (over)crowding during rush hours. This requires coordination with the private sector, schools and universities.

Textbox 7.5 What could a pandemic-resistant mega-city look like?

An important improvement would be to see and restructure mega-cities as a segmented yet connected structure. Each segment should have essential facilities such as open-air markets, shopping malls and office space (both traditional and providing individualized services for tele-working) in combination with housing, schools and health care and possibly with a green circle of public parks and sport facilities. The lockdowns have shown that the green in mega-cities is even more important than we had previously thought.

Under normal circumstances connections would be open and the parks and facilities would be shared, but the interfaces would be semipermeable as they could be monitored and if necessary closed down during an epidemic. It may at first sight seem odd, overly costly and impossible to have such structures or circles in place while we need them so infrequently, but this line of defence based on connected but separable circles is how many countries actually arrange protection against flooding.

City design could also enable alternatives for public transportation. Walking is not a bad alternative at all, but it means that roads need to be closed down at least partially to enable social distancing for pedestrians. Biking also requires a different use of city roads and dedicated lanes need to be organized as well as parking facilities. Biking in some mega-cities has always been the preferred mode of transportation for large parts of the population and in other places it is being (re)discovered as such.

Pandemic preparedness of cities requires more than bricks, mortar and greens. Helsloot and Quinn (2009) argue that citizen and community engagement is an important determinant of pandemic resilience, also in order to build trust between, on the one hand, government and, on the other hand, marginalized groups, immigration populations and minorities. The need to involve civil society and NGOs is often overlooked in planning, playbooks and outbreak management teams. Especially at the local level citizen engagement can be better organized since the local conditions are better known and this will also help to increase awareness.

One of the key pandemic challenges that needs to be addressed at the local level and could in principle be done quickly and at relatively low investment is the organization of the access to health care facilities. During a pandemic there is a sudden and sharp overflow of patients with the new disease. The serious cases that cannot be cured at home will seek treatment. This puts the health infrastructure at risk. Doctors, nurses and workers at the emergency services get infected reducing the capacity of the health care sector in general. The outbreak creates the risk that the capacity of hospitals is dominated by patients with the new disease and we have learned that this limits normal care and creates unnecessary life-threatening situations. E-health has worked remarkably well and can be expected to remain an important means of consultation and diagnosis, but it cannot offer solutions for situations in which physical examination, treatments with expensive equipment and/or operations are necessary. The only solution is to designate specific institutions the task of taking care of the new disease and to select at the gates. It is efficient to ensure this division of tasks also because it reduces the demand for protective masks and clothing since they do not need to be changed and/or sterilized between patients all the time. This all requires a reallocation of patient flows and that means that an integrated approach to health care provision needs to be designed where the rules of engagement are identical and where the distinction between privileged and universal health care cannot be made. This is a new emergency structure that does not need investment but requires political will and determination – and may need coordination and adjustments of health care financing at a national level.

7.3 BE PREPARED: NATIONAL

Some things are better organized at the national level. Organizing and maintaining strategic stocks of drugs and medical equipment is often more costly at the local level (Wilgis, 2008). Local decisions on stock size may be suboptimal: they may lead to quantities that are too large if local authorities over stock or alternatively to local stocks that are too low, for example, because cost considerations are dominant.[7] The necessary medical and commercial expertise may only be available at the national level. The bargaining position of one national buyer is stronger than fragmented local demand, both under normal conditions and especially during a pandemic when scarcity soars because everyone is chasing after the same products.[8] Organizing and training sufficient medical professionals is also a national rather than a local task because labour mobility may undercut efforts in some parts of the country.

There are many issues that need reconsideration in the light of the Corona experience. Is it necessary to have national production facilities? The answer depends, first of all, on the type of product. For drugs and medical protection gear stockpiling offers a relevant alternative and the decision (that needs to take the possible direction of international value chains into account) can be based on economic principles. For testing free national facilities are necessary (Serra-Garcia and Szech, 2020) and the same is true for vaccines, depending on the availability of alternatives. Governments need to oversee these facilities and develop industry and labour market policies to ensure pandemic resilience.

Textbox 7.6 Multidisciplinary pandemic management teams

A stronger basis in all relevant sciences is key for the outbreak management teams and scientific councils that advice governments on pandemic response (Jenny, 2020). Narrowly composed teams and councils are not equipped to analyse the longer-term trade-offs between direct medical impact and indirect impact via the economy. An important step forward would be to make sure that teams in charge of non-pharmaceutical interventions publish scenario analyses with associated responses (Miller and Parent, 2012, p. 58), because

> [t]hese will allow for more optimal preparation by state and local public health agencies and departments and related NGOs, industries and interested stakeholders. [...] Publishing likely or anticipated responses forces a recognition and consideration of all the complexities prior to an outbreak.

The teams also need to organize their own in-team opposition. They need specialists to understand the medical technicalities and to run the epidemiological models that are necessary for planning purposes. They also need the input of other disciplines, because the inputs to the model and the impact on society should not be considered from one disciplinary perspective only. A more generalist approach to forecasting is conducive for the analysis because counteracting forces and contradictions are less likely to be overlooked by such teams (Epstein, 2019).

Economic preparation for the pandemic has been difficult, because the interaction between health policy makers and economic policy makers apparently has not been sufficient. Pandemics are a multidisciplinary problem. The solution must be multidisciplinary as well (Textbox 7.6). An important issue is that the analysis of contagious diseases structurally needs to become more multidisciplinary than before – with a much stronger component for the social sciences – and needs to be ingrained in the research agendas of the top-notch knowledge institutes.

One specific economic issue to reconsider is the use of helicopter money, that is, emergency money-financed fiscal interventions that are distributed widely amongst the population (Galí, 2020). We have seen several methods to support households and firms. The more or less general distribution of government checks that was used in the United States, where the social safety net is underdeveloped, and the unconditional income support for business owners at the start of lockdown in many European countries. The argument for unconditional support is that it needs to be delivered very quickly without red tape and as an emergency measure has initially been accepted by mainstream economics. The unconditional cash transfer of the century is, however, hardly something to repeat because it creates moral hazard, that is, an incentive to increase the exposure to risk because one does not have to bear the full costs of that risk. In view of the importance of individual preparedness that we discussed in Section 7.1 moral hazard is a serious problem.

Moreover, alternative measures to have a social safety net for emergencies are available or can be designed. Gray Molina and Ortiz Juarez (2020), for example, have floated the idea of a basic income in developing countries and, like other elements of the welfare state, the social safety net may require further thought.

Textbox 7.7 Facilitate structural change

Adjustment of the economy is an important mechanism to reduce the costs of a pandemic. Structural change needs to be facilitated and here the problem is that support for industries with an outdated business model delays the necessary adjustment. With limited funding available society should refocus support from the dinosaurs to the mammals, the newly emerging crucial activities of testing and tracing, e-commerce and home delivery. The growth sectors of the Corona economy need the time and attention of policy makers rather than business firms with limited prospects to survive the medium term that will be dominated by the risk of a next wave. Even if COVID-19 were to be cured and a vaccine would be available for the population at large, these industries would not have a sustainable business model because a new pandemic will occur. Some sort of conditionality thus will have to be introduced, legislation has to be prepared and the new approach needs to be transparently communicated.

National governments hold the keys to solving the big inequalities that have been the breeding cultures for the COVID-19 outbreaks. Low income earners, often in essential services that were not organized to meet the requirements of social distancing, with neither paid sick leave nor health insurance, living in crowded places without ventilation and travelling in mass public transportation are a recipe for pandemic disaster. The first key is workplace regulation. Working conditions in meat processing, distribution centres, overcrowded

factories and the like need to be improved, if not as a matter of human decency
then in order to prevent the spread of contagious diseases. Market forces will
create a drive to the bottom because the external health effects are not
incorporated in market prices. Housing conditions are the second key.
Affordable and good housing cannot be organized overnight, but housing
programmes would be a very good way to stimulate effective demand and
create jobs threatened and destroyed by the Corona crisis. The third key is paid
sick leave and health care for those that keep society running during a
pandemic.[9]

Textbox 7.8 What extras do essential workers need?

During a pandemic the list of essential services with employees that risk
their health is long: health care, emergency services, garbage collection,
public transportation, cleaning, distribution, retail, the military, prison
guards, journalism, and even politicians. All these professions keep society
going during a pandemic and cannot work from home. Estimates of the
share of essential workers are in the range of one fifth to one-third of the
working population.[10] We want these workers to do their jobs under difficult
and risky conditions and we want them to stay at home if they are sick.
Some would argue that we owe them medical care and financial
compensation if they get infected, and we owe them decent living
conditions. Such social policies can expect political opposition, so it is
better to investigate the business case.

We do not need to be altruistic to argue for health insurance, sick pay and
a decent wage. The essential workers essentially are the part of the
population that unavoidably connects people during a pandemic – also those
sheltering and in lockdown. A lockdown would be much more effective and
shorter if the working and living conditions of the essential workers were
no longer conducive to spreading contagious diseases. The business case
rests on the reduced risk of spreading the disease. Health/life insurance, sick
pay and a decent wage implies a redistribution of income, but this time not
based on social considerations: these measures are necessary and efficient
from the perspective of managing pandemic risks.

Other sectors are also essential – energy, ICT, telecom and the public
services directly involved in crisis management come spontaneously to
mind. Workers in these sectors also often had to work extremely hard, but
their jobs are less risky and often better paid. There is also a case for better
reward and secondary benefits here, but the priority is somewhat lower.

The fourth key is needed for an often-forgotten door. Behind that door are the
marginally poor, the homeless and the people in care and correction facilities.
The people behind that door live in places that have formed hotspots of new
cases and high per capita levels of deaths (Roberts and Tehrani, 2020). These

places are known to form reservoirs or pools of contagious viruses but tended to be ignored. An example is Chile that after initial apparent success of the lockdown in April 2020 was hailed as an exemplar for Latin America, but where the success was limited to higher income municipalities and continued to rage in low income areas characterized by informality, poverty, poor housing and limited testing capacities (Bennett, 2020). Moreover, Chilean government support stood out 'for its stinginess towards the most vulnerable' (Blofield et al., 2020). Reducing the vulnerability of the vulnerable is a very important stepping stone to improving resilience against pandemic outbreaks (Busso et al., 2020). Reducing inequalities is a key policy to which governments are already committed by accepting the Sustainable Development Goals. The pandemic does not change this – it only proves the urgency of explicit consideration of inequality and the need for concrete action plans (van Bergeijk and van der Hoeven, 2017; van der Hoeven, 2020; Murshed, 2020).

The most important task of the government during a pandemic, however, is to set uniform standards and rules that govern access to health care at a national level. It is necessary to clarify what can be provided, where investment is necessary and also to be realistic: the next pandemic may be more deadly, more contagious and require a longer stay in the hospital. Realistically, we need to accept that care cannot be provided to all during a pandemic, for example, because

> (…) actually deploying and using such high volumes of mechanical ventilators would be challenging in terms of having enough hospital space and staff to support additional ventilator use. Thus, during moderate and severe pandemics, a higher level of unmet demand might need to be expected. Attending physicians will have to determine who gets access to the limited number of ventilators and who does not (Meltzer and Patel, 2019, p. 1021).

This is an observation that holds for other medical equipment and care in general as well. Therefore it is unavoidable and necessary to set guidelines for triage and rules for access to scarce lifesaving equipment once admitted into a health care facility. These guidelines should be based on the established facts of the COVID-19 pandemic (and it may take quite a while before the picture is complete), while at the same time being sufficiently open to be applicable to the unknown characteristics of the next pandemic. The key principle is that the rationing of health care access needs to be accepted as a rational, ethical and moral solution during a pandemic of a highly contagious disease. Such a change in the general approach to health care issues can only be arrived at after a broad consultation and an open discussion. The ultimate aim of the procedures should be codification in legislation rather than leaving the ethical problems for the medical professionals to solve. Such guidelines would be an essential part of the social contract that has not been written yet and it may be necessary also to revise other pillars of the social fabric. Societies need to do this before the next pandemic, because many trade-offs need to be considered. It is better to do this without the stress and panic of an outbreak that gets out of control. The settings that we discussed in Chapter 6 can provide a useful framework of alternative ways to organize that social contract.

7.4 BE PREPARED: INTERNATIONAL

It seems almost imperative that health policies are national and it seems unquestionable that pandemics will rise on the agenda for homeland security, much in line with a trend that already existed before COVID-19 – Elbe (2011) already speaks about the 'medicalisation' of national security. National measures, however, can only provide partial solutions and, moreover, only during the pandemic. Prevention and preparation require cooperation. There is a strong mutual interest in early detection, information sharing, and attempts to contain the pandemic as early as possible. Containment is costly and burden-sharing mechanisms need to be designed so that an outbreak country can take the strictest measures possible.

Textbox 7.9 The case of Ischgl

Local authorities may hide or play down a local outbreak for commercial reasons as appears to have happened in Ischgl in Austrian Tirol where the après ski became a super spreading event among tourists that transmitted the disease to Denmark, Norway, Iceland, Germany, the United Kingdom and the Netherlands (Felbermayr et al., 2020; Correa-Martínez et al., 2020). Early March 2020 the state medical director commented on the emerging cases abroad: 'aus medizinischer Sicht wenig wahrscheinlich, dass es in Tirol zu Ansteckungen gekommen ist' (from a medical point of view it is unlikely that the infections occurred in Tirol).[11] The case of Ischgl does not only show the need for full transparency, which is much more difficult to achieve and adhere to for local authorities under pressure from local commercial and local political interests, but also illustrates the danger that an outbreak is missed due to registration and reporting on too low a level of aggregation: Austria 'exported' the ski tourist cases effectively, erroneously reducing its own number of reported cases and fatalities as well as the estimates of the speed and severity of the pandemic that raged within its borders. At the European level of aggregation these cases would have been picked up without the distortion introduced by reporting at a sub-optimal national level.

During the outbreak medical cooperation is essential, both regarding medical supplies (testing materials and protective gear) and medical staff, and, if possible, sharing of medical infrastructures in neighbouring countries could be considered. Medical aid creates goodwill and enables an environment in which information can be shared. International medical cooperation builds and spreads knowledge of treatment and policy. In essence an emerging pandemic is a humanitarian disaster unfolding and there is no reason why we should not generously provide aid and support for the people that are hit by the outbreak, much like we do with earthquakes, floods and famines.

One reason why we have not seen solidarity during pandemics is a lack of preparedness and low levels of national stocks and supply. It is, however, also a matter of mentality. We tend to see sickness differently – that is in our DNA: we cannot get infected by earthquake or famine when we travel to those hot spots of disaster. We can in the same vein receive refugees from natural disasters without importing the floods and droughts from which they flee. A pandemic is different on both counts. Some cross-border cooperation did still occur. The EU, for example, has Guidelines in place since April 2020 but the effective use of cross border cooperation has been limited.[12]

At another level, nations need to recognize that the nation state is often not the optimal health care area. Perhaps Europe is the best example. While the markets of the European Union have been highly integrated and the movement of people within the union is free, health policy had remained on a strictly national level, with some coordination, but clear and ultimate national decision making. It makes no sense to have only national policies in a highly integrated economy.

7.5 BE PREPARED: GLOBAL

Sometimes the scale of preparations cannot be international (that is involving many countries) but needs to be global – so involving all countries. This has been recognized by the move from 'international health' to 'global health' (Brown et al., 2006).[13] Pandemics, however, have not yet received the explicit attention they need in the Sustainable Development Goals (SDGs). The SDGs (and in particular, the SDG 3 'Ensure healthy lives and promote wellbeing for all at all ages') do not mention prevention of pandemics *per se*. Health target 3.3 'By 2030, end the epidemics of AIDS, tuberculosis, malaria and neglected tropical diseases and combat hepatitis, water-borne diseases and other communicable diseases' could be easily adjusted. Target 3.d 'Strengthen the capacity of all countries, in particular developing countries, for early warning, risk reduction and management of national and global health risks' looks satisfactory at first sight but misses the point that the 'in particular' is equally relevant for the advanced countries. What we have learned from COVID-19 is that every Earthling is at risk so we cannot afford the luxury of focussing on groups that are particularly vulnerable to infections only. Handwashing, for example, is only possible if clean water, sink facilities and soap are available to everyone. Since a pandemic is global, the approach needs to be global. Handwashing facilities in developing countries are a cheap, significant and necessary precaution for the advanced economies. The realization that poverty is a breeding ground for pandemics implies that income inequality between and within countries is much more important than the SDGs seem to acknowledge (van Bergeijk and van der Hoeven, 2017). Also from this perspective, a reformulation of SDGs may be necessary.

For economists the task is especially to rethink global governance and the role of international organizations. Several authors (Gallagher et al., 2020; Griffith-Jones et al., 2020) have suggested major changes in international finance and development cooperation and even in the international financial architecture especially with a view to providing financial support to developing countries and emerging markets. The development and strengthening of a global financial safety net to meet the fallout of the COVID-19 pandemic certainly is important. It is, however, from a longer term perspective crucial that the international organizations make the assessment of pandemic preparedness a standard element of country studies and monitoring.

Textbox 7.10 Economic policy preparation

Flagship products of the international organizations that should cover pandemic preparedness include the OECD's *Economic Outlook* and the Economic and Development Review Committee (EDRC) peer pressure system based on the OECD country reports that are regularly published and the IMF's annual Article IV consultations that are the core of IMF surveillance of individual countries. The Article IV consultations already cover a full range of macroeconomic policies and performance as well as microeconomic and structural policies and issues, such as trade policies, labour market policies and pension systems. The IMF also provides regional surveillance (for example, of the Euro Area) and global surveillance (the *World Economic Outlook*, the *Global Stability Report* and whitepapers for the meetings of the G7 and the G20). All these products and peer processes should consider the issue of pandemic preparedness as a regular item.

If anything, COVID-19 proves that a WHO is a necessary global public good in today's world. Ideas on what kind of WHO is necessary may differ but the need for a global evidence-based institution is not really a point for discussion – the discussion is about authority, independence and enforcement (Fidler, 2020). In a sense, however, the WHO is stuck with the pandemic trilemma setting that we discussed in Section 6.2 as the *International Health Regulations* (World Health Organization, 2005) require that 'The implementation of these

Regulations shall be with full respect for the dignity, human rights and fundamental freedoms of persons' (Article 3) and has recognized that a health rights approach requires poverty reduction and needs to address 'the linkages between health and other areas, including macroeconomic policies and relevant sectors such as water and sanitation' (World Health Organization 2008, p.2) as well as to 'evaluate trade-offs between health spending needs, inflation, debt and growth' (*ibid.*, p. 43). With countries positioned in different corners of the globalization–freedom policy space (Diagram 6.2) and the hollowing out of world leadership during a phase of contested hegemonism, it is no surprise that the WHO position in the pandemic trilemma is a permanent challenge as adjustment to the reality of the pandemic and to geopolitical pressures involves significant trade-offs along many dimensions. This trilemma puts the multi-faceted criticism of the WHO into perspective. The criticism on the WHO's lack of opposition to human rights violations (for example, the harsh and forced isolations) and the tsunami of travel bans (that are setting clear limits to globalization) ignore the third pole of the pandemic trilemma. The third pole happens to be the WHO's core business: universal access to health care. Any critique that does not take the need to universal access to healthcare as its point of departure cannot be taken seriously.

This does, of course, not mean that the WHO is without faults. Like everybody, it made mistakes and that is, as argued before, in itself not problematic because it means that opportunities exist to learn. The WHO has not used to the full its independence and authority to investigate when national authorities are not sufficiently forthcoming. Moreover, the time required to arrive at the formal establishment of a Public Health Emergency of International Concern – in layman's terms: a pandemic – may have been too long. It is important to recognize that this is a consequence of the binary character of the decision and the grave implications of that decision. There is considerable merit in the restrictive use of the term pandemic, because of the possibility of creating panic. These criticisms are not new and were earlier voiced by the independent Panel on the Global Response to Ebola (Moon et al., 2015). The panel also proposed

the creation of a Global Health Committee as part of the UN Security Council to expedite high-level leadership and systematically elevate political attention to health issues, recognising health as essential to human security (Moon et al., 2015, p. 2205)

Given the track record of the UN Security Council and the fact that pandemics have a geopolitical impact as well and are thus 'high politics', it is doubtful that a Global Health Committee would improve on the speed of reaction. A practical solution could be to enable the WHO with the option to give a warning that the planet may be close to meeting the standard for a pandemic.

The start of a Procedure to Investigate A Potential Public Health Emergency of International Concern could provide the strong signal and in a much shorter period with less political pressure. The start of the Procedure would also offer a solution to reduce the impact of one of the factors that over the last century has made it so much easier to cross over from epidemic to pandemic, that is, the ease of diseases to travel across the globe in airplanes (Textbox 7.11).

Textbox 7. 11 Could we help air travel to be the safest industry again?

The air industry has invested enormous amounts to improve safety: its 10-year average fatality rate decreased from about 1500 at the turn of the Millennium to a little over 400 per year (2019 recorded 179 deaths).[14] Given this commitment to making air travel one of the safest modes of transportation, the industry could be expected to contribute to reducing the external effect of being a pandemic channel. But the industry cannot do that on its own; it needs guidance and protection in a highly competitive environment that if left alone would go for the cheapest solution driving down safety and quality. The key point of the increased safety record is therefore regulation and standards that apply to a global market.

The problem during an outbreak is that international aviation connectivity allows global travel times that are much shorter than the incubation period of infectious diseases in combination with a multitude of hubs and destinations (Christidis and Christodoulou, 2020). In-travel contamination at airports occurs due to problems with social distancing. The infrastructure in other words does not allow for the pre-pandemic flows to be handled from the perspective of national health, and the flows, moreover, from an international perspective need to be significantly reduced. The traditional approach to prohibit arrivals from specific countries has not worked. It is extremely costly and threatens the very existence of an industry that under normal conditions contributes significantly to positive global interaction.

A possible solution that requires further investigation is to have a global regulation in place that strictly limits the number of passengers per airplane during Public Health Emergency of International Concern and allows airline companies to increase prices accordingly during the pandemic.

The point that strengthening global governance is an elementary step in pro-active pandemic preparedness is certainly not new (Bloom et al., 2017; Bloom and Cadarette, 2019). The Panel on the Global Response to Ebola is fair in its criticism and points out the lack of global governance, the lack of preparedness and the need to invest in pandemic preparedness. Any evaluation of the WHO will need to take these gaps in global governance as its point of departure.

7.6 THE FUTURE VERDICT OF HISTORY

How will future generations judge the way we handled the 2020 COVID-19 pandemic? I have no doubt that the verdict will be negative about our preparedness at the time of the outbreak and it is also very likely that the slowness by which some of the measures (especially the easy measures such as using mouth caps and masks) were introduced will be met with disbelief if not disapproval. We have now ourselves experienced what it means to be unprepared or, as I argued in Chapter 2, unequipped. We can only win back the respect of future generations if we take preparation seriously and act massively to prepare and equip for the next pandemic. We should do this on short notice, we should devote a very significant share of our income and we should do more than merely catching up. This will be an exceptionally large, challenging and global societal project and it is one of the best ways to get the economy started again.

Regarding the use of the non-pharmaceutical interventions, including the monetary and fiscal bazookas, it is probably too early to call the jury in. The further development of the pandemic, the long-run health impact of the Corona virus, the direct and indirect health impact of the non-pharmaceutical interventions and the much hoped-for vaccine (also in view of possible mutations of the virus) are important unknowns that make it impossible to already assess the costs and benefits for the world community.

The choices regarding differences in the extent of social distancing and/or the strictness of the lockdown can also not yet be assessed at this stage. Relaxed lockdowns may, for example, be more resilient to fatigue and rebellion than strict lockdowns with curfews and the population might therefore be more willing and capable to take the medicine again if the need arises during a next wave. Imposition of a lockdown too early may spoil the social capital that is needed for the lockdown while the instrument may be needed later in the pandemic. Lifting the lockdown measures may be more orderly with intelligent lockdowns. Alternatively, a bad start may provide the incentive to do better during the revival of the pandemic. Or perhaps the countries that opened 'too early' arrive quicker at the endemic end-state of the pandemic. All these issues can only be evaluated after a number of years. Current evaluations are by definition based on incomplete information and may guide policy in the wrong direction.

The economics and economic policies of the pandemic period also cannot be evaluated yet. It is unclear whether the bazookas worked or if governments and Central Banks have simply shot their bolt and will be unable to provide the stimulus to kickstart the economy. But it is not too early to conclude that the international economic organizations and the global scientific community have let the world down by not engaging with a clearly identified risk for the world economy.

Therefore, in the end, I opted for a cartoon of an economics professor for the cover of this book, because the message of this book is a message from and for the economic profession.[15] The reader should, however, also know that the cartoon below ranks first *ex aequo*. The non-pharmaceutical interventions introduced in this pandemic saved national COVID lives but threaten other livelihoods. Further economic analysis is necessary to ensure a more rational approach to the next pandemic.

Key takeaways of Chapter 7

- Pandemic preparedness starts at home.
- Firms cannot rely on bailouts and need to adjust their business strategies to pandemic risk.
- Financial pandemic preparedness can help with other disasters and vice versa.

- Cost-efficient adjustment and investments in preparedness require a sustained long-term approach.
- City planning and (re)construction should be focussed on resilience and based on citizen and community engagement.
- The organization of the access to health care facilities during pandemics is a local task; national governments need to set uniform standards and rules that govern access to health care.
- Governments should use the adjustment potential of the economy and focus support on sectors that need to and can grow.
- Outbreak management teams and scientific councils that advise governments on pandemic response need a stronger basis in all relevant sciences.
- The nation state is only the optimal health care area in very special cases.
- International organizations should make the assessment of pandemic preparedness a standard element of country studies, monitoring and surveillance.
- Pandemics have not yet received the explicit attention they need in the Sustainable Development Goals (SDGs).
- Strengthening global governance is an elementary step in pro-active pandemic preparedness.

ENDNOTES

[1] The perception that this is discrimination based on gender simply is wrong. I met people in Zanzibar that were for religious reasons only allowed to shake hands (touch) with parents, brothers, sisters and children.

[2] This was true not only when I was in Zambia, so close to the hotspots of Ebola, but also at international meetings in the Global North during this period.

[3] Midões (2020) estimates that a third of Europeans live in households that cannot cover two months of basic expenses.

[4] In Switzerland a shelter-in-house room with emergency supplies that would enable survival during nuclear accidents used to be required. Like most of our Swiss friends, we used the mini bunker practically as a wine cellar and storage facility.

[5] An example is Bohle and Warner (2008) that offer a comprehensive view on resilience of mega-cities and many aspects of social vulnerability but not on the potential for breakdown of the health care system. In the same vein Daffara (2011) discussing macro trends mentions pandemic risk *in passim*

but then ignores it in his overview of critical issues and vision goals. Hoornweg and Freire (2013) likewise mention pandemic risk on page one, but leave the issue untouched. The Corona crisis has acted as a wake-up call; see Honey-Roses et al. (2020) and the impact of several waves of the COVID-19 pandemic on public space is starting to get recognized, but the point that we need to prepare for the next pandemic hasn't made it yet.

6   See Fisher (2010) for an inspiring discussion based on an art and architecture project 'Landscapes of Quarantines'.

7   An interesting example is Texas, where a 2017 analysis estimated the required number of ventilators between 1.2 to 15.7 thousand in a mild to severe scenario. The 2009 stockpile of ventilators was 3.7 thousand (Huang et al. 2017). In April 2020 the Texas stock was 2.4 thousand ventilators (*Click2Houston*): https://www.click2houston.com/health/2020/04/10/texas-medical-center-data-shows-icu-ventilator-capacity-vs-usage-during-coronavirus-outbreak/ accessed July 4, 2020.

8   It can be even worse. The US Federal government was bidding against US states; see A. Sherman 'Are states in a bidding war over medical gear with the feds?', *Politifact* https://www.politifact.com/article/2020/apr/01/are-states-bidding-war-over-medical-gear-feds/.

9   Paid sick leave in general is important because it reduces contagious presenteeism (Pichler and Ziebarth, 2017).

10   See Office for National Statistics (2020), Redmond and McGuinness (2020) and Rho et al. (2020).

11   'Franz Katzgraber, der Hüter der Gesundheit Tirols, steht in der Kritik' *Der Standard*, March 16, 2020.

12   *Guidelines on EU Emergency Assistance in Cross-Border Cooperation in Healthcare related to the COVID-19 crisis C(2020) 2153 final*, available at https://ec.europa.eu/info/sites/info/files/guidelines_on_eu_emergency_assistance_in_cross-bordercooperationin_heathcare_related_to_the_covid-19_crisis.pdf.

13   See Holst (2020) for a more critical analysis of the Global Health concept.

14   Aviation Safety Network, accessed June 28, 2020 and available at: https://news.aviation-safety.net.

15   See https://youtu.be/f5lcTucOXro.

References

Abraham, K.G., 2005, 'Distinguished lecture on economics in government –
what we don't know could hurt us: some reflections on the
measurement of economic activity', *Journal of Economic Perspectives*
19 (3), pp. 3–18.

Adda, J., 2016, 'Economic activity and the spread of viral diseases: evidence
from high frequency data', *Quarterly Journal of Economics* **131** (2), pp.
891–941.

Ager, P. et al., 2020, 'How the other half died: immigration and mortality in
US cities', *CEPR Discussion Paper No.14949*, Centre for Economic
Policy Research: London.

Alfani, G., 2015, 'Economic inequality in northwestern Italy: a long-term
view (fourteenth to eighteenth centuries)', *Journal of Economic History*
75 (4), pp.1058–96.

Algaba, A. et al., 2020, 'Econometrics meets sentiment: an overview of
methodology and applications', *Journal of Economic Surveys* doi:
10.1111/joes.12370.

Alimohamadi, Y. et al., 2020, 'The estimate of the basic reproduction
number for novel Coronavirus disease (COVID-19): a systematic
review and meta-analysis', *Journal of Preventive Medicine and Public
Health* **53** (3), pp. 151–7.

Álvarez Nogal, C. et al., 2020, 'Economic effects of the Black Death: Spain
in European perspective', *Working Papers in Economic History 2020-
06*, University of Madrid: Madrid.

ANV Netherlands Network of Safety and Security Analysts, 2016, *National
Risk Profile 2016: An all hazard overview of potential disasters and
threats in the Netherlands*, RIVM: Bilthoven, accessed 31 July 2020 at
www.rivm.nl/documenten/dutch-national-risk-profile-2016.

Apuzzo, M. et al., 2020, 'How the world missed COVID-19's silent spread',
New York Times, June 27.

Aum, S. et al., 2020, 'COVID-19 doesn't need lockdowns to destroy jobs: the
effect of local outbreaks in Korea', *NBER Working Paper No. 27264*,
National Bureau of Economic Research: Cambridge MA.

Avery, C. et al, 2020, 'Policy implications of models of the spread of Coronavirus: perspectives and opportunities for economists', *CESifo Working Paper No. 8293*, Center for Economic Studies and Ifo Institute: Munich.

Azomahou, T.T. et al., 2016, 'HIV/AIDS and development: a reappraisal of the productivity and factor accumulation effects', *American Economic Review* **106** (5), pp. 472–7.

Bairoliya, N. and A. Imrohoroglu, 2020, 'Macroeconomic consequences of stay-at-home policies during the COVID-19 pandemic', *Covid Economics* Issue 13, pp. 71–90.

Baker, S.R. et al., 2020, 'How does household spending respond to an epidemic? Consumption during the 2020 COVID-19 pandemic', *NBER Working Paper 26949*, National Bureau of Economic Research: Cambridge MA.

Baldwin, R. and B. Weder di Mauro (eds), 2020a, *Economics in the Time of COVID-19*, Centre for Economic Policy Research: London.

Baldwin, R. and B. Weder di Mauro, 2020b, 'Macroeconomics of the flu', in: R. Baldwin and B. Weder di Mauro (eds), 2020a, pp. 31–5.

Baldwin, R. and B. Weder di Mauro (eds), 2020c, *Mitigating the COVID Economic Crisis: Act Fast and Do Whatever It Takes,* Centre for Economic Policy Research: London.

Barro, R.J. et al., 2020, 'The coronavirus and the great influenza pandemic: lessons from the "Spanish Flu" for the coronavirus's potential effects on mortality and economic activity', *NBER Working Paper No. 26866*, National Bureau of Economic Research: Cambridge MA.

Barrot, J.-N. et al., 2020, 'Sectoral effects of social distancing', *Covid Economics* Issue 3, pp. 85–102.

Bell, C. and H. Gersbach, 2009, 'The macroeconomics of targeting: the case of an enduring epidemic', *Journal of Health Economics* **28** (1), pp. 54–72.

Bell, C. and M. Lewis, 2005, 'Economic implications of epidemics old and new', *Center for Global Development Working Paper* CGD: Washington DC.

Bello, W., 2017, 'Globalization and deglobalization: a retrospective', keynote Global (Dis)Order and Development, University of Gothenborg, Department of Economics, November 6.

Belot, M. et al., 2020, 'Six-country survey on Covid-19', *IZA Discussion Paper No. 13230*, Institut zur Zukunft der Arbeit: Bonn.

Benmelech, E. and N. Tzur-Ilan, 2020, 'The determinants of fiscal and monetary policies during the Covid-19 crisis', *NBER Working Paper No. 27461*, National Bureau of Economic Research: Cambridge MA.

Bennett, D. et al., 2015, 'Learning during a crisis: the SARS epidemic in Taiwan', *Journal of Development Economics* **112**, pp. 1–18.

Bennett, M., 2020, 'All things equal? Heterogeneity in policy effectiveness against COVID-19 spread in Chile', *mimeo*, accessed 31 July 2020 at https://www.magdalenabennett.com/files/sub/mbennett_covid.pdf

Bentzen, J.S., 2019, 'Acts of God? religiosity and natural disasters across subnational world districts', *Economic Journal* **129** (622), pp. 2295–321.

Bergeijk, P.A.G. van, 1995, 'The accuracy of international economic observations', *Bulletin of Economic Research*, **47** (1), pp. 1–20.

Bergeijk, P.A.G. van, 2010, *On the Brink of Deglobalization: An Alternative Perspective on the World Trade Collapse*, Edward Elgar: Cheltenham.

Bergeijk, P.A.G. van, 2012, Opârg fitfara eft ksvurf, *Ekonomiy ur Ďônopros*, **72** (8), p. 6.

Bergeijk, P.A.G. van, 2013, *Earth Economics: An Introduction to Demand Management, Long-Run Growth and Global Economic Governance*, Edward Elgar: Cheltenham.

Bergeijk, P.A.G. van, 2017, 'Making data measurement errors transparent: the case of the IMF', *World Economics* **18** (3), accessed 31 July 2020.

Bergeijk, P.A.G. van, 2019, *Deglobalization 2.0: Trade and Openness during the Great Depression and the Great Recession*, Edward Elgar: Cheltenham.

Bergeijk, P.A.G. van (ed.), 2021, *Research Handbook on Economic Sanctions*, Edward Elgar: Cheltenham.

Bergeijk, P.A.G. van and J.M. Berk, 2001, 'European Monetary Union, the term structure, and the Lucas Critique', *Kyklos* **54** (4), pp. 547–56.

Bergeijk, P. A.G. van et al., 2017, 'Heterogeneous economic resilience and the great recession's world trade collapse', *Papers in Regional Science* **96** (1), pp. 3–12.

Bergeijk, P.A.G. van and M. Mennen, 2014, 'De economische betekenis van nationale veiligheidsrisico's' (The economics of national security risks; in Dutch), *Tijdschrift voor Veiligheid* **13** (2), pp. 35–51.

Bergeijk, P.A.G. van and R. van der Hoeven (eds), 2017, *Sustainable Development Goals and Income Inequality*. Edward Elgar: Cheltenham.

Berlemann, M. and E. Haustein, 2020, 'Right and yet wrong: a spatio-temporal evaluation of Germany's COVID-19 containment policy', *Covid Economics* Issue 36, pp. 80–104.

Berloffa, G. and S. Giunti, 2019, 'Remittances and healthcare expenditure: human capital investment or responses to shocks? Evidence from Peru', *Review of Development Economics* **23**(4), pp.1540–61.

Betsch, C., 2020, 'How behavioural science data helps mitigate the COVID-19 crisis', *Nature Human Behaviour* **4** (5), p. 438.

Bhagwati, J.N., and T.N. Srinivasan, 1969, 'Optimal intervention to achieve non-economic objectives', *Review of Economic Studies* **36** (1), pp. 27–38.

Binder, C., 2020, 'Coronavirus fears and macroeconomic expectations', *Review of Economics and Statistics*, doi.org/10.1162/rest_a_00931.

Bloem, J.R. and C. Salemi, 2020, 'COVID-19 and conflict', *HiCN Working Paper 332*, The Institute of Development Studies: Brighton.

Blofield, M. et al., 2020, 'Assessing the political and social impact of the COVID-19 crisis in Latin America', *GIGA Focus Lateinamerika*, German Institute of Global and Area Studies: Hamburg.

Bloom, D.E. et al., 2017, 'Emerging infectious diseases: a proactive approach', *Proceedings of the National Academy of Sciences of the United States of America* **114** (16), pp. 4055–9.

Bloom D.E. et al., 2018, 'Epidemics and economics: new and resurgent infectious diseases can have far-reaching economic repercussions', *Finance and Development* **55** (2), pp. 46–9.

Bloom, D.E. et al., 2019, 'Health and economic growth: reconciling the micro and macro evidence', *NBER Working Paper, No. 26003*, National Bureau of Economic Research: Cambridge MA.

Bloom, D.E. and D. Cadarette, 2019, 'Infectious disease threats in the twenty-first century: strengthening the global response', *Frontiers in Immunology* **10** article 549, doi: 10.3389/fimmu.2019.00549.

Bodenhorn, H., 2020, 'Business in a time of Spanish influenza', *NBER Working Paper No. 27495*, National Bureau of Economic Research: Cambridge MA.

Bohle, H.G. and K. Warner (eds), 2008, *Megacities: Resilience and Social Vulnerability*, UNU Institute for Environment and Human Security (UNU-EHS): Bonn.

Boissay, F. et al., 2020, 'Dealing with Covid-19: understanding the policy choices', *BIS Bulletin No. 19*, Bank for International Settlements: Basel.

Boldog, P., et al., 2020, 'Risk assessment of novel coronavirus COVID-19 outbreaks outside China', *Journal of Clinical Medicine* **9** (2), doi:10.3390/jcm9020571.

Bonadio, B. et al., 2020, 'Global supply chains in the pandemic', *CEPR Discussion Paper 14766*, Centre for Economic Policy Research: London.

Bonnel, R., 2000, 'HIV/AIDS: does it increase or decrease growth in Africa?', ACT, Africa Department, Washington DC, World Bank, doi: 10.1.1.201.8357.

Bos, F., 2003, *The National Accounts as a Tool for Analysis and Policy: Past, Present and Future*, PhD thesis University of Twente: Enschede.

Boucekkine, R. et al., 2008, 'Growth economics of epidemics: a review of the theory', *Mathematical Population Studies* **15** (1), pp. 1–26.

Brahmbhatt, M. and A. Dutta, 2008, 'On SARS type economic effects during infectious disease outbreaks', *Policy Research Working Paper 4466*, World Bank: Washington DC.

Brainerd, E. and M. V. Siegler, 2003, 'The economic effects of the 1918 influenza epidemic', *Discussion Paper No. 3791*, Centre for Economic Policy Research: London.

Brake, E., 2019, 'Rebuilding after disaster: inequality and the political importance of place', *Social Theory and Practice* **45** (2), pp. 179–204.

Brakman, S. et al., 2004, 'The strategic bombing of German cities during World War II and its impact on city growth', *Journal of Economic Geography* **4** (2), pp. 201–18.

Brata, A.G. et al., 2018, 'Shaking up the firm survival: evidence from Yogyakarta (Indonesia)', *Economies* **6** (2), doi: 10.3390/economies6020026.

Bridgman, B. et al., 2018, 'Structural transformation, marketization, and household production around the world', *Journal of Development Economics* **133**, pp. 102–26.

Brown, T.M. et al., 2006, 'The World Health Organization and the transition from "international" to "global" public health', *American Journal of Public Health* **96** (1), pp. 62–72.

Buchheim, L. et al., 2020, 'Sudden stop: when did firms anticipate the potential consequences of COVID-19?', *IZA Discussion Paper No. 13457*, Institute of Labor Economics (IZA): Bonn.

Busso, M. et al., 2020, 'The challenge of protecting informal households during the COVID-19 pandemic: evidence from Latin America', *Discussion Paper IDB-DP-780*, Inter-American Development Bank: Washington DC.

Caggiano, G. et al., 2020, 'The global effects of Covid-19-induced uncertainty', *Research Discussion Paper 11/2020*, Bank of Finland: Helsinki.

Calvo, R.A. et al., 2020, 'Health surveillance during Covid-19 pandemic', *BMJ* **369**, doi:10.1136/bmj.m1373.

Carlitz, R.D. and R. McLellan, 2020, 'Open data from authoritarian regimes: new opportunities, new challenges', *Perspectives on Politics*, doi:10.1017/S1537592720001346.

Caruso, R., 2020, 'What post COVID-19? Avoiding a «twenty-first century general crisis»' *Peace Economics, Peace Science and Public Policy,* doi: 10.1515/peps-2020-9013.

Castle, J.L. et al., 2009, 'Nowcasting is not just contemporaneous forecasting', *National Institute Economic Review* **210** (1), pp. 71–89.

Cavallino, P. and F. De Fiore, 2020, 'Central banks' response to Covid-19 in advanced economies', *BIS Bulletin No. 21*, Bank for International Settlements: Basel.

CGHRFF (Commission on a Global Health Risk Framework for the Future), 2016, *The Neglected Dimension of Global Security: A Framework to Counter Infectious Disease Crises*, doi: 10.17226/21891.

Chang, C.C. et al., 2007, 'The potential economic impact of avian flu pandemic on Taiwan', Paper for the American Agricultural Economics Association 2007 Annual Meeting, Portland, Oregon, July 28–August 1, 2007, https://ageconsearch.umn.edu/record/9803/files/sp07ch03.pdf, accessed May 12, 2020.

Chang, R. and A. Velasco, 2020, 'Economic policy incentives to preserve lives and livelihoods', *Covid Economics* Issue 14, pp. 33–56.

Chen, S. et al., 2020, 'Tracking the economic impact of COVID-19 and mitigation policies in Europe and the United States', *IMF Working Paper WP/20/125*, IMF: Washington DC.

Chernozhukov, V. et al., 2020, 'Causal impact of masks, policies, behavior on early COVID-19 pandemic in the US', *Covid Economics* Issue 35, pp. 116–75.

Cho, S.W., 2020, 'Quantifying the *Impact of Non-pharmaceutical Interventions* (NPI) during the COVID-19 outbreak: the case of Sweden', *Covid Economics* Issue 35, pp. 70–95.

Christidis, P. and A. Christodoulou, 2020, 'The predictive capacity of air travel patterns during the global spread of the COVID-19 pandemic: risk, uncertainty and randomness', *International Journal of Environmental Research and Public Health* **17** (10), doi: 10.3390/ijerph17103356.

Cicala, S., 2020, 'Early economic impacts of COVID-19 in Europe: a view from the grid', *mimeo*, University of Chicago: Chicago.

Cinelli, M. et al., 2020, 'The covid-19 social media infodemic', *arXiv preprint*, accessed 31 July 2020 at https://arxiv.org/pdf/2003.05004.pdf.

Cirillo, P. and N.N. Taleb, 2020, 'Tail risk of contagious diseases', *Nature Physics,* pp. 1–8.

Claeys, G., 2000, 'The "Survival of the Fittest" and the origins of social Darwinism', *Journal of the History of Ideas* **61** (2), pp. 223–40.

Coibion, O. et al., 2020, 'Does policy communication during COVID work?', *Chicago Booth Research Paper 20-15*, University of Chicago: Chicago.

Committee for the Coordination of Statistical Activities, 2020, *How COVID-19 is Changing the World: A Statistical Perspective*, UNCTAD: Geneva.

Committee for Development Policy, 2020, *Development Policy and Multilateralism after COVID-19*, United Nations, New York.

Correa-Martínez, C.L. et al., 2020, 'A pandemic in times of global tourism: superspreading and exportation of COVID-19 cases from a ski area in Austria', *Journal of Clinical Microbiology* **58** (6), doi: 10.1128/JCM.00588-20.

Correia, S. et al., 2020a, 'Pandemics depress the economy. Public health interventions do not: evidence from the 1918 Flu', *mimeo*, https://www.sbmfc.org.br/wp-content/uploads/2020/03/SSRN-id3561560.pdf, accessed 31 July 2020.

Correia, S. et al., 2020b, 'Fight the pandemic, save the economy: lessons from the 1918 Flu', *The Economic Historian*, accessed 31 July 2020 at https://economic-historian.com/2020/05/1918-flu/.

Council of Economic Advisers, 2019, *Mitigating the Impact of Pandemic Influenza through Vaccine Innovation*, Government of the United States: Washington DC.

CPB Netherlands Bureau for Economic Analysis, 2010, 'Effect Mexicaanse Griep op economie valt waarschijnlijk mee' (Likely impact of Mexican Flu is small; in Dutch), *Macroeconomische Verkenningen 2010*, CPB Netherlands Bureau for Economic Analysis: The Hague, https://www.cpb.nl/sites/default/files/mev2010_kader_p15.pdf, accessed 31 July 2020.

CPB Netherlands Bureau for Economic Analysis, 2020, 'World Trade Monitor April', CPB: The Hague.

Cunha, B.A., 2004, 'Influenza: historical aspects of epidemics and pandemics', *Infectious Disease Clinics* **18** (1), pp. 141–55.

Daffara, P., 2011, 'Rethinking tomorrow's cities: emerging issues on city foresight', *Futures* **43** (7), pp. 680–89.

Dahl, C.M. et al., 2020, 'The 1918 epidemic and a V-shaped recession: evidence from municipal income data', *Covid Economics* Issue 6, pp. 137–62.

Daszak, P., 2012, 'Anatomy of a pandemic', *Lancet* **380** (9857), pp.1883–84.

Davis, S.L., 2020, *The Uncounted: Politics of Data in Global Health*, Cambridge University Press: Cambridge MA.

Delamater, P.L. et al, 2019, 'Complexity of the basic reproduction number (R_0)', *Emerging Infectious Diseases* **25** (1), pp. 1–4.

Delatte, A.L. and A. Guillaume, 2020, 'Covid 19: a new challenge for the EMU', *CEPR Discussion Paper No. DP14848*, Centre for Economic Policy Research: London.

Dempsey, W., 2020, 'The hypothesis of testing: paradoxes arising out of reported coronavirus case-counts', *arXiv preprint*, accessed 31 July 2020 at https://arxiv.org/pdf/2005.10425.pdf.

Derriks, H.M. and P.M. Mak, 2007, *IRTAD Special Report Underreporting of Road Traffic Casualties*, ITF and OECD, accessed 31 July 2020 at https://www.itf-oecd.org/sites/default/files/docs/road-casualties-web.pdf.

Deslandes, A. et al., 2020, 'SARS-COV-2 was already spreading in France in late December 2019', *International Journal of Antimicrobial Agents*, doi: 10.1016/j.ijantimicag.2020.106006.

De Vito, A. and J.-P. Gomez, 2020, 'Estimating the COVID-19 cash crunch: global evidence and policy', *Journal of Accounting and Public Policy* **39** (2), doi: 10.1016/j.jaccpubpol.2020.106741.

Dingel, J.I. and B. Neiman, 2020, 'How many jobs can be done at home?', *NBER Working Paper 26948*, National Bureau of Economic Research, Cambridge MA.

Dixon, P.B. et al., 2010, 'Effects on the U.S. of an H1N1 epidemic: analysis with a quarterly CGE model', *Journal of Homeland Security and Emergency Management* **7** (1), Article 7.

Dixon, S. et al., 2001, 'AIDS and economic growth in Africa: a panel data analysis', *Journal of International Development*, **13** (4), pp. 411–26.

Dixon, S. et al., 2002, 'The impact of HIV and AIDS on Africa's economic development', *BMJ* **324** (7331), pp. 232–4.

Djankov, S. and U. Panizza (eds), 2020, *COVID-19 in Developing Economies*, Centre for Economic Policy Research: London.

Drake, T. et al., 2013, 'Buy now, saved later? The critical impact of time-to-pandemic uncertainty on pandemic cost-effectiveness analyses', *Health Policy and Planning* **30** (1), pp. 100–10.

Dreher, A. et al., 2008, *Measuring Globalisation – Gauging its Consequences*, Springer: New York.

Drouhin, N. et al., 2003, 'Aids and economic growth in Africa: a critical assessment of the "base-case scenario" approach', in: J.P. Moatti et al. (eds), *Economics of AIDS and Access to HIV/AIDS Care in Developing Countries: Issues and Challenges*, ANRS, Collection Sciences Sociales et Sida: Paris, pp. 383–413.

Duffey, R.B. and E. Zio, 2020, 'Analysing recovery from pandemics by Learning Theory: the case of CoVid-19', *medRxiv* 020.04.10.20060319.

Dunn, F.L., 1958, 'Pandemic influenza in 1957: review of international spread of new Asian strain', *Journal of the American Medical Association* **166** (10), pp. 1140–8.

Ecks, S., 2020a, 'Coronashock capitalism: the unintended consequences of radical biopolitics', *Medical Anthropology Quarterly* accessed 31 July 2020 at http://medanthroquarterly.org/2020/04/06/coronashock-capitalism-the-unintended-consequences-of-radical-biopolitics.

Ecks, S., 2020b, 'Lockdowns save, lockdowns kill: valuing life after coronashock', *Somatosphere*, (April 24, 2020) accessed 31 July 2020 at http://somatosphere.net/2020/lockdowns-save-lockdowns-kill-valuing-life-after-coronashock.html/.

Eichenbaum, M.S. et al., 2020, 'The macroeconomics of epidemics', *NBER Working Paper No. 26882*, National Bureau of Economic Research: Cambridge MA.

Elbe, S., 2007, 'Our epidemiological footprint: the circulation of avian flu, SARS, and HIV/AIDS in the world economy', *Review of International Political Economy* **15** (1), pp. 116–30.

Elbe, S., 2011, 'Pandemics on the radar screen: health security, infectious disease and the medicalisation of insecurity', *Political Studies*, **59** (4), 848–66.

El Turabi, A. and P. Saynisch, 2016, 'Modeling the economic threat of pandemics', in: CGHRFF, 2016, pp. 111–4.

Elmahdawy, M. et al., 2017, 'Ebola virus epidemic in West Africa: global health economic challenges, lessons learned, and policy recommendations', *Value in Health Regional Issues* **13**, pp. 67–70.

Epstein, D., 2019, *Range: Why Generalists Triumph in a Specialized World*, Pan Macmillan: Basingstoke.

Eubank, S. et al., 2020, 'Commentary on Ferguson, et al., "Impact of non-pharmaceutical interventions (NPIs) to reduce COVID-19 mortality and healthcare demand"', *Bulletin of Mathematical Biology* **82**, pp. 1–7.

European Centre for Disease Prevention and Control, 2009, *Guide to Public Health Measures to Reduce the Impact of Influenza Pandemics in Europe: 'The ECDC Menu'*, ECDC: Stockholm.

European Commission, 2020, *European Economic Forecasts* (winter 2020), EU: Brussels.

Fan, E.X., 2003, 'SARS: economic impacts and implications', *ERD Policy Brief No. 15*, Asian Development Bank Manila, accessed 31 July 2020 at https://www.adb.org/sites/default/files/publication/28073/pb015.pdf.

Fan, V.Y. et al., 2017, 'The loss from pandemic influenza risk', *Disease Control Priorities: Improving Health and Reducing Poverty*, 3rd edition, The International Bank for Reconstruction and Development/The World Bank, pp. 347–58.

Fan, V.Y et al., 2018, 'Pandemic risk: how large are the expected losses?', *Bulletin of the World Health Organization* **96** (2), pp. 129–34.

Farzanegan, M.R. et al., 2020, 'Globalization and outbreak of COVID-19: an empirical analysis', *Joint Discussion Paper Series in Economics, No. 18-2020*, Philipps-University Marburg, School of Business and Economics: Marburg.

Felbermayr, G. et al., 2020, 'Apres-ski: the spread of coronavirus from Ischgl through Germany', *Covid Economics* Issue 22, pp. 177–204.

Ferguson, N. et al., 2020, 'Impact of non-pharmaceutical interventions
      (NPIs) to reduce COVID-19 mortality and healthcare demand'
      https://spiral.imperial.ac.uk/handle/10044/1/77482.
Fidler, D.P., 2020, 'The World Health Organization and pandemic politics',
      thinkglobalhealth.org April 10, accessed 31 July 2020 at
      https://www.thinkglobalhealth.org/article/world-health-organization-
      and-pandemic-politics.
Fisher, T., 2010, 'Viral cities: urban design and public health from the
      medieval plague to H1N1', *Places Journal*, accessed 31 July 2020 at
      https://placesjournal.org/article/viral-cities.
Flaxman, S. et al., 2020, 'Estimating the effects of non-pharmaceutical
      interventions on COVID-19 in Europe', *Nature*, doi: 10.1038/s41586-
      020-2405-7.
Fleurbaey, M., 2020, 'Must governments choose between saving lives and
      saving the economy?', in: Committee for Development Policy, 2020,
      pp. 29–33.
Forster, M., 2011, 'The debate between Whewell and Mill on the nature of
      scientific induction', *Handbook of the History of Logic* (Vol. 10),
      North-Holland: Amsterdam and New York, pp. 93–115.
Frey, C.B. et al., 2020, 'Democracy, culture, and contagion: political regimes
      and countries responsiveness to Covid-19', *Covid Economics* Issue 18,
      pp. 222–38.
Galí, J., 2020, 'Helicopter money: the time is now', in: R. Baldwin and B.
      Weder di Mauro (eds), 2020c, pp. 57–70.
Gallagher, K.P., 2020, 'IMF Special Drawing Rights: a key tool for attacking
      a COVID-19 financial fallout in developing countries', in: Committee
      for Development Policy, 2020, pp. 41–4.
Gardner, L. 2020. 'Modeling the spreading risk of 2019-nCoV, Center for
      Systems Science and Engineering, Johns Hopkins University,
      https://systems.jhu.edu/research/public-health/ncov-model-2, accessed
      11 May 2020.
Garrett, T.A., 2009, 'War and pestilence as labor market shocks: US
      manufacturing wage growth 1914–1919', *Economic Inquiry* **47** (4), pp.
      711–25.
Gaudecker, H.M. von et al., 2020, 'Labour supply in the early stages of the
      covid-19 pandemic: empirical evidence on hours, home office, and
      expectations', *IZA Discussion Papers, No. 13158*, Institute of Labor
      Economics (IZA): Bonn.
Gilman, S.L., 2010, 'Moral panic and pandemics', *The Lancet* **375** (9729),
      pp. 1866–7.

Givens, A.D. et al., 2018, 'Going global: the international dimensions of US homeland security policy', *Journal of Strategic Security* **11** (3), pp. 1–34.

Global Fund, 2020, *Mitigating the Impact of Covid-19 On Countries Affected by HIV, Tuberculosis and Malaria*, Global Health Campus: Geneva.

Goenka, A. and L. Liu, 2019, 'Infectious diseases, human capital and economic growth', *Economic Theory*, pp. 1–47.

Goodhart, C.A. and J. Ashworth, 2020, 'Coronavirus panic fuels a surge in cash demand', *CEPR Discussion Paper 14910*, Centre for Economic Policy Research: London.

Gopinath, G., 2020, 'Foreword', in: *IMF World Economic Outlook*, April 2020, IMF: Washington DC, pp. *v–vi*.

Gourinchas, P.E., 2020, 'Flattening the pandemic and recession curves' in: R. Baldwin and B. Weder di Mauro (eds), 2020c, pp. 31–40.

Gray Molina, G. and E. Ortiz-Juarez, 2020, *Temporary Basic Income: Protecting Poor and Vulnerable People in Developing Countries*, UNDP: New York.

Griffith-Jones, S. et al., 2020, 'Mobilizing development banks to fight COVID-19', in: Committee for Development Policy, 2020, pp. 50–5.

Gupta Strategists, 2020, 'COVID goes cuckoo: how the March–April 2020 COVID-19 surge overwhelmed Dutch hospitals and undermined regular care', https://gupta-strategists.nl/storage/files/200521-COVID-goes-Cuckoo.pdf, accessed 31 July 2020.

Gutierrez, E. et al., 2020, 'Delays in death reports and their implications for tracking the evolution of COVID-19', *Covid Economics* Issue 34, pp. 116–44.

Hai, W. et al., 2004, 'The short-term impact of SARS on the Chinese economy', *Asian Economic Papers* **3** (1), pp. 57–61.

Hale, T. et al., 2020, Oxford COVID-19 Government Response Tracker, Blavatnik School of Government, accessed 31 July 2020 at https://www.bsg.ox.ac.uk/research/research-projects/coronavirus-government-response-tracker.

Harari, M., 2020, 'Cities in bad shape: urban geometry in India', *American Economic Review* **110** (8), pp. 2377–421.

Hartley, J.S. and A. Rebucci, 2020, 'An event study of COVID-19 Central Bank quantitative easing in advanced and emerging economies', *NBER Working Paper. No. 27339*, National Bureau of Economic Research: Cambridge MA.

Hays, J.N., 2005, *Epidemics and Pandemics. Their Impacts on Human History*, ABC-Clio: Santa-Barbara.

Helsloot, I. and S.C. Quinn, 2009, 'Citizen response to pandemics: authorities' nightmare or daydream?' Paper for the 2009 American

Political Science Conference Toronto September 3–6, accessed 31 July 2020 at https://papers.ssrn.com/id=1450740.

Hendricks, V.F., 2019, 'Why statistical offices should hire a comedian', *OECD Observer*, July 29.

Hernandez, J.B. and P. Kim, 2019, *Epidemiology Morbidity and Mortality*, StatPearls, https://www.statpearls.com/sp/ms/473/21202/ accessed 31 July 2020.

Hoeven, R. van der, 2020, 'Multilateralism, employment and inequality in the context of COVID-19', in: Committee for Development Policy, 2020, pp. 45–9.

Holst, J., 2020, 'Global Health – emergence, hegemonic trends and biomedical reductionism', *Globalization and Health* **16**, pp. 1–1, doi: 10.1186/s12992-020-00573-4.

Horbach, S.P.J.M., 2020, 'Pandemic publishing: medical journals drastically speed up their publication process for Covid-19', *Quantitative Science Studies*, pp.1–16.

Hördahl, P. and I. Shim, 2020, 'EME bond portfolio flows and long-term interest rates during the Covid-19 pandemic', *BIS Bulletin No. 18*, Bank for International Settlements: Basel.

Honey-Roses, J. et al., 2020, 'The impact of COVID-19 on public space: a review of the emerging questions', doi: 10.31219/osf.io/rf7xa.

Hoornweg, D. and M. Freire, 2013, *Building Sustainability in an Urbanizing World*, World Bank: Washington DC.

Hsieh, Y.-C. et al., 2006, 'Influenza pandemics: past, present and future', *Journal of the Formosan Medical Association* **105** (1), pp. 1–6.

Huang, H.C. et al., 2017, 'Stockpiling ventilators for influenza pandemics', *Emerging Infectious Diseases* **23** (6), pp. 914–21.

Huber, C. et al., 2018, 'The economic and social burden of the 2014 Ebola outbreak in West Africa', *Journal of Infectious Diseases* **218** (suppl. 5), pp. S698–S704.

IMF 2018, *World Economic Outlook: Challenges to Steady Growth*, IMF: Washington DC.

IMF 2020a, *World Economic Outlook: The Great Lockdown*, IMF: Washington DC.

IMF 2020b, *Fiscal Monitor: Policies to Support People During the COVID-19 Pandemic*, IMF: Washington DC.

International Telecommunication Union, 2020, *Measuring Digital Development: Facts and Figures*, ITU: Geneva.

International Working Group on Financing Preparedness, 2017, *From Panic and Neglect to Investing in Health Security: Financing Pandemic Preparedness at a National Level*, accessed 23 January 2021, at https://documents.worldbank.org/en/publication/documents-reports/documentdetail/979591495652724770/from-panic-and-neglect-to-investing-in-health-security-financing-pandemic-preparedness-at-a-national-level.

Jackson, C., 2009, 'History lessons: the Asian Flu pandemic', *British Journal of General Practice*, **59** (565), pp.622–3.

Jaravel, X. and M. O'Connell, 2020, 'Inflation spike and falling product variety during the Great Lockdown', *IFS Working Paper W20/17*, Institute for Fiscal Studies: London.

Jedwab, R. et al., 2019, 'Pandemics, places, and populations: evidence from the Black Death', *CESifo Working Paper, No. 7524*, CESifo: Bonn.

Jenny, F., 2020, 'Economic resilience, globalisation and market governance: facing the Covid-19 test', *Covid Economics* Issue 1, pp. 64–78.

Jetter, M. et al., 2019, 'The intimate link between income levels and life expectancy: global evidence from 213 Years', *Social Science Quarterly* **100** (4), pp. 1387–403.

Johnson, N.P.A.S. and J. Mueller, 2002, 'Updating the accounts: global mortality of the 1918-1920 "Spanish" influenza pandemic', *Bulletin of the History of Medicine* **76** (1), pp. 105–15.

Jonas, O.B., 2013, 'Pandemic Risk', *Background Paper*, World Bank: Washington DC.

Jonung, L., 2020, 'Sweden's constitution decides its exceptional Covid-19 policy', *Voxeu* (June 18), accessed 31 July 2020 at: https://voxeu.org/article/sweden-s-constitution-decides-its-exceptional-covid-19-policy

Jonung, L. and W. Roeger, 2006, 'The macroeconomic effects of a pandemic in Europe. A model-based assessment', *European Economy – Economic Papers 251*, European Commission: Brussels.

Jordà, Ò. et al., 2020, 'Longer-run economic consequences of pandemics', *NBER Working Paper No. 26934*, National Bureau of Economic Research: Cambridge MA.

Kamwela, V.K. and P.A.G. van Bergeijk, 2020, 'The border walls of (de) globalization', *ISS Working Paper. No. 651*, International Institute of Social Studies of Erasmus University: The Hague.

Karesh, W.B. et al., 2012, 'Ecology of zoonoses: natural and unnatural histories', *The Lancet* **380** (9857), pp. 1936–45.

Karlsson, M. et al., 2014, 'The impact of the 1918 Spanish flu epidemic on economic performance in Sweden: an investigation into the consequences of an extraordinary mortality shock', *Journal of Health Economics* **36**, pp. 1–19.

Keane, M.P. and T. Neal, 2020, 'Consumer panic in the COVID-19 pandemic', *Covid Economics* Issue 19, pp. 115–42.

Kearney, A. and C. Muñana, 2020, Taking stock of essential workers, *KFF*, (May 1), accessed 31 July 2020 at https://www.kff.org/coronavirus-policy-watch/taking-stock-of-essential-workers/.

Keogh-Brown, M.R., 2014, 'Macroeconomic effect of infectious disease outbreaks', *Encyclopedia of Health Economics*, pp. 177–80.

Keogh-Brown, M.R. and R.D. Smith, 2008, 'The economic impact of SARS: how does the reality match the predictions?', *Health Policy* **88** (1), pp. 110–20.

Keogh-Brown, M.R. et al., 2010, 'The macroeconomic impact of pandemic influenza: estimates from models of the United Kingdom, France, Belgium and The Netherlands', *European Journal of Health Economics* **11** (6), pp. 543–54.

Kilbourne, E.D., 1976, 'National immunization for pandemic influenza', *Hospital Practice*, **11** (6), pp. 15–21.

Kindleberger, C.P., 1986, 'International public goods without international government', *American Economic Review* **76** (1), pp. 1–3.

Kotsopoulos, N. and M.P. Connolly, 2014, 'Is the gap between micro- and macroeconomic assessments in health care well understood? The case of vaccination and potential remedies', *Journal of Market Access & Health Policy* **2** (1), doi: 10.3402/jmahp.v2.23897.

Kotsopoulos, N. et al., 2019, 'Estimating the money flow in the economy attributed to rotavirus disease and vaccination in the Netherlands using a Social Accounting Matrix (SAM) framework', *Journal of Expert Review of Pharmacoeconomics & Outcomes Research*, doi: 10.1080/14737167.2020.1693269.

Kozlowski, J. et al., 2020, 'Scarring body and mind: the long-term belief-scarring effects of Covid-19', *FRB St. Louis Working Paper 2020-009,* Federal Reserve Bank of St. Louis: St. Louis.

Krueger, D. et al., 2020, 'Macroeconomic dynamics and reallocation in an epidemic', *NBER Working Paper No. 27047*, National Bureau of Economic Research: Cambridge MA.

Kuchler, T. et al., 2020, 'The geographic spread of COVID-19 correlates with structure of social networks as measured by Facebook', *NBER Working Paper No. 26990*, National Bureau of Economic Research: Cambridge MA.

Kügelgen, J. von et al., 2020, 'Simpson's paradox in Covid-19 case fatality rates: a mediation analysis of age-related causal effects', *arXiv*:2005.07180 (2020).

Kupferschmidt, K., 2020, 'Case clustering emerges as key pandemic puzzle', *Science* **368** (5693), pp. 808–9.

Kuznets, S., 1950, 'On the Accuracy of Economic Observations (review)' *Journal of the American Statistical Association* **45** (252), pp. 576–79.

Kyle, J. and B. Meyer, 2020, *High Tide? Populism in Power, 1990–2020*, Tony Blair Institute: London.

Lazzaroni, S. and P.A.G. van Bergeijk, 2014, 'Natural disasters' impact, factors of resilience and development: a meta-analysis of the macroeconomic literature', *Ecological Economics* **107**, pp. 333–46.

Lederberg, J., 1988, 'Pandemic as a natural evolutionary phenomenon', *Social Research* **55** (3), pp. 343–59.

Lee, J.-W. and W.J. McKibben, 2004, 'Globalization and disease: the case of SARS', *Asian Economic Papers* **3** (1), pp. 113–31.

Levin, A.T. et al., 2020, 'Assessing the age specificity of infection fatality rates for covid-19: meta-analysis & public policy implications', *NBER Working Paper No. 27597*, National Bureau of Economic Research: Cambridge MA.

Li, C. and P.A.G. van Bergeijk, 2019, 'Do natural disasters increase international trade?', in: T. Besedeš and V. Nitsch (eds), *Disrupted Economic Relationships: Disasters, Sanctions, Dissolutions*, MIT Press: Cambridge MA, pp. 169–90.

Lilley, A. et al., 2020, 'Public health interventions and economic growth: revisiting the Spanish Flu evidence', *mimeo*, (May 2, 2020), doi: 10.2139/ssrn.3590008.

Lin, P.Z. and C.M. Meissner, 2020, 'A note on long-run persistence of public health outcomes in pandemics', *NBER Working Paper No. 27119*, National Bureau of Economic Research: Cambridge MA.

Lipton, E. and J. Steinhauer, 2020, 'The untold story of the birth of social distancing', *New York Times*, April 22, 2020, accessed 31 July 2020 at https://www.nytimes.com/2020/04/22/us/politics/social-distancing-coronavirus.html

Lucas, R.E., 1976, 'Econometric policy evaluation: a critique', in: *Carnegie-Rochester Conference Series on Public Policy* Vol. 1, No. 1, pp. 19–46.

Lührmann, A. et al., 2019, 'State of the world 2018: democracy facing global challenges', *Democratization* **26** (6), pp. 895–915.

MacKellar, L., 2007, 'Pandemic influenza: a review', *Population and Development Review* **33** (3), pp. 429–51.

Maddison, A., 2006, *The World Economy: Volume 1: A Millennial Perspective and Volume 2: Historical Statistics*, OECD: Paris.

Madhav, N. et al., 2017, 'Pandemics: risks, impacts, and mitigation', in: *Disease Control Priorities: Improving Health and Reducing Poverty*, 3rd edition, The International Bank for Reconstruction and Development/The World Bank: Washington DC, pp. 315–45.

Mahbubani, K., 2020, 'The world after Covid-19 – by invitation: Kishore Mahbubani on the dawn of the Asian century', *The Economist*, April 20, https://www.economist.com/by-invitation/2020/04/20/kishore-mahbubani-on-the-dawn-of-the-asian-century, accessed 31 July 2020.

Maijama'a, D. et al., 2015, 'HIV/AIDS and economic growth: empirical evidence from Sub-Saharan Africa', *Research in Applied Economics* **7** (40), pp. 30–47.

Maliszewska, M. et al., 2020, 'The potential impact of COVID-19 on GDP and trade: a preliminary assessment', *Policy Research Working Paper 9211*, World Bank: Washington DC.

Malthus, T.R., 1798, *Essay on the Principle of Population*, Reprints of Economic Classics: New York.

Manski, C.F., 2019, 'Communicating uncertainty in policy analysis', *Proceedings of the National Academy of Sciences* **116** (16), pp. 7634 – 41.

Mariani, L. et al., 2020, 'Words can hurt: how political communication can change the pace of an epidemic', *Covid Economics* Issue 12, pp. 104– 37.

Marrewijk, C. van and P.A.G. van Bergeijk, 1990, 'Trade uncertainty and specialization: social versus private planning', *De Economist*, **138** (1), pp. 15–32.

Marrewijk, C. van and P.A.G. van Bergeijk, 1993, 'Endogenous trade uncertainty: why countries may specialize against comparative advantage', *Regional Science and Urban Economics* **23** (5), pp. 681–94.

Marshall, M.G. et al., 2011, *POLITY IV PROJECT: Dataset Users' Manual*, https://data.nber.org/ens/feldstein/ENSA_Sources/CSP/Polity%20Score/p4manualv2015.pdf, accessed 23 January 2021.

Martin, I.W.R. and R.S. Pindyck, 2019, 'Welfare costs of catastrophes: lost consumption and lost lives', *NBER Working Paper 26068*, National Bureau of Economic Research: Cambridge MA.

Mavalankar, D.V., 1995, 'Indian 'plague' epidemic: unanswered questions and key lessons', *Journal of the Royal Society of Medicine* **88** (10), pp. 547–51.

McDonald, M. et al., 2008, 'The macroeconomic costs of a global influenza pandemic', Global Trade Analysis Project 11th Annual Conference on Global Economic Analysis, Helsinki, available at: https://www.gtap.agecon.purdue.edu/resources/res_display.asp?RecordID=2755 and accessed January 23, 2021.

McDonald, S. and J. Roberts, 2006, 'AIDS and economic growth: a human capital approach', *Journal of Development Economics* **80** (1), pp. 228– 50.

McKibbin, J.W. and R. Fernando, 2020, 'The global macroeconomic impacts of COVID-19: seven scenarios', *CAMA Working Paper 19/2020,* Australian National University: Canberra.

McKibben, J. W. and A. Sidorenko, 2006, *Global Macroeconomic Consequences of Pandemic Influenza*, Lowy Institute for International Policy: Sydney.

McKinley, K., 2020, 'How the rich reacted to the bubonic plague has eerie similarities to today's pandemic', *The Conversation*, accessed 31 July 2020 at https://theconversation.com/how-the-rich-reacted-to-the-bubonic-plague-has-eerie-similarities-to-todays-pandemic-135925.

Melone, M.R.S. and S. Borgo, 2020, 'Rethinking rules and social practices. The design of urban spaces in the post-Covid-19 lockdown', *TeMA-Journal of Land Use, Mobility and Environment*, pp. 333–41.

Meltzer, M.I. and A. Patel, 2017, 'Stockpiling ventilators for influenza pandemics', *Emerging Infectious Diseases* **23** (6), pp. 1021–22.

Midões, C., 2020, 'Who can live without two months of income?', *Covid Economics* Issue 18, pp. 157–69.

Miller, G.Y. and K. Parent, 2012, 'The economic impact of high consequence zoonotic pathogens: why preparing for these is a wicked problem', *Journal of Reviews on Global Economics* **1**, pp. 47–61.

Milne, G.J. et al., 2013, 'The cost effectiveness of pandemic influenza interventions: a pandemic severity based analysis', *PloS one* **8** (4), e61504.

Moon, S. et al., 2015, 'Will Ebola change the game? Ten essential reforms before the next pandemic. The report of the Harvard-LSHTM Independent Panel on the Global Response to Ebola', *The Lancet* **386** (10009), pp. 2204–21.

Morens, D.M. and A.S. Fauci, 2007, 'The 1918 influenza pandemic: insights for the 21st century', *The Journal of Infectious Diseases* **195** (7), pp. 1018–28.

Morgenstern, O., 1963, *On the Accuracy of Economic Observations*, 2nd edition, Princeton University Press: Princeton NJ.

Moro, A. et al., 2017, 'Does home production drive structural transformation?', *American Economic Journal Macroeconomics*, pp. 116–46.

Morse, S.S. et al., 2012, 'Prediction and prevention of the next pandemic zoonosis', *The Lancet* **380** (9857), pp. 1956–65.

Murakami, E. et al., 2020, 'The potential impact of the Covid-19 pandemic on the welfare of remittance-dependent households in the Philippines', *Covid Economics* Issue 14, pp. 183–204.

Murshed, S.M., 2020, 'Capitalism and COVID-19: crisis at the crossroads', *Peace Economics, Peace Science and Public Policy*, in print.

Ng, W.L., 2020, 'To lockdown? When to peak? Will there be an end? A macroeconomic analysis on COVID-19 epidemic in the United States', *Journal of Macroeconomics* **65,** doi:10.1016/j.jmacro.2020.103230.

Niepelt, D. and M. Gonzalez-Eiras, 2020, 'Tractable epidemiological models for economic analysis', *Voxeu*, accessed 31 July 2020 at https://voxeu.org/article/tractable-epidemiological-models-economic-analysis.

Norman, J. et al. 2020, 'Systemic risk of pandemic via novel pathogens—Coronavirus: a note', accessed 31 July 2020 https://jwnorman.com/wp-content/uploads/2020/03/Systemic_Risk_of_Pandemic_via_Novel_Path .pdf.

Norris, P., 2020, 'Measuring populism worldwide', *Faculty Research Working Paper Series RWP20-002*, Harvard Kennedy School: Cambridge MA.

Noy, I. et al., 2020, 'Measuring the economic risk of COVID-19', *CESifo Working Paper No. 8373*, CESifo: Bonn.

Obstfeld, M. and A.M. Taylor, 1997, 'The Great Depression as a watershed: international capital mobility over the long run', in: M.D. Bordo, C. Goldin and E.N. White (eds), *The Defining Moment: The Great Depression and the American Economy in the Twentieth Century,* University of Chicago Press: Chicago, pp. 353–402.

O'Callaghan-Gordo, C. and J.M. Antó, 2020, 'COVID-19: the disease of the Anthropocene', *Environmental Research*, doi: 10.1016/j.envres.2020.109683.

OECD, 2011, *Reviews of Risk Management Policies – Future Global Shocks: Improving Risk Governance*, OECD: Paris.

OECD, 2014, 'Shifting gear: policy challenges for the next 50 years', *Economics Department Policy Note 24*, OECD: Paris.

OECD, 2020a, Interim Economic Assessment 2020 'Coronavirus: the world economy at risk', OECD, Paris, March 2020, accessed 31 July 2020 at http://www.oecd.org/berlin/publikationen/Interim-Economic-Assessment-2-March-2020.pdf.

OECD, 2020b, *OECD Economic Outlook*, Volume 2020b Issue 1, Preliminary version, accessed 31 July 2020 at https://www.oecd-ilibrary.org/economics/oecd-economic-outlook/volume-2020/issue-1_0d1d1e2e-en.

Office for National Statistics, 2020, *Coronavirus and Key Workers in the UK*, Office for National Statistics: London.

Okada, K., 2018, 'Health and political regimes: evidence from quantile regression', *Economic Systems* **42** (2), pp. 307–19.

Okubo, T., 2020, 'Spread of COVID-19 and telework: evidence from Japan', *Covid Economics* Issue 32, pp. 1–25.

Olson, M., 1965, *The Logic of Collective Action: Public Goods and the Theory of Groups*, Harvard University Press: Harvard.

Olson, M., 1982, *The Rise and Decline of Nations: Economic Growth, Stagflation, and Social Rigidities*, Yale University Press: New Haven.

Oppenheim, B. et al., 2019, 'Assessing global preparedness for the next pandemic: development and application of an Epidemic Preparedness Index', *BMJ Global Health* **4** (1).

Orwell, G., 1949, *Nineteen Eighty-Four: A Novel*, Secker & Warburg: London.

Ötker-Robe, I., 2014, 'Global risks and collective action failures: what can the international community do?', *IMF Working Paper WP/14/195*, IMF: Washington DC.

Panizza, E., 2020 'Europe's ground zero', in: R. Baldwin and B. Weder di Mauro (eds), 2020c, pp. 149–65.

Patton, M.Q., 2014, *Qualitative Research & Evaluation Methods: Integrating Theory and Practice*, Sage publications: London.

Pappas, G. et al., 2008, 'Insights into infectious disease in the era of Hippocrates', *International Journal of Infectious Diseases* **12** (4), pp. 347–50.

Peckham, R., 2013, 'Economies of contagion: financial crisis and pandemic', *Economy and Society* **42** (2), pp. 226–48.

Pei, S. et al., 2020, 'Differential effects of intervention timing on COVID-19 Spread in the United States', accessed 31 July 2020 at https://www.medrxiv.org/content/10.1101/2020.05.15.20103655v1.

Pen, J., 1985, *Amongst Economists: Reflections of a Neo-Classical Post-Keynesian,* Elsevier North Holland: Amsterdam and New York.

Petropoulos Petalas, P.D. et al., 2017, 'Forecasted economic change and the self-fulfilling prophecy in economic decision-making', *Plos one* **12** (3), e0174353.

Pezzani, M.D., 2020, 'COVID-19 outbreak: the gold rush and the responsibilities of the scientific community', *Clinical Microbiology and Infection*, https://doi.org/10.1016/j.cmi.2020.05.002.

Phlippen, S., 2020, 'Trilemma van afruilen kenmerkt afbouw coronamaatregelen' (Trilemma of trade-offs characterizes ending the Corona measures; in Dutch), *Economisch-Statistische Berichten* **105** (4785), pp. 220–21.

Pichler, S. and N.R. Ziebarth, 2017, 'The pros and cons of sick pay schemes: testing for contagious presenteeism and noncontagious absenteeism behavior', *Journal of Public Economics* **156**, pp. 14–33.

Pitt, C. et al., 2016, 'Economic evaluation in global perspective: a bibliometric analysis of the recent literature', *Health Economics* **25**, pp. 9–28.

Pohlman, A. and O. Reynolds, 2020, 'Why economic forecasting is so difficult in the pandemic', *Harvard Business Review* (May 18, 2020), accessed 31 July 2020 at https://hbr.org/2020/05/why-economic-forecasting-is-so-difficult-in-the-pandemic.

Pollack, T. et al., 2020, 'Vietnam's commitment to containment', *Exemplars*, accessed 1 July 2020 at https://www.exemplars.health/emerging-topics/epidemic-preparedness-and-response/covid-19/vietnam.

Posen, A.S., 2020, 'Containing the economic nationalist virus through global coordination', in: R. Baldwin and B. Weder di Mauro (eds), 2020c, pp. 203–11.

Prager, F. et al., 2017, 'Total economic consequences of an influenza outbreak in the United States', *Risk Analysis* **37** (1), pp. 4–19.

Pullano, G. et al., 2020, 'Novel coronavirus (2019-nCoV) early-stage importation risk to Europe', *Euro Surveillance* **25** (4) doi.org/10.2807/1560.

Qualls, N. et al., 2017, 'Community mitigation guidelines to prevent pandemic influenza – United States, 2017'. *Morbidity and Mortality Weekly R Recommendations and Reports* **66** (No. RR-1), pp.1–34, doi: 10.15585/mmwr.rr6601a1.

Rajaonah, B. and E. Zio, 2020, 'Contributing to disaster management as an individual member of a collectivity: resilient ethics and ethics of resilience', accessed 31 July 2020 at https://hal-uphf.archives-ouvertes.fr/hal-02533290v2.

Rasul, I., 2020, 'The economics of viral outbreaks', *AEA Papers and Proceedings* **110**, pp. 265–8.

Redmond, P. and S. McGuinness, 2020, 'Essential employees during the COVID-19 crisis', *ESRI Survey and Statistical Report Series Number 85*, Economic and Social Research Institute: Dublin.

Reinders, H.J., D. Schoenmaker and M.A. van Dijk, 2020, 'Is COVID-19 a threat to financial stability in Europe?', *CEPR Discussion Paper No. DP14922*, Centre for Economic Policy Research: London.

Rho, H.J. et al., 2020, *A Basic Demographic Profile of Workers in Frontline Industries*, Center for Economic and Policy Research: Washington DC.

Robalino, D.A., 2020, 'The COVID-19 conundrum in the developing world: protecting lives or protecting jobs?', *IZA Discussion Papers, No. 13136*, Institute of Labor Economics: Bonn.

Robert Koch Institute, 2020, 'Event Horizon - 2019-nCoV', Robert Koch Institute: Humboldt, March 5, accessed 31 July 2020 at https://web.archive.org/web/20200320133848/http://rocs.hu-berlin.de/corona/docs/model/import_risk/.

Roberts, J.D. and S.O. Tehrani, 2020, 'Environments, behaviors, and inequalities: reflecting on the impacts of the Influenza and Coronavirus Pandemics in the United States', *International Journal of*

Environmental Research and Public Health **17** (12), doi: 10.3390/ijerph17124484.

Rockefeller Foundation, 2010, *Scenarios for the Future of Technology and International Development*, www.nommeraadio.ee/meedia/pdf/RRS/ Rockefeller%20Foundation.pdf, accessed July 1, 2020.

Rodrik, D., 2011, *The Globalization Paradox: Democracy and the Future of the World Economy*, W.W. Norton & Company: New York.

Roser, M. et al., 2020, 'Coronavirus pandemic (COVID-19)', accessed 31 July 2020 at https://ourworldindata.org/coronavirus.

Rubin, H., 2011, 'Future global shocks: pandemics', *OECD International Futures Programme, IFP/WKP/FGS(2011)2*, OECD: Paris.

Ruggie, J.G., 1982, 'International regimes, transactions, and change: embedded liberalism in the postwar economic order', *International Organization* **36** (2), pp. 379–415.

Saltiel, F., 2020, 'Who can work from home in developing countries?', *Covid Economics* Issue 7, pp. 104–18.

Sands, P. et al., 2016, 'Assessment of economic vulnerability to infectious disease crises', *The Lancet* **388** (10058), pp. 2443–48.

Santos, J.R. et al., 2009, 'Pandemic recovery analysis using the dynamic inoperability input-output model', *Risk Analysis* **29** (12), pp. 1743–58.

Schnettler, S., 2009, 'A structured overview of 50 years of small-world research', *Social Networks* **31** (3), pp. 165–78.

Schumacher, E. F., 2011, *Small is Beautiful: A Study of Economics as if People Mattered*, Random House: London (original published in 1973).

Seiler, P., 2020, 'Weighting bias and inflation in the time of Covid-19: evidence from Swiss transaction data', *Covid Economics* Issue 35, pp. 96–115.

Semenza, J.C. et al., 2019, 'Systemic resilience to cross-border infectious disease threat events in Europe', *Transboundary and Emerging Diseases* **66** (5), pp. 1855–63.

Serra-Garcia, M. and N. Szech, 2020, 'Demand for COVID-19 antibody testing, and why it should be free', *CESifo Working Paper No. 8340*, Center for Economic Studies and Ifo Institute (CESifo): Munich.

Sheynin, O.B., 1982, 'On the history of medical statistics', *Archive for History of Exact Sciences* **26** (3), pp. 241–86.

Shim, E. et al., 2020, 'Transmission potential and severity of COVID-19 in South Korea', *International Journal of Infectious Diseases* **93**, pp. 339–44.

Shinde, G.R. et al., 2020, 'Forecasting models for Coronavirus disease (COVID-19): a survey of the state-of-the-art', *SN Computer Science* **1** (4), pp. 1–15.

Smeden, M. van et al., 2020, 'Reflection on modern methods: five myths about measurement error in epidemiological research', *International Journal of Epidemiology* **49** (1), pp. 338–47.

Smith, A., 1776, *An Inquiry into the Nature and Causes of the Wealth of Nations*, Canna's edition, Clarendon Press: Oxford (published in 1976).

Smith, D., 2017, 'Pandemic risk modelling', *The Palgrave Handbook of Unconventional Risk Transfer*, Palgrave Macmillan: Cham, pp. 463–95.

Smith, R.D. and M.R. Keogh-Brown, 2013, 'Macroeconomic impact of pandemic influenza and associated policies in Thailand, South Africa and Uganda', *Influenza and Other Respiratory Viruses* **7**, pp. 64–71.

Smith, R.D. et al., 2011, 'Estimating the economic impact of pandemic influenza: an application of the computable general equilibrium model to the UK', *Social Science & Medicine* **73** (2), pp. 235–44.

Snower, D., 2020, 'The socio-economics of pandemics policy', *CEPR Discussion Paper 14872*, Centre for Economic Policy Research: London.

Sorci, G. et al, 2020. 'Why does COVID-19 case fatality rate vary among countries?', *medRrvix,* 2020/04/22/2020.04.17.20069393.full.pdf.

Spinney, L., 2017, *Pale Rider: The Spanish Flu of 1918 and How It Changed the World*, Jonathan Cape: London.

Stevenson, J. et al., 2016, 'Economic and business recovery', *Oxford Research Encyclopedia of Natural Hazard Science*, doi: 10.1093/acrefore/9780199389407.013.19.

Stiglitz, J.E., 2018, *Globalization and its Discontents Revisited. Anti-Globalization in the Era of Trump*, Norton: New York and London.

Suijkerbuijk, A.W.M., 2018, *Costs of Infectious Diseases Outbreaks and Cost-Effectiveness Of Interventions*, PhD thesis Tilburg University: Tilburg.

Sumner, A. et al., 2020a, 'Estimates of the impact of COVID-19 on global poverty', *WIDER Working Paper 2020/43*, UN-WIDER: Helsinki.

Sumner, A. et al., 2020b, 'Precarity and the pandemic: COVID-19 and poverty incidence, intensity, and severity in developing countries', *WIDER Working Paper 2020/77*, UN-WIDER: Helsinki.

Suyker, W., 2020, 'De ramingen voor de schade aan de economie buitelen over elkaar heen' (Estimates for damage to the economy are tumbling over each other; in Dutch), ESB.nu, accessed 31 July 2020 at https://esb.nu/blog/20059395/de-ramingen-voor-de-schade-aan-de-economie-buitelen-over-elkaar-heen.

Swedberg, R., 2017, 'Colligation', in: H. Leiulfsrud and P. Sohlberg (eds), *Concepts in Action – Conceptual Constructionism*, Brill: pp. 63–78.

Taubenberger, J.K and D.M. Morens, 2006, '1918 influenza: the mother of all pandemics', *Emerging Infectious Diseases* **12** (1), pp. 15–22.

Thunström, L. et al., 2020, 'The benefits and costs of using social distancing to flatten the curve for COVID-19', *Journal of Benefit-Cost Analysis*, doi: 10.1017/bca.2020.12.

Tinbergen, J., 1952, *On the Theory of Economic Policy*, North Holland: Amsterdam.

Tognotti, E., 2009, 'Influenza pandemics: a historical retrospect', *Journal of Infection in Developing Countries* **3** (5), pp. 331–4.

Udovički, K., 2020, 'The fragility of global value chains: more reason to guide and develop productive capacity', in: Committee for Development Policy, 2020, pp. 14–17.

UNCTAD, 2020, *The Coronavirus Shock: A Story of Another Global Crisis Foretold*, https://unctad.org/system/files/official-document/gds_tdr2019_update_coronavirus.pdf, accessed 23 January 2021.

UN DESA, 2019, *World Population Prospects 2019*, United Nations, Department of Economic and Social Affairs, Population Division (custom data acquired via website June 30, 2020).

US Congressional Budget Office, 2005, *A Potential Influenza Pandemic: Possible Macroeconomic Effects and Policy Issues*, Congress of the United States, Congressional Budget Office.

Velasco, R.P. et al., 2012, 'Systematic review of economic evaluations of preparedness strategies and interventions against influenza pandemics', *PloS one* **7** (2), e30333.

Veldkamp, L. and A. Fogli., 2020, 'Germs, social networks and growth' *CEPR Working Paper DP13312*, Center for Economic Policy Research: London.

Verikios, G. et al., 2012, 'H1N1 influenza and the Australian macroeconomy', *Journal of the Asia Pacific Economy* **17** (1), pp. 22–51.

Verity, R. et al., 2020, 'Estimates of the severity of coronavirus disease 2019: a model-based analysis', *The Lancet Infectious Diseases* **20** (6), pp. 669–77.

Wei, S.J., 2020, 'Ten keys to beating back COVID-19 and the associated economic pandemic', in: R. Baldwin and B. Weder di Mauro (eds), 2020c, pp. 71–6.

Wallace, R. et al., 2020, 'COVID-19 and circuits of capital', *Monthly Review* **72** (1), pp. 1–13.

Wells, C.R. et al., 2020, 'Impact of international travel and border control measures on the global spread of the novel 2019 coronavirus outbreak', *Proceedings of the National Academy of Sciences* **117** (13), pp. 7504–509.

Whewell, W., 1847, *The Philosophy of the Inductive Sciences, Founded Upon Their History*, London: John W. Parker.

Wilgis, J., 2008, 'Strategies for providing mechanical ventilation in a mass casualty incident: distribution versus stockpiling', *Respiratory Care* **53** (1), pp. 96–103.

Woodford, M., 2005, 'Central-Bank communication and policy effectiveness', *Department of Economics Discussion Paper Series 0506-07*, Columbia University: New York.

World Bank, 2014a, *The Economic Impact of the 2014 Ebola Epidemic: Short- and Medium-Term Estimates for West Africa*, World Bank Group, 2014.

World Bank, 2014b, *World Development Report 2014: Risk and Opportunities. Managing Risk for Development*, World Bank: Washington DC.

World Bank, 2020a, 'COVID-19 crisis through a migration lens', *Migration and Development Brief 32*, World Bank, Washington DC.

World Bank, 2020b, *Global Economic Prospects*, World Bank, Washington DC.

World Health Organization, 2005, *International Health Regulations*, Third edition, World Health Organization: Geneva.

World Health Organization, 2008, 'Human rights, health and poverty reduction strategies', *Health and Human Rights Publications Series No 5*, World Health Organization: Geneva.

World Health Organization, 2019, *Pandemic Influenza Preparedness in WHO Member States: Report of a Member States Survey*, World Health Organization: Geneva.

World Travel and Tourism Council, 2020, *Economic Impact Report 2020*, WTTC: London.

Wyplosz, C., 2020, 'The good thing about coronavirus', in: R. Baldwin and B. Weder di Mauro (eds), 2020a, pp.113–5.

Young, A., 2005, 'The gift of the dying: the tragedy of AIDS and the welfare of future African generations', *Quarterly Journal of Economics* **120** (2), pp. 423–66.

Young, S.D. et al., 2000, *EVA and Value-Based Management*, McGraw-Hill Professional Publishing: Maidenhead.

Zimmermann, K.F. et al., 2020, 'Inter-country distancing, globalization and the Coronavirus pandemic', *World Economy*, doi:10.1111/twec.12969.

Index

individual freedom 139–40
individual preparedness 9, 149–52
individualism 126–7
Indonesia 54
inequalities 157, 159
infectious periods 75, 76
inflation 108–9
influenza pandemics 1–2, 23–6, 32–3,
        36–7
    morbidity levels 48
    preparedness 15–16, 21
informal sector 40
information pandemics 4
input output analyses 22, 32–3
insurance 23
Intensive Care facilities 21
interdependence of firms 33
interest rates 106
international cooperation 2
International Monetary Fund (IMF) 51,
        162
international organizations 132–3, 162
international preparedness 160–1
international trade 110, 112, 114, 133
internationalism 126
internet use 80, 152
Iran 115
Iraq 81
Ischgl 73, 160
ISLM model 105–8
isolationism 134
Israel 115, 137, 143
Italy 49, 81, 98, 137, 141, 143

Jackson, C. 149
Japan 26, 46, 55, 63, 80, 81, 94, 115

Keogh-Brown, M.R. 29–30, 35
Keynesian demand management 104
Kindleberger, C.P. 22
knowledge cycles 85
knowledge gap 38–9
Kügelgen, J. von 98

labour productivity 36, 100, 102
labour supply 32–3, 97–8
laissez faire attitude 127–8
Lee, J.-W. 30
Lewis, M. 26

Li Wenliang 146
Liberal Peace 133
Liberia 27
liberty 137, 139–40
liquidity trap 107–9, 118
local communities 130, 133
local preparedness 9–10, 152–5, 160
'lock step' scenario 145
lockdowns 6, 53, 85–6, 99, 104, 165
    advanced economies 128
    autocracies 127, 138
    city design 153–4
    classification errors 72
    economic numbers 78–9, 82
    essential workers and 158
    limitations of 37
    market democracies 126
    model predictions 88
    saving rate reduction 102
    supply effects 42
    trade shocks 111
London 153
long-run supply 96–103
Lucas Critique 34, 77

Macedonia 81
McKibben, W.J. 30
macroeconomics 22–36, 61, 70, 96–103
Mahbubani, K. 137
Maijama'a, D. 29
Malaysia 30
Malthus, Thomas 128
management teams 156
market democracies 126, 128, 141
market economy 87, 108–9, 158
market services 80–1
mask-wearing 150
mass surveillance 138
mass transportation 154
maximax decision rule 91
maximin decision rule 91
measurement 70, 72, 74, 78, 89
measurement error 70–1, 75
media coverage 78, 149
medical cooperation 160–1
medical reactions 53, 88, 147, 156, 159
mega-cities 152–4
MERS 17
Mexican Flu 110
Mexico 81